DEMOCRATIC
MARXISM

DEMOCRATIC MARXISM SERIES

Series Editor: Vishwas Satgar

The crisis of Marxism in the late twentieth century was the crisis of orthodox and vanguard-ist Marxism associated mainly with hierarchical communist parties, and imposed, even as state ideology, as the 'correct' Marxism. The Stalinisation of the Soviet Union and its eventual collapse exposed the inherent weaknesses and authoritarian mould of vanguardist Marxism. More funda-mentally, vanguardist Marxism was rendered obsolete but for its residual existence in a few parts of the world, including within authoritarian national liberation movements in Africa and in China.

With the deepening crises of capitalism, a new democratic Marxism (or democratic historical materialism) is coming to the fore. Such a democratic Marxism is characterised by the following:

- Its sources span non-vanguardist grassroots movements, unions, political fronts, mass parties, radical intellectuals, transnational activist networks and parts of the progres-sive academy;
- It seeks to ensure that the inherent categories of Marxism are theorised within constantly changing historical conditions to find meaning;
- Marxism is understood as a body of social thought that is unfinished and hence challenged by the need to explain the dynamics of a globalising capitalism and the futures of social change;
- It is open to other forms of anti-capitalist thought and practice, including currents within radical ecology, feminism, emancipatory utopianism and indigenous thought;
- It does not seek to be a monolithic and singular school of thought but engenders contending perspectives;
- Democracy, as part of the heritage of people's struggles, is understood as the basis for articulating alternatives to capitalism and as the primary means for constituting a transformative subject of historical change.

This series seeks to elaborate the social theorising and politics of democratic Marxism.

BRICS AND THE NEW AMERICAN IMPERIALISM

GLOBAL RIVALRY AND RESISTANCE

Edited by Vishwas Satgar

WITS UNIVERSITY PRESS

Published in South Africa by:

Wits University Press
1 Jan Smuts Avenue
Johannesburg 2001

www.witspress.co.za

First published 2020

http://dx.doi.org.10.18772/22020035287

978-1-77614-528-7 (Print)
978-1-77614-566-9 (Hardback)
978-1-77614-563-8 (PDF)
978-1-77614-564-5 (EPUB)
978-1-77614-565-2 (Mobi)
978-1-77614-576-8 (Open Access PDF)

The publication of this volume was made possible by funding from the Rosa Luxemburg Stiftung and through a grant received from the National Institute for the Humanities and Social Sciences.

Project manager: Inga Norenius
Copyeditor: Inga Norenius
Proofreader: Tessa Botha
Indexer: Margaret Ramsay
Cover design: Hothouse, South Africa
Typesetter: MPS
Typeset in 10 point Minion Pro

CONTENTS

TABLES AND FIGURES

ACKNOWLEDGEMENTS

This volume owes a special debt to the Rosa Luxemburg Foundation. Without their support it would have been impossible to hold a contributors' workshop in South Africa and to ensure the manuscript was prepared for publication. The use of the conferencing space at their office provided a conducive space for engagement during the contributors' workshop. We are also grateful for the support given by the Co-operative and Policy Centre (COPAC), which played a central role in organising the workshop convened with contributors and activists from various social movements and community organisations. The support given by the National Institute for the Humanities and Social Sciences has enabled the digitisation of this volume. Moreover, it is important to acknowledge the editorial assistance provided by Jane Cherry from COPAC. Her efforts were crucial for keeping things on track. The efforts of Courtney Morgan and Aaisha Domingo, working with Jane Cherry, are also appreciated. Special thanks to Professor Michelle Williams for her supportive feedback during this project. Finally, our sincerest appreciation to the team at Wits University Press, particularly Veronica Klipp, Roshan Cader and Corina van der Spoel, for supporting this volume and the Democratic Marxism series.

ACRONYMS AND ABBREVIATIONS

ACFI	Agreement on Cooperation and Facilitation of Investment
AfDB	African Development Bank
ANC	African National Congress
BNDES	Banco Nacional de Desenvolvimento Economico e Social (Brazilian Economic and Social Development Bank)
BRICS	Brazil, Russia, India, China and South Africa
CFM	Caminhos de Ferro de Moçambique
CRA	Contingent Reserve Arrangement
CSIR	Council for Scientific and Industrial Research
GATT	General Agreement on Trade and Tariffs
IMF	International Monetary Fund
IOCs	international oil companies
JICA	Japan International Cooperation Agency
MNC	multinational corporation
NAM	Non-Alignment Movement
NATO	North Atlantic Treaty Organization
NIEO	New International Economic Order
NOCs	national oil companies
OECD	Organisation for Economic Co-operation and Development
ONGC	Oil and Natural Gas Corporation
SDI	Spatial Development Initiative
TNC	transnational corporation
TTIP	Transatlantic Trade and Investment Partnership
UNCTAD	United Nations Conference on Trade and Development
UNCTC	United Nations Commission on Transnational Corporations
UNFCCC	United Nations Convention on Climate Change
Veja	Vaal Environmental Justice Alliance
WSF	World Social Forum
WTO	World Trade Organization

For Rosa Luxemburg who was murdered on 15 January 1919.

1

OLD AND NEW IMPERIALISM: THE END OF US DOMINATION?

Vishwas Satgar

For over three decades the main buzzword of development, international relations and policy making has been 'globalisation'. It is a descriptive concept used to characterise processes underway in the global political economy related to production, trade, finance, technology and labour. It has been an overworked term, sometimes evoking the metaphor of a happy 'global village' in which all countries are equal and in which there is smooth mobility not just of finance and goods, but also of labour and technology. The embrace of globalisation has also promised that all ships will rise as the tides of competition and winds of integration buttress the engines of national economies. Inequality and poverty will all be history in this global market utopia according to the promises and rhetoric of globalisation discourse. Or more poignantly, we would all be Americans and would all have been conscripted to the 'end of history' in which the US standard of liberal democracy was also our common standard. However, the realities of today's global political economy are much more complex. This fifth volume in the Democratic Marxism series seeks to explore the remaking of the global political economy over the past few decades in a world of deepening systemic crises (such as climate change and water crises), redistributions of economic power (with China today the largest economy), the rise of the Brazil-Russia-India-China-South Africa (BRICS) bloc and sharpening global rivalries. In this volume we unpack the new patterns of global power within the context of conjunctural and longer spans of history, the remaking of capitalism and the forms of resistance that are emerging. In short, this volume seeks to clarify the meanings of imperialism/anti-imperialism in the context of a crisis-ridden globalisation and the various social forces shaping our world, from above and below.

The concept of imperialism was central to Marxist theorising and political economy analysis in the twentieth century. It has important analytical strengths to uncover hierarchies of power and relations of oppression as part of the expansionary dynamics of capitalism. However, the mechanisms and material foundations of imperialism in the twentieth century are very different from those of imperialism in the twenty-first century. More sharply, twenty-first century imperialism is not the same as twentieth-century imperialism and merely reading the current historical period through a lens of the past (through Lenin's conception of imperialism, for instance) is not useful and will certainly miss nuance and historical specificity. To enable a twenty-first century perspective on the new imperialism, this volume brings together Marxists and critical thinkers from within some of the BRICS countries, in dialogue with scholars from the global north. The volume also builds on themes related to the emergence of a new imperialism that has featured in previous volumes, such as marketisation, passive revolution, capitalism's crises, the climate crisis and ongoing racism in the world order.

This chapter situates the origins of the term imperialism and highlights its place within Marxist theory. Instead of merely focusing on the contributions of Rudolf Hilferding, Vladimir Lenin and Nikolai Bukharin as the progenitors of the first Marxist theories of imperialism, this chapter looks more deeply into the history of Marxism to understand the debates after Karl Marx that gave rise to Marxist approaches to imperialism. More specifically, the chapter focuses on the contribution of Rosa Luxemburg, who provided an extremely original theory of imperialism, which was largely ignored after her murder in 1919 and after her thought was banned in the Soviet Union in 1925. The chapter highlights key aspects of Luxemburg's theory of imperialism and its contribution to our understanding of classical imperialism, but also traces the lineage of thought she inaugurated, which has drawn on her work to theorise and analyse the new imperialism of our times. Through a Luxemburg-inspired understanding of imperialism, this chapter locates the cycles of US hegemonic imperialism in the twentieth century and the challenges it faces in the twenty-first century. The Trump moment and the possible trajectories of US imperialism in relation to contemporary crisis dynamics are explored. The chapter concludes by reviewing the main contributions of the chapters in this volume, which together highlight the conditions informing contemporary global rivalries, the role of BRICS countries and the challenges for anti-imperial resistance.

ORIGINS OF THE TERM 'IMPERIALISM' AND THE DEVELOPMENT OF MARXIST THEORIES

It is patently clear in modern international relations thought that Marxists have played a pivotal role in providing an intellectual, theoretical and historical basis to imperialism as a conceptual category. However, the origins of the term are less well known. The original use of the term 'imperialism' cannot be ascribed to Marxism although Marxist-Leninists tend to believe that Lenin invented the term. For them, imperialism as a conceptual category derives from a post-competitive phase of capitalism and emerged with the rise of monopolies, the dominance of finance capital and recurrent crises at the end of the nineteenth century. Actually, the origins of the term imperialism, in the English language, goes back to the mid-nineteenth century (Day and Gaido 2011: 5). It was initially used to describe Louis Napoleon's Second French Empire (1852–1870) and was later used more widely in Britain with the passage of the Royal Titles Act of April 1876, which officially conferred the title 'Empress of India' on Queen Victoria. Only much later in the nineteenth century, and particularly after the publication of John Hobson's book on imperialism, which was inspired by the Boer War (1898–1902), did the English socialist press associate imperialism with the emerging imperatives of capitalist competition (Day and Gaido 2011: 7). In the US context, the term imperialism was initially used to describe, in positive ways, the expansionist turn in US foreign policy initiated by the 1898 Spanish-American War and the US annexation of the Philippines, which was then rejected by the American Anti-Imperialist League and the Democratic Party (Day and Gaido 2011: 7–8).

Most renderings of the historiography of Marxist theory related to imperialism focus merely on Hilferding, Bukharin and Lenin. Hobson, the liberal thinker, is also mentioned as being a forerunner. Rosa Luxemburg is treated as having serious flaws in her understanding of Marx and is generally dismissed (Brewer 1990). Lenin, on the other hand, is given undue importance due to his canonical place in sovietised Marxism–Leninism. Lenin's pamphlet (1917) *Imperialism: The Highest Stage of Capitalism* builds on the work of Hilferding and Bukharin. While recognising the uneven development of capitalism, the role of finance capital (combined banking and industrial capital) and colonial rivalries underpinned by monopoly capital and war, Lenin made several mistakes in how he situated imperialism. Moreover, the dogmatic reading of Lenin is given a trans-historical salience which inhibits how contemporary imperialism is understood. These problems have been specified by various Marxists in the course of the twentieth century.[1] First, imperialism has been central to the early expansion of proto-capitalism, mercantile capitalism, since the fifteenth and sixteenth centuries. Second, it was integral to the development of competitive capitalism (which preceded monopoly capitalism) in the nineteenth century, and British imperialism. Third, imperialism in the twenty-first century has been shaped by new dynamics such as the hegemonic role of the US, the global monopoly phase of techno-financial capitalism and the development of weapons of mass destruction. Fourth, Lenin did not fully appreciate the racist logics and practice of imperialism, both historically and in his own time. However, the dogmatic canonisation of Lenin's thought has presented it to the world as original and unsurpassed.

The unearthing of the actual history of Marxism reveals several important developments that unsettle the origins of Marxist thinking on imperialism. Marxist theorising about imperialism was contingent on and shaped by developments in the late nineteenth century related to colonialism – including the Boer wars, genocidal violence against the Herero peoples in what is known today as Namibia and the brutal US colonial conquest of the Philippines – but also related to rising nationalism and militarism among dominant European powers. A valuable archive of primary documents and original contributions capturing these debates, which exploded during the Second International, is contained in the 951-page *Discovering Imperialism: Social Democracy to World War 1* (Day and Gaido 2011). What follows draws on this material to highlight central contributions that shaped debates about imperialism within Marxism. Various themes run through these engagements, including the causes of imperialism, colonialism, imperialism and capitalist crisis, disarmament, and war and tactics. What follows focuses merely on the formative contributions to debates about the causes of imperialism and the relationship between imperialism and colonialism.

Marx did not have a developed theory of imperialism, nor did he write his planned volumes on the world market and the state. Although he recognised the tendency for capitalist accumulation to expand beyond nationally bounded spaces, the challenge of elaborating a causal theory of imperialism was left to subsequent generations. The pioneering analysis of imperialism, unknown to most historians, was by Max Beer (1864–1943), an Austrian émigré in London, and Paul Louis, a Frenchman whose real name was Paul Levi (1872–1955) (Day and Gaido 2011: 16). Both these socialists were thinking in a context characterised by the complexity of British imperialism, European colonialism and the role of the United States. They both attempted to elaborate an understanding of the economic foundations of imperialism and they certainly initiated the debate on imperialism that gave rise to more systematic theoretical analysis. Beer's analysis starts with *Modern English Imperialism* (November 1897) and proceeds to *The United States in 1898* (31 December 1898), *The United States in 1899* (19 November 1899) and then turns to *Reflections on England's Decline* (March 1901), *Social Imperialism* (8 November

1901), *Party Projects in England* (January 1902), *Imperialist Policy* (December 1902) and *Imperialist Literature* (December 1906).

In characterising the rise of British imperialism, Beer had this to say:

> Two factors were at work in Great Britain that made possible the erection and consolidation of the worldwide 'Second Empire': the powerful Industrial Revolution, which led to the development of gigantic productive forces, and the relatively free constitution, which enabled the Englishmen to take up the colonial policy again and continue it in the spirit of the new economic doctrines. The strong influence of Adam Smith's *Wealth of Nations* . . . Those factors enabled England to overcome the serious crisis and put together the elements of modern English imperialism. ([1897] 2011: 98–99)

Paul Louis's work covers *Anglo-Saxon Imperialism* (March 1899) and *An Essay on Imperialism* (April 1904). For Louis imperialism marked the epoch and shaped the life worlds of the majority, tied to chauvinistic nationalisms, militarism and economic expansion. He says:

> Imperialism appears as the result of an economic revolution, as the product of capitalism, industrialism, free competition and the universal struggle for markets. One can say that, like proletarian socialism, it had to result inevitably from all the phenomena caused by the growth of production and exchange in the last century, and that is why it is so engaging, general and appealing. If a people lapses into the imperialist conception, or, rather, if its leaders try to inculcate the imperialist spirit, that is a certain sign that the ruling class, which exploits and oppresses that people, feels threatened in its fortunes and hurt in its interests. Now, in which country are the bourgeoisie, the oligarchy of landowners and industrialists sure of their future and income? ([1904] 2011: 294)

The relationship between imperialism and colonialism was a serious and engaged debate in the Second International. It had many twists, turns and setbacks. To simplify, it was culturally inflected and racist in some instances on the one hand and, on the other, anti-imperialist. One of the main protagonists in this debate was the reformist theoretician Eduard Bernstein. Bernstein drew on the economistic and epistemological Eurocentrism in the early Marx and justified colonialism as based on the racial and civilisational superiority of Europeans (Day and Gaido 2011: 11). He argued his position from 1896 till 1907, continuing to argue his support for the civilising role of colonialism and pointing out that colonies would be inherited by socialism (Day and Gaido 2011: 41). On the other side of this debate stood many principled leftists, including Rosa Luxemburg. Luxemburg rebuffed the chauvinistic positions of Bernstein and his supporters. In the 1900 International Socialist Congress in Paris, Luxemburg sponsored a resolution, which was acclaimed. In this was framed a crucial rejection of imperialism as a necessary consequence of capitalism's contradictions: it led to colonial expansion; it excited chauvinism; it led to brutalisation and cruelties against natives of the colonies conquered by armed forces and it required united, anti-imperial resistance everywhere (Day and Gaido 2011: 20–21). These debates continued up to the eve of World War 1. It is in this context that we turn to Luxemburg's contribution to analysing the imperialism of her time.

ROSA LUXEMBURG AND CLASSICAL IMPERIALISM

Rosa Luxemburg (1871–1919) was an extremely prominent Marxist at the end of the nineteenth century and the beginning of the twentieth century. She held her own in a very male-dominated Social Democratic Party (SPD) of Germany. At the same time, she was also not a Leninist and forged a more humanist and radical democratic approach to revolutionary struggle. Her work *The Accumulation of Capital* (1913) shook up the SPD, increasingly degenerate as it became trapped in electoralism, nationalism and even, in the end, defending militarism. It is a sophisticated attempt to think through and ground a Marxist understanding of imperialism. Luxemburg's critics have foregrounded only certain aspects of her argument, distorted most of it or have merely rejected it as flawed. Many caricatures were invited by this ambitious work as it also took on Marx, while it also challenged the growing Eurocentric and nationalist chauvinism within the SPD.

There are three parts to *The Accumulation of Capital*. Part 1 deals with the problems of reproduction in Marx's work regarding the realisation of a part of the surplus product. Part 2 focuses on how bourgeois economic theory (from Sismondi to the Russian 'legal' Marxists) grappled with the problem, and Part 3 deals with the historical conditions of accumulation as it relates to enabling imperial expansion. From her 453-page text, four crucial aspects of her theory of imperialism are highlighted here. First, a literal reading of Luxemburg's critique of Marx's reproduction schemas in Volume 2 of *Capital* suggests that she argued underconsumption was the basis of the crisis in expanded reproduction and ultimately therefore also the basis for expansion to non-capitalist spaces. Put differently, the part of the surplus product which capital could not consume could only be realised by expansion to non-capitalist parts of the world. Many of her critics ascribe this argument to her and suggest that she had a simplistic argument contra Marx. For Riccardo Bellofiore (2004), Luxemburg had to also be read through her notes on the *Introduction to Political Economy* (published posthumously) which she used at the SPD school. This reading yields a much richer interpretation of Luxemburg's understanding of crisis in expanded reproduction. This includes (i) the internal link between value, abstract labour and money; (ii) the connection between dynamic competition, relative surplus value extraction and the 'law' of the falling tendency of the 'relative wage' and (iii) the realisation that her theory of the crisis is not underconsumptionist. Effective demand is reduced due to a fall in autonomous investment related to inter-sectoral disequilibria, which are related to innovation in methods of production, and the consequent relative reduction of workers' consumption. Ultimately, Bellofiore (2004: 289) suggests that Luxemburg recognised the importance of money in the reproduction process, more so than most Marxists, and posed the right questions. As a result, Bellofiore (2004: 290) concludes that 'what Kautsky or Lenin, Bauer or Bukharin dubbed as her "errors" now appear as what make Luxemburg a forerunner of a *macro-monetary* theory of exploitation, accumulation and crisis'.

Second, for Luxemburg the pre- or non-capitalist modes of production were what surrounded the heartland of capitalism. To her, this meant that primitive accumulation did not end with the development of capitalism in the European centre, it continued as part of colonial policy (Luxemburg [1913] 2003: 350). This, she argued, is about the conquest of natural economy (an economy in which there is production for personal need). An imperialist capitalism thus attempted ([1913] 2003: 349–350): '(1) To gain immediate possession of important sources of productive forces such as land, game in primeval forests, minerals, precious stones and ores, products of exotic flora such as rubber, etc. (2) To "liberate" labour power and to coerce it into service. (3) To introduce a commodity economy. (4) To separate trade and agriculture.'

Third, Luxemburg compellingly connected the role of money capital, as loan finance, to the imperial expansion of capitalism. She dedicated chapter 30 to providing historical examples and insights into how this had worked through building railways and funding wars, for example. However, for Luxemburg ([1913] 2003: 408) this was not just about commodity production overcoming the natural economy but also about remaking commodity production in existing capitalist economies, in some instances. Reading this chapter now draws out interesting parallels with how global financialisation works today. In summary this is how it works ([1913] 2003: 407):

> Realised surplus value, which cannot be capitalised and lies idle in England or Germany, is invested in railway construction, water works, etc. in the

7

Argentine, Australia, the Cape Colony or Mesopotamia. Machinery, materials and the like are supplied by the country where the capital has originated, and the same capital pays for them. Actually, this process characterises capitalist conditions everywhere, even at home. Capital must purchase the elements of production and thus become productive capital before it can operate. Admittedly, the products are then used within the country, while in the former case they are used by foreigners. But then capitalist production does not aim at its products being enjoyed, but at the accumulation of surplus value.

Fourth, Luxemburg was never blind to how the use of force is central to the expansion of capital and imperialism. In this regard she provided a dedicated chapter on militarism (chapter 32). She not only situated the historical role and significance of militarism in ongoing processes of primitive accumulation but also highlighted how militarism is connected to the realisation of surplus value by squeezing the consumption of the working class through taxation ([1913] 2003: 445). Her analysis also highlighted that the spread of imperialism – and ultimately capitalism – is contradictory and its full realisation also spells the demise of capitalism. Luxemburg ([1913] 2003: 447) put it as follows:

> The more ruthlessly capital sets about the destruction of non-capitalist strata at home and in the outside world, the more it lowers the standard of living for the workers as a whole, the greater also is the change in the day-to-day history of capital. It becomes a string of political and social disasters and convulsions, and under these conditions, punctuated by periodical economic catastrophes or crises, accumulation can go on no longer.

However, she argued for continued resistance and internationalist struggle for socialism, despite this possible eventuality.

LUXEMBURGIAN-INSPIRED PERSPECTIVES ON THE NEW IMPERIALISM

David Harvey, a well-known scholar of Marx's *Capital*, inaugurated the debate about a new imperialism with his crucial text, *The New Imperialism*, published after 9/11, after the declaration of the 'war on terror' and when the full-throttled invasion of Iraq was underway. Harvey wanted to respond to liberals and US neo-conservatives who suddenly felt it was time for the US to shift from empire 'lite' to a heavier imperial presence in the world. This was echoed by the British historian Niall Ferguson (2002) who called for the US to move away from informal empire to more direct forms of imperial rule in the world. The burden of the civilising mission of the US-led West was far from over. The US had to become like the British Empire according to Ferguson. At the same time, Harvey wanted to respond to the postmodern version of *Empire* (2000) by Michael Hardt and Antonio Negri, which gained a lot of attention for its attempts to think about imperialism as diffused and beyond the historical, material and geographic power of the US. Empire was everywhere and nowhere; it was the phantom appreciated only by the postmodern literate.

Harvey set out to clarify what is new about the US-led imperialism, how the conjuncture came together and how historical geographical materialism could unpack some of the deeper transformations occurring in our contemporary world. In his analysis and interpretation of these historical dynamics Harvey explicitly engages with and builds on Rosa Luxemburg's work on imperialism, particularly her deeper investigation of primitive accumulation and its links to imperialism. Harvey (2003: 137–182), like Luxemburg, observes the ongoing condition and presence of primitive accumulation. However, he goes further to theorise this in original ways. Harvey agrees with Luxemburg about the dual character of capital accumulation. On the one hand, surplus value extraction happens between capital and labour as part of expanded reproduction. On the other hand, the relationship between capitalist and non-capitalist modes of production are also crucial to capital accumulation. Harvey expands on this, suggesting that capital overaccumulation necessitates not only trade but also investment opportunities, which, Harvey (2003: 139–140) argues, means:

> The general thrust of any capitalistic logic of power is not that territories should be held back from capitalist development, but that they should be continuously opened up. From this standpoint colonial repressions of the sort that undoubtedly occurred in the late nineteenth century have to be interpreted as self-defeating, a case of a territorial logic inhibiting the capitalistic logic.

Harvey also develops a more expansive understanding of the inside-outside of capitalism. He argues, following Luxemburg, that capitalism always creates an outside. However, he avers that this outside is more than non-capitalist formations: 'The idea that some sort of "outside" is necessary for the stabilization of capitalism therefore has relevance. But capitalism can either make use of some pre-existing outside (non-capitalist social formations or some sector within capitalism – such as education – that has not yet been proletarianized) or it can actively manufacture it' (Harvey 2003: 141).

While he agrees with Luxemburg that primitive accumulation continues beyond the originary moments of capitalism, Harvey argues that primitive accumulation is not limited just to the 'outside of capitalism'. He also goes further to suggest that using the term 'primitive accumulation' to describe an ongoing condition of capitalism is not useful and hence he utilises the concept 'accumulation by dispossession' (2003: 144).

Luxemburg recognised primitive accumulation as referring to various processes in Marx's perspective. Harvey affirms, but also updates this understanding. He does not agree that capitalism completely wipes out pre-capitalist relations; instead he avers that actually, in some instances, capitalism engages in co-optation of these cultural and social achievements. Thus despite the universalisality of proletarianisation there will never be a homogenous working class (Harvey 2003: 147). Harvey also brings into view the role of the new, modernised financial system, the role of intellectual property rights, the commodification of nature, the depletion of the climate commons, privatisation and deregulation. All these dynamics are recognised as contingent, haphazard and complex processes that are part of contemporary accumulation by dispossession. Ultimately, Harvey argues that accumulation by dispossession does not solve the overaccumulation problem but merely moves it around, thus creating political management challenges and the risk of collapsing the system. Central to linking expanded reproduction and accumulation by dispossession is the role of finance (Harvey 2003: 152). Here Harvey is still on ground that Luxemburg covered in 1913.

Fifth, Luxemburg recognised the link between struggles within and outside capitalism. Harvey does the same and conceptually goes further to situate the classical wage-labour-versus-capital struggle within expanded reproduction on the one hand, and, on the other, new 'subaltern' struggles against accumulation by dispossession involving indigenous peoples, peasants and other victims of the neoliberal class project. He poses the challenge and dilemma of how to link these struggles, without resolving the issue.

Another important contemporary theorist who has worked with and built on Marx's and particularly Luxemburg's more expansive understanding of primitive accumulation is Nancy Fraser (Fraser and Jaeggi 2018: 43). Besides reworking Luxemburg's inside-outside approach to capitalism, through a new topographical theorisation of the foreground of exploitation and the background of structural divisions (production/reproduction, human/non-human nature, economy/polity) that enable exploitation, Fraser unpacks more sharply her structural conceptualisation of capitalism, imperialism and racism. In this regard, Fraser explicitly agrees with Harvey and Luxemburg about the continuities of primitive accumulation, beyond the initial moment of stockpiling capital through pillage, robbery, slavery and violence. However, Fraser also goes beyond Marx, Harvey and Luxemburg in two important respects regarding capitalism, imperialism and racism. First, she provides a more systematic theorisation of the notion of 'expropriation'. For Fraser, expropriation not only captures the genesis of the class divide in capitalist society between propertyless workers and capitalist owners of the means of production (referred to as primitive accumulation in Marx), it also highlights another social division: between 'free workers' that are exploited through wage labour, and unfree or dependent subjects that are also 'cannibalised' by capitalism. According to Fraser, 'Historically, that second division correlates roughly but unmistakenly with the colour line. In my view, the expropriation of racialized "others" constitutes a necessary background condition for the exploitation of "workers". In fact, I would say that "race" just *is* the mark that distinguishes free subjects of exploitation from dependent subjects of expropriation' (Fraser and Jaeggi 2018: 43).

Second, Fraser not only clarifies how exploitation depends on expropriation of racialised others, she also demonstrates how this works and has to be analysed at different levels in the context of imperialism and capitalism, and at different historical moments. Fraser argues:

> Capitalism's other, unofficial geography, its imperialist division of 'core' and 'periphery' is at work here as well. Historically, the capitalist core appeared as the emblematic heartland of exploitation, while the periphery seemed to be the iconic site of expropriation. And that geography was explicitly racialized from the get-go, as were the status hierarchies associated with it: metropolitan citizens versus colonial subjects, free individuals versus slaves, 'Europeans' versus 'natives', 'Whites' versus 'Blacks' . . . To understand the status divisions that underlie capitalism's racial formations, we need to attend simultaneously to all these levels: national/domestic, international/ 'Westphalian' and colonial/imperialist. (Fraser and Jaeggi 2018: 42–43)

Like Luxemburg, Fraser recognises the contingency and importance of struggles within her structural understanding of capitalism's divides (Fraser and Jaeggi 2018: 54). She theoretically innovates on her approach to struggles. She argues that contemporary struggles are boundary struggles to define the line as it relates to exploitation/expropriation, production/reproduction, human/non-human nature, economy/polity. These boundary struggles define the structural conditions of a

capitalist society and will ensue in different contexts and under variegated historical conditions.

Samir Amin, before his passing, was one of Africa's leading Marxists who, like
Rosa Luxemburg, came to similar conclusions about capitalism and imperialism.
A pioneering world-systems thinker, Amin focused on the causes of underdevelopment in his PhD during the mid-1950s (Amin 1970). Like Luxemburg, he
concluded that the world capitalist economy was based on a dynamic of global
polarisation: centres versus peripheries. Over the decades Amin sophisticated his
analysis as he engaged with the underdevelopment debate, Africa's challenges and
conjunctural developments in the world-system. Among his numerous and original Marxist contributions, three themes stand out that take us beyond Luxemburg
in thinking about contemporary global accumulation. First, Amin recognised that
unequal development laid the foundations on which centres could remake the basis
for domination and exploitation of the peripheries. As long as the imperial dynamic
prevailed, the peripheries would be subjects of domination. In the neoliberal conjuncture, adjustment to the centres and the needs of global monopolies became the
basis for restructuring southern economies. Globalisation was the new imperialism
(Amin 2001). Second, Amin (2004) was explicit about the imperial chaos a US-led
world-system would bring. According to Amin (2006), World War 3 began with the
first US invasion of Iraq and this kind of militarist supremacy required a new geopolitics of realignments, away from US hegemonic leadership, that would unmake
US supremacy and would also contribute to the renewal of socialism. Third, Amin
(2010) was consistent in his assertion that real change and the challenge to imperialism would come from the peripheries. This meant advancing delinking, even
at regional scales, which would enable the logics of capitalism, socialism and state
centrism to compete, contradict and shape the destiny of countries and regions in
the periphery as part of a long transition.

THE TWO CRISES OF US IMPERIAL HEGEMONY IN THE TWENTIETH CENTURY

Since the end of World War 2, the US has emerged on the world stage as the leading
Western capitalist power. The US had a highly industrialised war economy, led the
remaking of global institutions such as the World Bank, the International Monetary
Fund (IMF) and the General Agreement on Trade and Tariffs (GATT), shaped the
liberal format of the United Nations and opposed the continuity of direct colonial rule. In the period 1944–1972 the US-led world order was referred to as the

Pax Americana. During this time social democracy in the US and the West more generally enjoyed its golden years. The Marshall Plan opened up the European economy to US capital penetration; Japan was kept on a tight leash and the rest of the capitalist world was disciplined to follow its lead under the pretext of the Cold War. The latter was truly a hot war in parts of the peripheries of capitalism. Coups, assassinations, proxy wars and military juntas, and conventional warfare (Korea and Vietnam) characterised the frontiers of the Cold War. The US military-industrial complex grew and benefited from the economic logic of the Cold War. For Luxemburg this kind of militarism was intrinsic to the logic of imperialism and the US imperial role in the twentieth century merely confirms her thesis. The territorial logic of US imperialism served to ensure that the US controlled key geo-strategic resources such as fossil fuels (Iran and Venezuela, for example), access to minerals (South Africa), agricultural land (Guatemala) and key strategic trade choke points (such as the Panama Canal). In a Luxemburgian sense the 'natural economy' was subordinated to the needs of the imperial centre. Formally, colonialism might have ended after World War 2, but centre–periphery relations continued and were nonetheless shaped by US imperial power.

However, by the early 1970s the Pax Americana was in crisis. The 'golden years of social democracy' based on a social contract that ensured welfare benefits, Keynesian macro-economic management and mass production for mass consumption had reached its limits. Most orthodox Marxist readings of this moment ascribe it to the decline of profit rates and a generalised crisis of overaccumulation as a result. While there is compelling empirical evidence regarding this argument, a host of other factors contributed to the crisis of US hegemony. The military defeat in Vietnam was a major blow to US prestige and international leadership. Body bags of young soldiers, the anti-war movement and the Watergate scandal all fed into a deepening crisis of US leadership. Moreover, the emergence of communist China, the Cuban Revolution and the advance of national liberation struggles all placed immense geostrategic pressure on the US after World War 2. This expressed itself through the Non-Aligned Movement, the emergence of the United Nations Conference on Trade and Development (UNCTAD) in 1964, the '1968' moment in western Europe among students, workers and radical intellectuals, calls for a New International Economic Order in the 1970s by newly independent countries in the UN General Assembly and the squeeze of high oil prices through the Organisation of the Petroleum Exporting Countries. These developments, all of world historical significance, weakened US hegemony. In addition, the rise of Japan and western Europe by the 1970s, now also as high-tech industrial economies, placed immense pressure on the US to reorganise its relationship with the centres of capitalism.

13

Finally, the Cold War with the USSR was a costly affair, although the role of the North Atlantic Treaty Organization (NATO) and various theatres of conflict gave credence to the 'US domino theory', which was an elaborate red-threat conspiracy theory which suggested a 'red breakthrough anywhere will lead to more of the same'. This crude understanding of the world shaped geopolitical and national security calculations, including overstretch. All of these factors contributed to the crisis of the first hegemonic cycle of US leadership in the twentieth century (see figure 1.1).

However, the second cycle of US hegemony has its roots in the response of the US and internationalising monopoly capital to this conjuncture. In the 1980s Ronald Reagan and Margaret Thatcher unleashed the neoliberal offensive which mutated into the 'Third Way' across the centres of capitalism. As a class project it opened the way for greater financialisation, cutting back the welfare state and ending the social democratic social contract. Since then, labour has been further precariatised and unions pushed back. The remaking of the power of finance in the US political economy is crucial in this cycle of US hegemony. In 1980, what has come to be known as the 'Volcker shock' happened. Basically, the Federal Reserve, under the leadership of Paul Volcker, increased interest rates from 10.25 per cent to 20 per cent.[2] He inaugurated contractionary monetary policy to manage inflation. At the same time, the US experienced massive inflows of finance from around the world. Buying dollar-denominated bonds, investing on the US stock exchange and property markets became crucial for the dollar-Wall Street regime (Gowan 1999). The making of the dollar-Wall Street regime has a long history tied to the makings

Figure 1.1 US cycles of hegemony and crisis

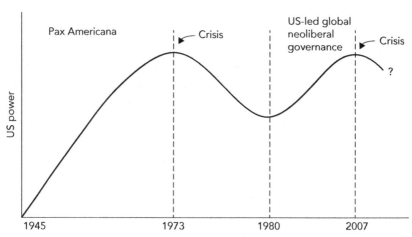

Source: Author.

of the US financial system, but when Nixon uncoupled the dollar from the gold standard, in the early 1970s, this laid the basis for the dollar to be crucial for global trade, debt and investment.

At the same time, Reagan renewed the Cold War with the objective of outspending the USSR in an arms race. In the global South the renewed Cold War continued being a hot war. Central America, Angola and Mozambique became crucial theatres of US intervention through proxy forces. Civil wars were intensified and sharp fault lines were drawn. At the same time, the Bretton Woods Institutions, particularly the World Bank and the IMF, became crucial in driving structural adjustment programmes that further deepened indebtedness and state failure in the global South. Over three decades of neoliberalisation has had limited impact on poverty rates, but has deepened inequality, entrenched an unequal division of labour and, in many instances, rolled back modest gains in industrial development. It has inaugurated what Samir Amin called 'lumpen development' in which ruling classes in the peripheries no longer have a development project but are merely about capturing resource rents and looting. From a Luxemburgian perspective the outside of the centres of capitalism has become part of the centres of capitalism, with growing poverty and inequality, and the outside of capitalism has become further marginalised as sites of continued primitive extraction under US imperial domination.

With the end of the Cold War, the US-led bloc intensified global financialisation and placed the neoliberal class project at the centre of US hegemony. This was globalised as the Washington Consensus and further entrenched within multilateral institutions, including the World Trade Organization (WTO). This process created global economic instability and global finance, centred on the dollar-Wall Street regime, became a structural feature of the global political economy. The 'global casino' destabilised currency markets, property markets and credit markets. Public and private debt increased. In the context of the US this reached its apogee with the collapse of the housing market in 2007, followed by the crash of Wall Street, and what has come to be known as the greatest financial crisis. Through a Luxemburgian political economy optic, the remaking of the US economy through financialisation allowed for deepening commodification, but it was also contradictory in producing its crisis-ridden limits.

The 2007–2009 crisis is a general crisis and part of a profoundly volatile and stagnating global economy. A globally financialised economy, deepening inequality, weak market democracies, water crises, resource peak (such as oil), climate crises and eco-systems collapse are all converging at this moment in history (Satgar 2015). The marketisation of planetary life under US imperial domination has reached a point of civilisational crisis for which the US is responsible and for which it does not have solutions. This is what the crisis of the second US hegemonic cycle is about. It is also in this context, and despite the US, that countries such as China, Russia, Brazil and India have found a place in the global political economy. For Jim O'Neill, the BRICs represented a new frontier of accumulation, with projected growth rates set to dominate by 2050, and in dollar terms larger than existing G6 economies (O'Neill 2001). Since the first BRICs summit in 2009, and with the addition of South Africa in 2010, the BRICS have been in existence for over a decade. Together they initiated the BRICS Development Bank and a contingent reserve arrangement in 2014. Moreover, the summitry of the BRICS has created an image of a rival bloc to the US-led Western bloc. But is this really the case? Do the BRICS have the capacity, institutional arrangements and ideational coherence to articulate an alternative world order? Do the domestic conditions in member countries lend themselves to advancing a consistent international relations policy that could give coherence to the BRICS?

For Giovanni Arrighi (2007), China has been the winner of the war on terror and embodies the Beijing Consensus, a new authoritarian, state-driven, high-growth-rates economic model for countries to follow. Consistent with his work on cycles of hegemonic domination and his observation of US decline, Arrighi argues China is a contender for hegemonic leadership of the contemporary world order. If one extends this argument to the BRICS, then in many ways this is a China-centred initiative and a calculated move by China to deepen its hegemonic leadership among semi-periphery states. However, China's own economic slowdown since 2015, its centrifugal impacts on accumulation processes within BRICS countries (see Bond in this volume), which it is not managing in a balanced way, highlights serious shortcomings in China-centred leadership. Pieterse (2018) reads the BRICS differently. He argues BRICS embodies 'multi-channel' politics that will contribute to rebalancing global power relations through being responsible 'stakeholders' in existing institutions, advancing the reform of existing institutions, initiating new institutions such as the BRICS Development Bank and developing cooperation frameworks outside existing networks. In a sense, for Pieterse, the BRICS represent a with-and-beyond approach to the US-led bloc. However, while this script has some purchase in comprehending some of the practices of the BRICS, Pieterse (2018: 74–84) also appreciates that domestic conditions, particularly how inequality is addressed, will certainly impact on the BRICS configuration.

However, the BRICS as a bloc, despite how it is characterised, faces the challenge of a civilisational crisis. Converging financialised inequality, climate change and water crises are also present in these countries. In the case of Brazil, Russia, India and South Africa marketised democracies are showing serious weaknesses and a growing tendency towards authoritarian practices. Political leadership in Brazil and

India are certainly adopting the Trumpian script for how politics is performed. As numerous chapters in this volume highlight, the BRICS fall very short of resolving the civilisational crisis and providing global leadership. It is in this context we turn to how US imperialism is being reframed and calibrated under Trump.

THE TRUMP MOMENT

Under Trump's leadership the renewal of US hegemony, as part of a third cycle of leadership of global capitalism, faces various challenges and uncertainties. On the surface, as has been widely pointed out, Trump seems to be out of step with the conventions of diplomacy, is very unpredictable, tweets his way across borders and at times comes across as a bumbling buffoon. However, underlying this is a concerted and purposeful national security strategy seeking to reposition the US in the world order and make it 'great again'. Reading Trump's *National Security Strategy* (adopted in December 2017),[3] the following stands out starkly:

- US market democracy is still the standard for the world;
- There are costs to be incurred to access the US market;
- Accumulation will be innovation driven;
- US strength will be maintained through counterbalancing any threats;
- Asymmetric threats such as the 'war on terror' are no longer centre stage; instead, threats from countries such as China and Russia are prioritised;
- The US will seek to also deal with Iran and North Korea.

These national security priorities mean that the US under Trump will support a diverse range of ideological forces rising in the world through weak market democracies. This will not only affirm Trump's own rise through such a flawed democratic system but will further valorise illiberal forces just like Trump. Absent from the national security strategy is the climate crisis. This silence further underlines the commitment of the Trump regime to climate change acceleration and carbon extraction (Satgar 2018). This has been confirmed through a raft of policy measures, executive orders and nefarious appointments to key parts of the US state bureaucracy. Carbon capital's interests are paramount for Trump and his administration.

Moreover, current rivalries with China are clearly informed by the national security priorities of the Trump administration. This includes the current trade war with China and the attacks on Huawei, a Chinese information and communications transnational. In many ways the Trump administration is seeking to squeeze

China economically and push back its innovation capacity. At the same time the US military budget is now over US$700 billion, clearly underlying a firm commitment to full spectrum dominance, which has initiated a new arms race with China and Russia. The US military-industrial complex is a major beneficiary of Trump's fiscal policy, laying the basis for aggressive militarism and conflict in the world. For Rosa Luxemburg this kind of militarism and jingoistic nationalism was the embodiment of barbarism and could only be destructive for workers, the poor and those outside capitalism. It was her opposition to the militarism of World War 1 and the nationalist fervour sweeping through Germany that earned her three and a half years in prison. In the context of our contemporary civilisational crisis the US bid for global domination is nothing short of an assertion of imperial chaos.

GLOBAL CRISIS AND POSSIBLE TRAJECTORIES OF US IMPERIALISM

Informed by a Luxemburg-inspired reading of US hegemonic cycles and Trump's national security strategy there are four possible trajectories for the US.

In the first possible trajectory, it takes on the role of hegemonic cycle breaker and intensifies rivalries to block contenders. This is what it did during the Cold War. In the 1980s this contributed to bankrupting the Soviet Union through the arms race and military spending. Today this means the US does everything from the standpoint of full-spectrum dominance to undermine China as a possible hegemonic contender. This has already begun in terms of rebalancing trade relations with China. There is a lot at stake for China in this: access to the US market, trade surpluses, the value of dollar-denominated debt it holds, intellectual property rights and even technology. This trajectory openly intensifies rivalries and has the potential to escalate on various fronts of conflict, from cyber warfare to open military confrontation, including through proxy states. In this context Russia would have to be neutralised or realigned around US geopolitical interests.

In the second scenario the US-led bloc, through the G7, NATO, the IMF, the World Bank, WTO and other institutions, increasingly builds a consensus to incorporate China into the global power structure. This would be similar to the contender challenges faced by the US in the 1970s, with the rise of western Europe and Japan as renewed hi-tech and industrial powers after World War 2. Through the Trilateral Commission, the G7, the Cold War and other forms of diplomatic engagement, the US increasingly incorporated western Europe and Japan into its sphere of influence and ensured this triadic relationship was the backbone of its leadership role in the world. However, whereas China has been brought into the IMF (its voting quota recently increased from 3.8 in 2010 to 6.1 in 2019, see Bond in this volume) and the World Bank, and has positioned itself inside the WTO (since 2001) it does not have a seat at the G7. It also is not considered an ally of the US-led triad. Bringing China into the US-led triad would mean placing it at the centre of coordinating, managing and leading global capitalism. This might be too far a leap for US ruling classes to consider, thus China gets incorporated to a degree into global neoliberal governance while it is weakened in other ways. Tensions with China continue but rivalries are muted and managed.

The third possibility is a trajectory in which the US plunges the world into worsening climate chaos. Trump is already accelerating carbon extraction and use. This will bring major disruptions, debt and even socio-ecological collapse to parts of the planet – even inside the US. In this trajectory the US-led bloc weakens dramatically, despite the endless 'war on terror' and Euro-American civilisational alignments against the 'Oriental other', and the US becomes increasingly supremacist. Europe, Japan and China realign the global interstate system in terms of climate emergency imperatives and transitions. Technology, resources and political will are marshalled in order to build systems to sustain life, while the US is isolated as a climate pariah. In turn the US retreats into its own 'lifeboat', polices zones of 'potential chaos' where its geopolitical interests are threatened, and becomes increasingly authoritarian and eco-fascist to contain popular discontent among its citizens. Collateral damage to the US working poor, other peoples and species in the world is rationalised as necessary to maintain the American way of life.

The fourth trajectory sees an intensification of the New Cold War with Russia and China. Instead of open military conflict, destabilisation of cyber networks and infrastructure central to the functioning of all societies intensifies. The internet is geopolitically balkanised and completely securitised. The US effectively uses the war on terror to manage its European allies; US support is also given to ethno-nationalist and neo-fascist forces like those in Ukraine and the US generally underwrites the rise of a new right wing against Russia, China and any social forces it perceives as threats. These countries respond in a similar vein, with Russia already seeking such alignments in parts of western Europe. In short, a neo-fascist US comes to the fore and engenders forces in this mould to advance proxy wars of destabilisation. The standard of liberal democracy exists only as a thin veneer, while the US plunges the world into various forms of ethno-nationalist conflict which it resources, instrumentalises and uses to its advantage. Climate shocks exacerbate such conflicts and this further strengthens US reach and leverage over conflict-ridden socio-ecological orders. The human cost is nothing short of genocidal.

BRICS AND GLOBAL RIVALRY

The contemporary global political economy is defined by fault lines and flashpoints within and between BRICS countries, between the BRICS and the US-led bloc, and within and between the US-led bloc. The dialectic of conflict and cooperation runs through these institutional configurations, conditioning contradictory international relations. An institutionalised multilateral system, treaty organisations and a web of institutionalised alliances assists to some extent to manage the escalation of tensions. However, the crisis of US hegemony, the lack of ideological coherence, deepening contradictions and shallow convergence in the BRICS and the dynamics of systemic crisis in the global political economy all impact on the character of global rivalry today. The geometry of such global rivalry is complex and cuts across the interstate system and global political economy more generally.

In chapter 2, William Carroll provides a political economy analysis of fossil capital, imperialism and the BRICS. Carroll highlights the centrality of fossil capital to the development of imperialism. He provides a periodisation of imperialism: (i) Pax Britannica, mid to late nineteenth century, which was centred on coal; (ii) classic imperialism, twentieth century to 1945, based on the rise of big oil and automobility; (iii) Pax Americana, after World War 2, premised on carbon democracy, automobility and the centrality of oil in mass consumer capitalism; and (iv) neoliberal governance, late 1970s to the present, characterised by a decline in US hegemony, rapid growth of national oil corporations mainly in the global South and a worsening climate crisis. Taking his analysis further, Carroll provides a network analysis of the top 50 fossil fuel corporations in the world and their location in relation to the global corporate elite. What is striking about this analysis is that while Northern-based fossil fuel corporations, owned by investors, dominate this network, Southern-based capital is still marginal and mainly tied to state-owned corporations.

At least two Chinese oil corporations are among the top fossil fuel corporations in the world. Excluding Norway's state-owned oil corporation, state-owned oil companies in the global South – at least 24 – control about 77 per cent of oil and gas reserves, which marks a major geopolitical shift from the second and third phases of imperialism, despite these corporations being marginal to the global corporate elite network. Carroll concludes from his analysis that China is a player in global fossil fuel geopolitics but really is about a regional accumulation strategy, through the Belt and Road Initiative (BRI), backed up by investments and coordination through the Shanghai Cooperation Organisation (SCO), formed in 2001. BRICS in his view, with its multiple fault lines and performative summitry, and given the objective process of regional accumulation, is not at the forefront of contending with the US-led bloc, nor for that matter is it the most pivotal mechanism to advance Chinese interests. Moreover, bearing the climate crisis in mind, China is positioning itself in partnership with Europe to isolate Trump's rearguard action to shore up fossil capital, and is also developing an edge regarding renewable energy.

In chapter 3, Ferrial Adam provides an argument to conceptually understand water conflicts as water wars both globally and within countries. Empirically, she highlights the constraints and pressures facing the water needs of societies and human beings. She utilises poignant data from the International Water Association, which suggest that almost 4 billion people lack proper access to water; 4.5 billion human beings do not have access to a proper sewage system and at least 5.5 billion drink untreated water. Her chapter foregrounds increasing subnational and inter-state conflicts over water. With climate change, poor governance, privatisation and geopolitical monopolisation of water resources, conflicts are on the rise. Within and even between BRICS countries such as China and India, serious water-related tensions are coming to the fore, while domestically, micro-level water wars are on the increase. South Africa, a water-scarce country with a failing mode of water governance, widespread water-related pollution and now climate change induced droughts, is an example of a country that is ill-prepared to meet the water needs of its citizens. Numerous social protests around water provisioning in both urban and rural areas have occurred. State repression and violence have also led to the death of one activist. Water wars have arrived and this has geopolitical salience within countries, between countries and on a planetary scale within the global political economy.

In chapter 4, Patrick Bond provides an analysis of the BRICS as an ersatz bloc of subimperial countries. The concept of subimperialism has been explained by Ruy Mauro Marini and David Harvey, using characteristics ranging across class structure, geopolitics and the displacement of overaccumulated capital, to which Bond adds a vital component: select middle-income countries' contributions to neoliberal global governance. One of the best examples of the phenomenon is the BRICS bloc, which for a decade since 2009 has rhetorically asserted an 'alternative' strategy to key features of Western imperialism, while in reality fitting tightly within it. This fit works through amplified neoliberal multilateralism serving both the BRICS and the West, the regional displacement of overaccumulated capital, financialisation and persistent super-exploitative social relations. In short, in spite of what some term the 'schizophrenic' character of subimperialism, the BRICS *all* generally promote extreme spatio-temporal fixes and the predatory condition known as accumulation-by-dispossession. They thus amplify the world's 'centrifugal' capitalist crisis tendencies, instead of providing a coherent bloc and the purported alternative to Western power. While Xi Jinping and Vladimir Putin remain Washington's most durable potential competitors, the other BRICS countries are splintering in unpredictable ways. Narendra Modi's Hindu-nationalist defeat of the Congress Movement in 2014, Cyril Ramaphosa's replacement of Jacob Zuma in 2018 and Brazilian president Jair Bolsonaro's ascension in 2019 together confirm the rightward political drift. The 'anti-imperialist' potential of the BRICS, if it ever existed, is exhausted, although fierce debate continues over the merits of subimperial theory. Bond takes on this debate to provide a strong defense of subimperial analysis. All told, he concludes that a much more brutal period appears on the horizon – in social, political, economic and ecological respects – unless 'BRICS from below' forces can make their resistance more coherent.

In chapter 5, Ana Garcia and Karina Kato draw on Rosa Luxemburg's inside-outside model of capitalism and the subjection of the natural economy to capitalist accumulation, and Harvey's innovation of accumulation by dispossession to explore a detailed case study of Brazilian and global interests in the development of the Nacala Corridor in Mozambique. Their study reveals increasing expansion and penetration of Brazilian capital, in a symbiotic relationship with the global power structure, to deepen resource extraction in Mozambique. This spans massive investments in coal, gas, construction and food production as part of the Nacala Corridor. Brazil's leading corporations, like Vale, are at the vanguard of this and have invested heavily to create an export pipeline that brings together coal and gas extraction, transport infrastructure (including an export terminal) and external markets. At the same time, the ProSavana farming programme pushes a model of export-led agriculture that also connects with this value chain. The dispossession, social conflict and violence associated with this necessitates thinking in terms of the subimperial dynamics shaping Brazil–Mozambique relations. In response to this subimperial accumulation by dispossession, Garcia and Kato, like Bond, make the argument for a 'BRICS-from-below' approach to resistance.

NEW FORMS OF ANTI-IMPERIAL RESISTANCE AND CHALLENGES

In the contemporary world, resistance and struggles are taking on diverse forms and are expressed through different social forces within the expanding realm of the sovereignty of capital. Over the past three decades, neoliberalisation and global restructuring have remade the working class; precariatisation has increased; greater atomisation of social agency has emerged in the context of rampant possessive individualism, and populist crowd politics has substituted for mass counter-hegemonic struggles. Old forms of resistance, such as Bandung solidarity among Third World countries, have been defeated and the World Social Forum (WSF) is in deep crisis and seems exhausted. At the same time, struggles against exploitation and accumulation through dispossession of all forms of life are certainly ongoing but fragmented and limited. The world is in transition, facing difficult challenges, including the threat of human extinction, systemic collapse and growing authoritarianism, but the conjuncture of crisis and transformative resistance has not yet provided a breakthrough.

In chapter 6, Christopher Chase-Dunn proposes a diagonal political organisation for the global Left that will link local and national networks and prefigurational communities to contend for power in the world-system during the next few decades of the twenty-first century. He describes the reasons why the global Left can no longer be content with the amorphous 'movement of movements' structure that has characterised the WSF process. Instead of repeating the hierarchical patterns of the earlier Internationals, he proposes a diagonal structure that promotes and supports self-organisational and prefigurational projects while providing a democratic global organisational instrument for coordinating challenges to the states, firms, NGOs and international organisations that are the organisational instruments of global capitalism. He describes the contemporary multicentric structure of the global justice movement and the culture of the new global Left as it emerged in the movement. Further, he argues, the WSF process needs to be reinvented in order to deal with the demise of neoliberalism, the decline of US hegemony and the rise of neo-fascist and reactionary populist nationalism. He discusses the implications for the global Left of the decline of the Latin American pink tide, the Arab Spring, the rise of a new global Right and the arrival of another period of competitive multipolarity in the core of the world-system. This chapter is also a contribution to the emerging discourse on global party formation while being cognisant of the context of the economic, cultural and political evolution of the world-system and recent developments among social movements.

In chapter 7, Samir Amin, who was one of Africa's leading independent Marxists, deepens the debate about internationalist institutional forms. In his work he has been a consistent critic of various forms of imperialism within the world-system. As a pioneer of world-systems thinking and as an African Marxist, Amin has also been conscious of the universals of capitalism; its expansion, albeit uneven; its polarising logic on a global scale to make profits for capital and the consequent need to build a requisite anti-imperial resistance among the 'people'. Amin has always understood that the abstract 'capital-labour' dialectic was never adequate to understand the variegated social relations imbricated in anti-imperial resistance. As part of his non-Eurocentric Marxism he always accepted that in the peripheries various victims of capitalism would come to the fore, from peasants to a segmented working class. He never believed a 'Third World Bourgeoisie' could lead the 'people's revolutions' and resistance in the peripheries. He also accepted that in the centres, nationalism and the competitive role of nation-states conscripted historical blocs (including the working class) to an imperialist project. However, in his chapter, first published in French and translated for a global audience in 2008, he makes a case for renewing internationalism by reflecting on the lessons of nineteenth and twentieth century internationalism, including the limits of the Bandung project (1955–1980). He sets out the case for a new International of Workers and Peoples. Even before he died, on 12 August 2018, Amin continued to make his case to the global Left. In 2017 he provided a summary of his argument in a piece entitled 'It is imperative to reconstruct the Internationale of workers and peoples'[4] and put out an email call on 24 June 2018 titled 'Letter of intent for an inaugural meeting of the International of Workers and Peoples'.[5] Samir Amin's argument deserves to be examined and engaged with given its relevance to contemporary resistance. Hence we have published his original contribution on the issue in this volume.

In chapter 8, Keamogetswe Seipato foregrounds a crucial campaign to confront and dismantle transnational corporate power. The Global Campaign to Reclaim Peoples Sovereignty, Dismantle Corporate Power and Stop Impunity was formed in 2012 and is a network of over 200 social movements, networks, organisations and affected communities resisting land grabs, extractive mining, exploitative wages and environmental destruction caused by transnational corporations (TNCs). The campaign's work focuses on developing a virtual observatory on TNCs, advancing global legal instruments to limit their power and strengthening grassroots campaigns. Seipato traces the emergence of TNCs within global capitalist accumulation, the facilitating role of neoliberalisation and the role of multilateral institutions in fostering their centrality. She also locates the resistance from the global South, including UNCTAD and the calls for a New International Economic Order. However, Seipato highlights that these were defeated attempts. Crucial in her analysis is the emergence of a global architecture of impunity which entrenches the sovereignty of TNCs against states, peoples and nature. She uses important case studies, such as the Marikana massacre of mineworkers in South Africa in their struggles against Lonmin mine, to illustrate how this impunity has worked. The chapter concludes with the challenges facing these courageous efforts to limit the power of TNCs in the southern African region.

In chapter 9, Alexander Gallas provides an explicit Luxemburgian analysis of mass strikes in the current global conjuncture of crisis. He frames his analysis on a reading of Luxemburg's pamphlet *The Mass Strike*, written as part of the run up to the first critical moment in the Russian revolutionary process of 1905, and brings to the fore parallel forms of power such as that of the Soviets. Gallas eschews thinking through historical analogy but provides a reading of Luxemburg's pamphlet that focuses on similarities to our contemporary period. He starts by conceptually clarifying the notion of the mass strike and its characteristics. Thereafter he affirms Luxemburg's methodological approach in thinking through the relevance and political necessity of the mass strike. Luxemburg did not view the mass strike as producing the revolution. Rather, she stressed that it was conjunctural conditions that gave rise to the mass strike; it was a weapon of struggle that could not be advanced under all circumstances. Moreover, conjunctural crisis conditions, particularly modes of politically managing the crisis, also posed a challenge for an adequate response from the working class. With this approach Gallas unpacks key features of the current global conjuncture of crisis, which includes an onslaught on trade unions and worker rights. He provides a rough sketch of defensive mass strikes that have registered in different parts of the world in the conjuncture of crisis and then grounds this in a comparison of mass defensive strikes in the US and India.

In chapter 10, Nivedita Majumdar resituates the Indian novel in the context of neoliberal capitalism. To do so, she engages critically with the commentary of two acclaimed literary texts, Kiran Desai's *The Inheritance of Loss* (2006) and Arvind Adiga's *The White Tiger* (2008). Both these texts have been vaunted as challenging the enduring scourge of neo-colonialism. Majumdar argues this is a misreading related to how the field of cultural studies has developed, which does not read or conceive of neoliberal capitalism as a phenomenon distinct from colonialism. Moreover, she argues that prominent theorists such as Gaytri Spivak and Partha Chatterjee have also elided the distinctions between neo-colonialism and neoliberal capitalism. Instead, they conflate Western domination with neoliberal capitalism. On the other hand, theorists like Walter Mignolo also provide an understanding of coloniality as continuing under neoliberal capitalism. Both conceptual understandings undermine a reading of the historical specificity of capitalism in the global South, including the role of neoliberalism. This critique allows Majumdar to re-read the critical commentary of the two novels from the standpoint of contemporary neoliberal capitalism and the dialectic capital versus labour in contemporary India. From this perspective culture and the literary form also have a crucial place in resistance against the brutalisation and inhumanity of neoliberal capitalism, both by domestic capitalists and imperial forces.

NOTES

1 In this regard, the extensive works of world-systems thinkers are useful.
2 See https://www.thebalance.com/who-is-paul-volcker-3306157 (accessed 29 May 2019).
3 See https://www.whitehouse.gov/wp-content/uploads/2017/12/NSS-Final-12-18-2017-09 05.pdf (accessed 2 August 2019).
4 See https://www.globalresearch.ca/it-is-imperative-to-reconstruct-the-internationale-of-workers-and-peoples/5601602 (accessed 3 August 2019).
5 See https://www.pambazuka.org/global-south/letter-intent-inaugural-meeting-international-workers-and-peoples (accessed 3 August 2019).

REFERENCES

Amin, S. 1970. *Accumulation on a World Scale: A Critique of the Theory of Underdevelopment*. New York and London: Monthly Review Press.

Amin, S. 2001. 'Imperialism and globalization', *Monthly Review* 53 (2). Accessed 29 May 2019, https://monthlyreview.org/2001/06/01/imperialism-and-globalization/.

Amin, S. 2004. *The Liberal Virus: Permanent War and the Americanization of the World*. New York: Monthly Review Press.

Amin, S. 2006. *Beyond US Hegemony? Assessing the Prospects for a Multipolar World*. Beirut: World Book Publishing.

Amin, S. 2010. *From Capitalism to Civilization: Reconstructing the Socialist Perspective*. New Delhi: Tulika Books.

Arrighi, G. 2007. *Adam Smith in Beijing: Lineages of the Twenty-first Century*. New York: Verso.

Beer, M. (1897) 2011. 'Modern English imperialism'. In R.B. Day and D. Gaido (trans. and eds) *Discovering Imperialism: Social Democracy to World War I*. Chicago, IL.: Haymarket Books, pp. 95–108.

Bellofiore, R. 2004. '"Like a candle burning at both ends": Rosa Luxemburg and the critique of political economy', *Research in Political Economy* 21: 279–298.

Brewer, A. 1990. *Marxist Theories of Imperialism: A Critical Survey*. London and New York: Routledge.

Day, R.B. and Gaido D. (trans. and eds). 2011. 'Introduction'. In *Discovering Imperialism: Social Democracy to World War I*. Chicago, IL.: Haymarket Books, pp. 1–94.

Ferguson, N. 2002. *Empire: The Rise and Demise of the British World Order and the Lessons for Global Power*. New York: Basic Books.

Fraser, N. and Jaeggi, R. 2018. *Capitalism: A Conversation in Critical Theory*. Cambridge and Medford: Polity.

Gowan, P. 1999. *The Global Gamble: Washington's Faustian Bid for Global Dominance*. New York: Verso Books.

Harvey, D. 2003. *The New Imperialism*. Oxford: Oxford University Press.

Louis, P. (1904) 2011. 'An essay on imperialism'. In R.B. Day and D. Gaido (trans. and eds) *Discovering Imperialism: Social Democracy to World War I*. Chicago, IL: Haymarket Books, pp. 291–300.

Luxemburg, R. (1913) 2003. *The Accumulation of Capital*. London and New York: Routledge.

O'Neill J. 2001. *Building Better Global Economic BRICS*. Global Economics Paper No. 66. New York: Goldman Sachs Economic Research Group. Accessed 29 May 2019, https://www.goldmansachs.com/insights/archive/archive-pdfs/build-better-brics.pdf.

Pieterse, J.N. 2018. *Multipolar Globalization: Emerging Economies and Development.* Oxon and New York: Routledge.

Satgar, V. 2015. 'From Marx to the systemic crises of capitalist civilisation'. In V. Satgar (ed.) *Capitalism's Crises: Class Struggles in South Africa and the World.* Johannesburg: Wits University Press, pp. 20–49.

Satgar, V. 2018. 'The climate crisis and systemic alternatives'. In V. Satgar (ed.) *The Climate Crisis: South African and Global Democratic Eco-Socialist Alternatives.* Johannesburg: Wits University Press, pp. 1–27.

GLOBAL CRISIS, BRICS AND RIVALRY

2

FOSSIL CAPITAL, IMPERIALISM AND THE GLOBAL CORPORATE ELITE

William K. Carroll

mperialism – a rich concept in the geopolitical economy of monopoly capital and a key theme of this volume – bears multiple meanings. My own research programme, which has centred upon the social organisation of corporate power, has drawn primarily upon the Hilferding-Bukharin-Lenin interpretation of imperialism as the 'highest stage' of capitalism (Lenin 1917). Under imperialism, giant corporations and financial institutions, based (initially) in the advanced capitalist states but accumulating capital internationally, and controlled by an elite of finance capitalists, come to dominate the world economy (Bukharin 1973; Hilferding 1981). Imperialism brings a massive concentration of economic power, as large-scale industrial and financial capitals become more integrated in symbiotic relations, evident in elite networks of interlocking directorates. Imperialism also implies geopolitical economic relations *among* imperialist powers (ranging from rivalry to cooperation and recently, 'global governance'), *between* imperialist ruling classes and dominant classes on capitalism's periphery (the articulation of modes of production) and *between* ruling classes and oppressed peoples (national oppression/liberation) (Weeks 1981: 121–122). Imperialism does not stand still, but is continually developing through the capital-logic of accumulation and the statist logic of territorialisation (Harvey 2003), most recently as 'neoliberal imperialism' (Rahnema 2017).

The imperialism of the twenty-first century's second decade is indeed distinct from what Lenin declared to be capitalism's 'highest stage'. To make sense of it, and of corporate power's organisation within it, we need first to take account of the changes. One has to do with the (uneven) industrialisation of the global South and the associated transnationalisation of markets, which Lenin (following Marx) predicted as an outcome of imperialism. In consequence, 'in today's global capitalism, the "home market" for big capital is the world market. Capital moves from one location to another to maximise profits and minimise costs, and globalisation has, in a sense, made notions like "export of capital" and "surplus capital" irrelevant' (Rahnema 2017). And in contrast to the classic imperialist division of the world among rivals, 'a major feature of the imperialism of the twenty-first century is the existence of a super-imperialist, the United States, on the one hand, and inter-imperialist collaborations on the other . . . The G7 is the clear example of inter-imperialist collaboration' (Rahnema 2017).

Indeed, since 1945, imperialism has been US-led, but never a purely American project. Yet given the existential crisis humanity now faces – the prospect of runaway global warming – we must complicate the narrative further. Staying momentarily with Lenin, his 1920 declaration 'Communism is Soviet power plus the electrification of the whole country' (Lenin 1920) did not anticipate the implications of burgeoning carbon emissions from electricity generation.[1] If, as Trotsky (1936) held, Stalin's abolition of workers' councils – the defeat of Soviet power – was a decisive blow to socialism in the USSR, industrialisation there followed exactly the same logic as elsewhere, converting the 'buried sunshine' of fossil fuels into massive quantities of energy and ever-growing carbon emissions. Indeed, with imperialism, 'fossil capital' – companies that extract and refine oil, natural gas, bitumen and coal – became both prime mover and a leading industrial sector worldwide. 'The connection between increased fossil fuel use and imperialist adventures in oil-rich countries is an obvious one. One of the primary reasons for US imperial expansion [was], of course, to control access to, and the marketing of oil (the other being US capitalist hegemony). This, in turn, creates further environmental degradation and destruction, both in the US, and worldwide' (Cole 2017: 162). Fossil capital has driven both climate change and imperialism. This sector counts among its ranks many of the world's largest corporations – some state-owned, others controlled by (groups of) capitalists.

Reflecting the extractivist logic of imperialism, until recently, the pattern has been for Northern-based international oil companies (IOCs) to be 'resource seeking' while Southern-based national oil companies (NOCs) have been 'market seeking'. Yet rapid economic growth in Brazil-Russia-India-China-South Africa (BRICS) and elsewhere heralds 'an emerging world political order defined less by the economic and political power of the USA. The growing transnational activity of resource-seeking, state-owned oil firms – like PetroChina, the Oil and Natural Gas Corporation (ONGC) and Petrobras – is a powerful expression of these geo-economic and geopolitical shifts' (Le Billon and Bridge 2017: 46). The state-owned status of these firms (sometimes in combination with a distribution of shares to private investors) is significant, as is their strategy of transnationalisation in competition with the IOCs for access to resources (Le Billon and Bridge 2017). In 2005 NOCs controlled approximately 77 per cent of global oil and gas reserves, in contrast to 1949, when the Seven Sisters controlled 88 per cent of the entire oil trade (World Energy Council 2016: 19). Shifts of this sort suggest that the power structure of imperialism, as it has been organised in and around the carbon energy sector, has also been shifting.

This chapter maps the transnational network of fossil capital as a formation of leading capitalists and their advisors, embedded within a global corporate elite. That elite forms one part of a wider imperialist order. I first bring a political ecology of fossil capital into a brief reconstruction of the eras through which imperialism has moved since the late nineteenth century. This sets the stage for a network analysis that explores how capitalist interests based in different locales, North and South, participate in the transnational network of fossil capital, and what the pattern of participation implies for imperialism today.

ERAS OF IMPERIALISM

Eras of imperialism have been interdependent with epochal shifts in fossil capitalism (see table 2.1). Broadly, we can distinguish an emergent phase, during Pax Britannia (covering the latter half of the nineteenth century), a classic phase from the early twentieth century to 1945, a post-war phase termed Pax Americana (Cox 1987), and a post-1970s phase as American hegemony gave way to 'global governance', partially integrating high-growth Southern countries (notably, the BRICS). During each phase, fossil capital has played a pivotal role within a changing global political economy and ecology.

Pax Britannia was the era of King Coal, and of transition from competitive capitalism organised around national markets to monopoly capitalism. As 'Victorian Britain scanned the planet for coal' (Malm 2016: 230), establishing extractive facilities in Asia, British North America, Trinidad, Tasmania and elsewhere, Pax Britannia created a Lockean heartland governed by market society and a burgeoning world market (Van der Pijl 1998), alongside deepening colonisation. From the 1860s onward, late-industrialisers like Germany and Japan developed state-centred

Table 2.1 Historical eras of imperialism

Era	Geopolitical economy	Political ecology of fossil capital
Pax Britannia Mid to late nineteenth century	Free trade, the end of competitive capitalism, colonisation of the South	King Coal; steam-powered industrialisation and transport
Classic imperialism Twentieth century to 1945	Great-power rivalry for control of colonies, resources and markets, finance capital and monopoly capitalism	Rise of Big Oil; Seven Sisters develop oilfields in the Middle East, Sumatra, Mexico etc.; emergence of automobility
Pax Americana Post World War 2 to 1970s	US Open Door policy within Cold War, transnational corporations, Fordism, neocolonialism and national liberation	Carbon democracy; full-throttle automobility; oil becomes lifeblood of consumer capitalism; burgeoning CO_2 emissions
Neoliberal global governance Late 1970s – today	Decline of US hegemony and state socialism; neoliberal globalisation via 'global governance'; rise of BRICS and the global South	Rapid growth of NOCs; gathering climate crisis; increasing resort to extreme oil; looming carbon bubble; emergence of 'climate capitalism'

Source: Author.

capitalist regimes – 'challenger states' designed to catch up with the Lockean formations (Van der Pijl 1998).

The second era witnessed the rise and then consolidation of Big Oil and modern imperialism. Within each major power (including Japan), giant corporations and banks controlled by financial-industrial elites, aligned closely with their national states, dominated the economy, generating voluminous economic surpluses that could not be fully absorbed by the domestic market. Finance capital internationalised a world divided among the major powers, engendering pitched rivalries over control of colonies (including the oil-rich Middle East) as zones of cheap labour, resource extraction and capital export, and leading to two world wars. Yet it would soon become clear that modern imperialism is about more than the geopolitical economy of monopoly capital. The success of the Russian Revolution spurred into existence the second dimension of imperialism: the containment of socialist possibilities worldwide. Embodied in the first 'coalition of the willing' (including Britain, France, the US, Italy and Japan), which attempted to put down the Bolshevik regime, this refers to the fact that, alongside rivalry, leading capitalist powers have a common interest in preventing socialist transformation, particularly in the global South.

During Pax Americana (1945–1970s) – an era of unprecedented growth stoked by the massive destruction of capital during World War 2 – oil displaced coal as the fossil fuel of choice and the Middle East overtook the US as the leading producing region. As the defeated Axis powers were brought into a dramatically enlarged Lockean heartland under American hegemony, colonial empires were supplanted by a system of global governance revolving around the US Open Door policy, the Bretton Woods Agreement, and the United Nations. Transnational corporations thrived amid an increasing international circulation of financial capital. But if in this Cold War era inter-imperialist rivalries ebbed, imperialist efforts to repress socialist regimes in the South and the East were redoubled, channelling national-liberation into passive revolutions, and repressing radical developments when necessary.

In the North, as a Fordist regime of 'carbon democracy' integrated workers into a class compromise backstopped by consumerism (Mitchell 2011), fossil capitalism expanded 'into every aspect of life and every part of the globe' (Angus 2016: 152), with petroleum products as its 'lifeblood' (Huber 2013). So began a sharp increase in global carbon emissions.[2] This was also an era of anti-imperialist struggles in the global South and resource nationalism. Iran's nationalisation of the forerunner to BP provoked a 1953 CIA-orchestrated coup which restored control of Iranian oil to the private companies, but Iran retained ownership of oil resources – a first in the Middle East. Brazil's Petrobras was established in 1953, followed by India's ONGC in 1956. In 1960 Saudi Arabia and Venezuela established the Organization of the Petroleum Exporting Countries (OPEC) in response to a unilateral move by northern-based IOCs to cut prices. A second nationalisation wave occurred around the time of the 1973 Arab Oil Embargo, with Iraq (1972), Qatar (1974), Malaysia (1974), Venezuela (1975), Kuwait (1975), Nigeria (1977) and finally Saudi Arabia (1980) forming national oil companies (De Graaff 2013: 67–75). In tandem with all this was the increasing reach of TNCs and of global finance.

The 1970s brought transition to a fourth era as the Northern Fordist accumulation regime unravelled while technological advances in transportation and (later) information processing stimulated transnationalisation of production and finance. In place of the classic articulation of capitalist and pre-capitalist modes of production, the new imperialism effected a selective industrialisation of the periphery, which globalised mass consumerism and its carbon footprint, yet continued imperialism's super-exploitation of low-wage labour on the periphery (Chesnais 2016: 170–172) while collaterally dragging working-class subsistence in the core downward (Carroll 2003). At the same time, neoliberalisation and financialisation accentuated accumulation by dispossession (Harvey 2003) through International

Monetary Fund (IMF)-mandated 'structural adjustment', land grabs and the commodification of nature in the global South.

Concomitantly, in the face of declining US hegemony (already signalled by the 1971 abrogation of the Bretton Woods sanctioned dollar standard and the 1973 military loss in Vietnam), the tendency toward collective imperialism through 'global governance' was further cemented. Neoliberalism's flowering in the 1980s and 1990s brought new institutions and frameworks (the World Trade Organization and investor-rights agreements such as the North American Free Trade Agreement) and repurposed familiar ones (such as the World Bank) to suit neoliberal logic. The Soviet bloc's collapse and China's turn to state capitalism allayed imperial concerns with the red menace, although developments such as South African liberation and, later, the Latin American 'pink tide' continued to require attention.

Most tellingly for the essays in this volume, the era witnessed the rise of BRICS, posing the challenge of their integration through expanded global governance arrangements (such as the G20, and the Conference of the Parties [COP]). Although the wave of resource nationalism receded in neoliberalism's heyday, the past quarter century has witnessed a resurgence. BRICS and other resource-holders renegotiated terms of trade while their NOCs (most dramatically China's), which formerly sought control over resources within their territories, looked outward, as the motors of capital accumulation shifted from the Triad to the global South (De Graaff 2013: 84–87; cf. Stephen 2014: 928).

Finally, declining reserves of high-grade petroleum have led to the mining of 'extreme carbon' (Pineault 2018) – tar sands, fracking and deep water drilling – entailing lower energy return on investment, greater ecological risk and in the case of bitumen extraction, higher carbon emissions. But the deepening climate crisis has also inspired political gestures toward climate mitigation and new accumulation strategies around 'clean energy', jeopardising the value of carbon reserves, which now appear as potentially stranded assets, and creating momentum within monopoly capital toward fossil-fuel divestment.

Whether recent developments such as the 2008 global financial meltdown and its aftermath in 'new austerity' and resurgent authoritarian-populist movements, including Trumpism, herald the beginning of a fifth imperialist era is unclear. Currently the US does double duty as both dominant imperialist and rogue state. Geopolitical rivalries have sharpened, placing global governance under stress. The climate crisis appears to be approaching tipping points sooner than (conservatively) projected by the Intergovernmental Panel on Climate Change, putting fossil capital under challenge from activist and even scientific communities. Yet carbon continues to power capitalism, and since carbon is extracted from specific places, imperialist practices in the control of territory (mines as well as transport infrastructures) form part of the accumulation process – whether in the river deltas of Nigeria or the coalfields of Columbia.

Meanwhile, globalisation proceeds in massive efforts to build infrastructure mega-corridors to 'annihilate space by time' as Marx once put it (Hildyard and Sol 2017: 19). Most ambitiously, China's Belt and Road Initiative (BRI), launched in 2013, endeavours to create free trade areas along transportation corridors that will link China to West Asia, Europe and Africa, where it is an increasingly significant foreign investor (*ChinaPower* 2018). How such initiatives fit into the structures of imperialism is an important issue. Many of the global oligopolies of BRICS countries are state owned; indeed, such companies account for 80 per cent of stock market capitalisation in China and 62 per cent in Russia, and 'everywhere oil and natural gas companies are important (PetroChina, Gazprom, Petrobras, Indian Oil Corporation)' (Chesnais 2016: 149).

THE TRANSNATIONAL NETWORK OF FOSSIL CAPITAL AND ITS NEIGHBOURS

In this context, I map fossil capital's leading 50 firms as a segment of corporate business still central in geopolitical economy, and integral to a 'regime of obstruction' that blocks urgently needed transformations that could usher in a post-imperial energy democracy. The regime has many threads and colours – from lobbying and policy planning focused on market-based remedies, through research into technological solutions such as geoengineering, to media power in framing discourse, and so on. But at its core is a global corporate elite in which fossil capital remains a strong force (Carroll 2020; Wright and Nyberg 2015).

The research literature shows that in the late phase of Pax Americana, a transnational network of bankers and industrialists, connected through their interlocking corporate directorships, was consolidated (Fennema 1982). In the era of neoliberal global governance the network expanded (Carroll 2010), and was preserved through the 2008 global financial meltdown (Heemskerk et al. 2016b). The global network of five million corporations is clustered into 14 geographically centred corporate communities, with ties spanning across them (Heemskerk et al. 2016a). Reflecting the structure of imperialism and Northern-based finance capital, the global corporate elite has centred upon the North Atlantic (Carroll 2018; Van der Pijl 1984). Yet with the uneven development of capitalism's semi-periphery, corporate interests based in high-growth Southern states have gained position on the margins. The elite network provides a command structure for transnational finance capital, even as geopolitical changes have been underway, as in the rise of BRICS.

The network analysis that follows explores how fossil capital is positioned within that structure, both geographically and vis-à-vis other economic sectors. It builds upon Naná de Graaff's research on transnational oil elites and the rise of NOCs based mainly in the global South. Mapping the interlocking directorates among the world's largest oil corporations in 1997 and 2007, she distinguishes between companies based in Organisation for Economic Co-operation and Development (OECD) countries (most of them privately owned IOCs) and companies based in the global South (most of them state-owned NOCs) and finds that in the decade spanning the turn of the last century,

- There was very little elite integration between the two segments;
- Interlocking directorates were much less common among the non-OECD-based firms;
- OECD-based companies, while centred in national corporate communities, engaged in extensive transnational interlocking, while non-OECD-based firms rarely engaged;
- Whereas OECD-based oil elites often sit on the boards of transnational policy-planning organisations such as the World Economic Forum, non-OECD NOCs do not participate in these sites of global capitalist governance. Instead, their boards tend to be 'intimately linked' to their respective owning states, with NOC directors often holding ministerial or vice-ministerial state positions (2013: 149).

De Graaff concludes that the shift in ownership of reserves from IOCs to NOCs has transformed the global energy order, in a 'contradictory dynamic' of capitalist transnationalisation and in the reassertion of state power. Yet, as NOCs increasingly take up 'roles previously reserved for IOCs by expanding beyond their borders', they have not established many elite ties to the old order (2013: 198). A key question for us is whether the state-owned oil companies of Southern-based fossil capital have become more integrated with the Northern-centred corporate power structure, or if there are signs that they are forming their own elite.

METHOD

This study builds on and extends De Graaff's in several ways. De Graaff analysed the directorates of five leading NOCs and five leading IOCs and mapped their board affiliations with other major corporations as of 2007. This study examines the world's 50 largest carbon-capital corporations and the entire network of interlocking directorates in which they are embedded, as of 2018.

The current research required a two-step, snowball sampling of corporations. First, the Top 50 fossil-capital corporations (hereafter, fossils) were identified, using *Fortune* magazine's Global 500 (published in 2017) as the main source. Five of *Fortune's* Top 12 are oil and gas giants (Sinopec ranked 3, China National Petroleum ranked 4, Royal Dutch Shell ranked 7, ExxonMobil ranked 10, BP ranked 12), underlining the continuing global importance of fossil capital. Data on the directors and executives of Top-50 firms were downloaded from the online database ORBIS which, despite some discrepancies, meets basic research standards (Heemskerk et al. 2017).

In the second step, corporations with revenue at least as large as that of the smallest Top-50 fossils ($16 billion US), whose boards interlock with any of the Top-50 fossils, were added to the sample, yielding 111 additional corporations. The revenue filter ensures that we include only the world's largest corporations – no corporation in the analysis is smaller than the 50th largest fossil. Twelve of the Top-50 fossils showed no interlocks with any of the 111 non-fossil firms; thus our network mapping proceeds on the basis of 149 firms: 38 carbon-extractive companies and their immediate neighbours in the elite network. This snowball sample enables us to map the network of *overlapping neighbourhoods* that surround the world's largest fossil-capital companies, each neighbourhood being comprised of all the large corporations that directly interlock with a given fossil. The composition of those neighbourhoods, and how they are configured into the wider network, can illuminate the state of play at the commanding heights of fossil capitalism.

FINDINGS

Overall, the Top 50 is split between state-owned (NOC) and investor-owned (IOC) enterprises, in a striking, if predictable, regional differentiation (table 2.2). With the exception of Moscow-based Lukoil, the IOCs are all domiciled in countries of the Triad, including the US (nine firms), Canada (three), Japan (three), Britain (two), South Korea (two) and various European states. With the exception of Norway's Statoil, all NOCs are domiciled in the global South. This category includes BRICS, other Latin American countries and Middle-East petro-states, some of which rank among the world's wealthiest according to GDP per capita. BRICS contribute five firms based in China, four based in India, three in Russia and one in Brazil. The

Table 2.2 Composition of the Top 50 fossil corporations, 2018

Region	Ownership		Total
	Private: IOC	State: NOC	
North America	12	0	12
Europe	7	1	8
Rich Asia-Pacific	6	0	6
Asia, including Middle East	0	17	17
Russia	1	2	3
Latin America	0	4	4
Total	26	24	50

Source: Author.

NOCs of the United Arab Emirates, Kuwait, Saudi Arabia, Iran and Qatar in the Middle East, Indonesia, Malaysia and Thailand in East Asia and Columbia, Mexico and Venezuela in Latin America complete the list.[3] The 25 IOCs based in countries of the Triad claim 51.4% of total Top-50 revenue (most of which is split between companies based in the US [21.7%] and Europe [23.1%]); the 23 NOCs based in the global South claim 43.9% (most of which is split between the Middle East [17.1%] and China [11.3%]).

Centrality, neighbourhoods and fringes

To discern how fossil capital is articulated with the contemporary structure of finance capital, I now consider which fossils are most central in the elite network. In this analysis, two companies are considered to be directly linked if their boards of directors or top executives are interlocked – if they share one or more directors or executives. A basic measure of a firm's centrality in the elite network is the size of its immediate neighbourhood, that is, the number of other firms with which it is interlocked (also known as its neighbours in the network). I also consider, as a related measure, 'two-step reach': how many other companies a given firm is linked to at one remove, as its directors or top executives and those of another firm sit on a common third directorate (table 2.3). Two-step reach measures the size of the fringe that immediately surrounds a firm's neighbourhood. Companies whose neighbours are especially central in the network will show elevated two-step reach.

The most central fossil-fuel firms are, with two exceptions, Triad-based. The leading six include the continuing versions of the Seven Sisters (ExxonMobil,

Table 2.3 The most central fossil corporations in the global interlock network

Name	ICO or NOC	Domicile	Size of neighbourhood	Two-step reach (fringe)
1. Total	ICO	France	19	23
2. ExxonMobil	ICO	US	16	44
3. ConocoPhillips	ICO	US	14	33
4. Shell	ICO	UK/Netherlands	13	33
5. BP	ICO	UK	13	30
6. Chevron	ICO	US	11	30
7. Marathon Petroleum	ICO	US	6	24
8. PetroChina	NOC	China	6	11
9. Phillips 66	ICO	US	5	17
10. Rosneft	ICO	Russia	4	12
11. Statoil	NOC	Norway	4	11
12. Valero	ICO	US	3	13
13. BHP Billiton	ICO	Australia/UK	3	5
14. Cosmo Energy	ICO	Japan	3	1
15. China Shenhua	NOC	China	3	0

Source: Author.

ConocoPhillips, Shell, BP, Chevron), plus Paris-based Total (excluded from the original Seven Sisters because it was state-owned at the time). Although Total has the largest immediate neighbourhood, five of the six most central companies are US- or UK-based.[4] These also have extensive fringes: each is embedded in a well-integrated subnetwork, so that its directors sit on other boards that are themselves well-connected. The nine other firms have much smaller neighbourhoods and, with the exception of US-based Marathon Petroleum and Phillips 66, much smaller fringes. They include three US-based ICOs (Marathon, Phillips 66, Valero); thus, half of the Top 12 are American. PetroChina's neighbourhood is 8th largest, although its fringe is modest; the same holds for Moscow-based Rosneft and Norway's Statoil, each of them state-owned (although Rosneft is partly owned by BP). The next three, whose neighbourhoods rank 13 to 15, include two major coal producers (Melbourne-based BHP Billiton and Beijing-headquartered China Shenhua) plus Tokyo-based Cosmo Energy. Although these have three immediate neighbours, their fringes are small: they interlock with companies on the margins of the network.

The other 35 fossils have neighbourhoods of two (seven companies) or one (16), or are entirely isolated from the elite network (12). Except for ExxonMobil's majority-owned Canadian subsidiary Imperial Oil, their fringes are small.[5] Clearly, network participation is highly selective, and the corporate interests that dominated oil imperialism throughout the twentieth century continue to be centrally positioned. In our Top 50, the 35 firms with neighbourhoods of two or fewer account for only 20 per cent of all interlocks involving any of the 50 fossils, while the six most central companies (all veteran IOCs) account for 50 per cent.

A key factor shaping how extensively corporations participate in the elite network is whether they are state owned or owned by private investors. In the latter case, each corporate board brings together associated capitalists and their advisors in the quest for profit; in the former, the firm is more likely to be managed by state officials, to take on projects of 'national development' (often identical to profit-maximisation, but sometimes carrying distinct mandates), and to be less engaged with capital markets – all of which may contribute to network marginality (Carroll 2010). Among the Top 50, ten of the 12 that showed no interlocks with sizeable corporations are NOCs based in the South. The two non-state-owned isolates are based respectively in Japan and Poland.[6] On the other hand, among the 38 fossils in the transnational elite network, 24 are based in the Triad (including Australia and South Korea with Japan as its Asia-Pacific corner), and 22 of those are owned by investors, not states. Northern-based fossil capital has developed under the control of associated capitalists, who form a transnational business community, with investments often spread across many venues. Southern-based fossil capital tends to be state-owned and detached from or marginal in the network (though these companies may be prominent in their state-society complexes).

Communities in the network

A second issue is, how is the network differentiated into subnetworks and communities? If Southern-based fossil capital is relatively marginal in the transnational network, one reason is apparent in the results of a component analysis. For our purposes, a component is a set of companies whose boards/executives are all either directly or indirectly interlocked, forming a connected network. The 149 companies that interlock with other major corporations are actually arrayed in 13 distinct network components (each one detached from all the others). Most firms belong to the *dominant component* of 113 (examined below), but 36 (20 of them fossil-fuel firms) participate only in 12 minor components ranging in size from two to five. Figure 2.1 displays these isolated mini-networks, with the Triad-based components on the left and the Southern-based ones on the right.

In figure 2.1, all 15 of the Southern-based corporations are state-owned enterprises; all but two of the 21 Triad-based companies are investor-owned. The two exceptional cases are also instructive. S-Oil of Seoul is a 64 per cent owned subsidiary of Saudi Aramco, with which it is interlocked; Cepsa of Madrid is majority owned by Abu Dhabi state investor Mubadala Investment Company, and shares a director with Abu Dhabi Oil. Mubadala also owns a 21 per cent stake in Tokyo-based Cosmo Oil, and since 2014 Cepsa has had a 'strategic partnership' with Cosmo, reinforced by an interlocking directorship.[7] Departing from the classic structure of imperialism, these exemplify Middle Eastern petro-states recycling earnings into strategic investments that offer control and influence in Northern-based fossil firms.

On the right-hand side of figure 2.1, the remaining Southern firms are all based in the BRIC countries. Six are state-owned Chinese firms (two of them fossils – CNOOC and China Shenhua) that link among themselves in components of four and two; four are state-owned Indian firms (all of them fossils) configured as a chain. Giant Russia-owned investment bank Sberbank interlocks with Rome-based Eni SpA, while Brazil's Petrobras shares a director with London hotelier Compass. On the left-hand side of the sociogram, 20 of the 36 firms detached from the dominant component are investor-controlled corporations, all based in the Triad (five

Figure 2.1 Twelve minor components in the network

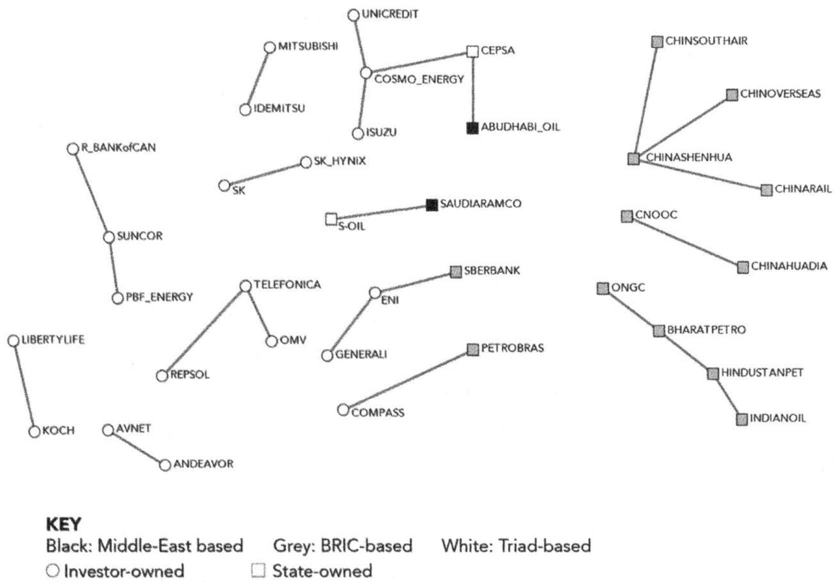

KEY
Black: Middle-East based   Grey: BRIC-based   White: Triad-based
○ Investor-owned   □ State-owned

Source: Author.
Note: See the appendix for explanations of the abbreviations.

in the US, four in Japan, three in Italy, two in South Korea, two in Canada, two in Spain, one in the UK, one in Austria).

Turning to the dominant component of 113 connected corporations (including 18 fossil-fuel companies), two factors seem important in shaping its structure: the geopolitical and the economic-sectoral (distinguishing between fossil capital, financial capital and other industries). *All but ten of the 113 corporations are based in the Triad.* Fully 43 are US-based; 15 are based in the UK, 12 in France, ten in Canada, four in Germany, 14 elsewhere in the North Atlantic region, one in Japan, four in Australia, six in China, two in Russia and two in Latin America. As for economic sectors, besides the 18 fossil-capital corporations, the dominant component includes 27 financial institutions and 68 companies in other industries. Its ten Southern members are evenly split between fossil-fuel firms and their neighbours, (the latter includes three China-based financial institutions).

The geopolitical stands out in an analysis of the relatively cohesive 'communities' embedded in the dominant component. For present purposes, a community is a subnetwork in which interlocking occurs predominantly among its members rather than between members and non-members.[8] Figure 2.2 groups the 113 firms into three communities. Node size is proportionate to neighbourhood size. Fossil-capital firms are black, financials white and other industries grey.

Geographically, the network is divided between a large community of 52 mainly American corporations (at the top right of figure 2.2), a smaller Franco-German-Canadian configuration of 31 (at the bottom), and a third, loosely-knit, diverse community of 30 in which British capital predominates (at the top left). Fully 91.1 per cent of the 257 interlocks in the dominant component occur *within* the three communities, underlining their coherence as distinct formations. Only nine interlocks link the US-centred community to the French-German-Canadian one; eight link the latter to the UK-centred community; 12 connect the US and UK-centred communities.

The US-centred community includes 41 of the 43 US-based corporations in the dominant component, plus a smattering of British, Canadian, other European, Latin American and Chinese companies.[9] Organised around five US-based fossils, notably ExxonMobil, ConocoPhillips and Chevron – all descendants of Standard Oil – this community also includes ExxonMobil's majority-owned Canadian subsidiary Imperial Oil as well as the Columbia-based NOC, Ecopetrol. Most other participants are US-based industrial corporations, such as GE, Boeing and Caterpillar, and major US-based financial institutions such as Morgan Stanley, Morgan Chase and Amex. *The community's American composition, its tightly knit organisation and its comparatively sparse ties to the other communities suggest that fossil capital continues to occupy a central position in the American corporate community.*

43

44

Figure 2.2 Three communities in the fossil-capital network

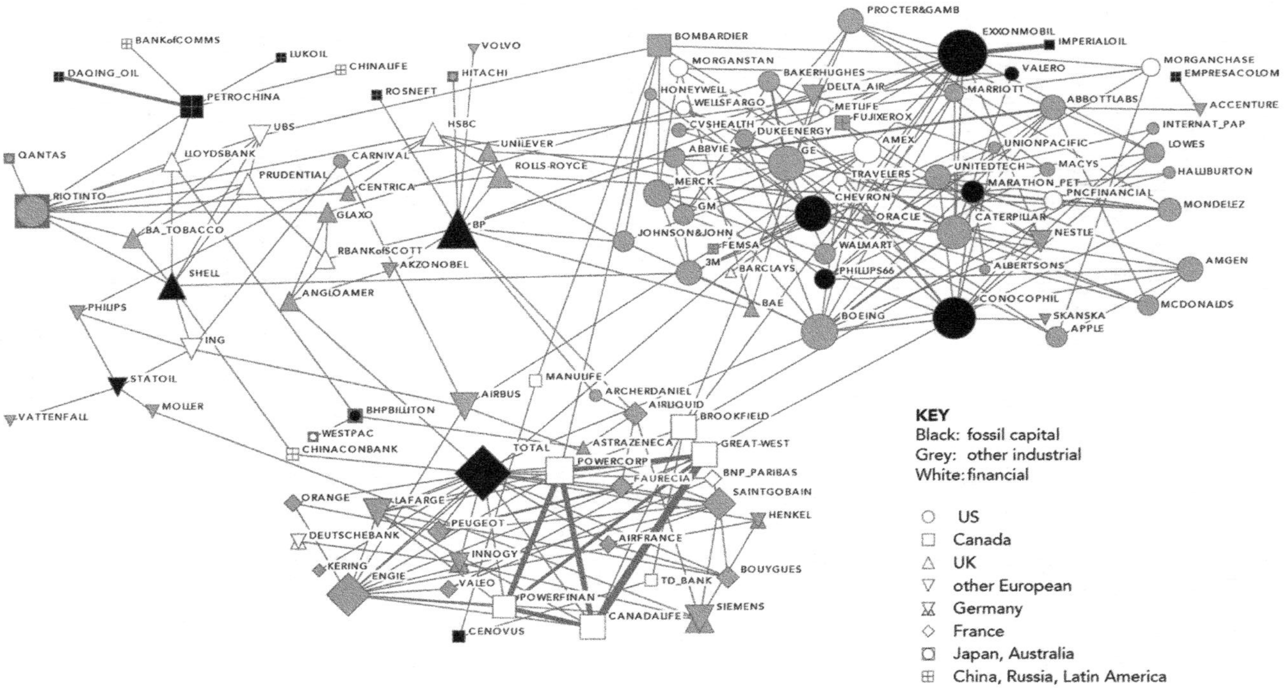

KEY
Black: fossil capital
Grey: other industrial
White: financial

○ US
□ Canada
◁ UK
▽ other European
⋈ Germany
◇ France
▭ Japan, Australia
⊞ China, Russia, Latin America

Source: Author.
Note: See the appendix for explanations of the abbreviations.

In the Franco-German-Canadian configuration fossil capital is much less prominent. Total of Paris plays an integrative role, but the community includes only two other fossil-fuel companies, Australia-based BHP Billiton (which is co-managed in London) and Canada-based Cenovus Energy. Yet it includes 11 financial institutions and 17 other industrials. Power Corporation of Canada has major investments in both Canadian and European companies, accounting for its multiple-director interlocks with three other Canadian financial institutions as well as its interlocks with cement maker LafargeHolcim and Total, in which Power Corporation holds stakes. BNP Paribas, Deutsche Bank, natural gas utility Engie, Airbus and Siemens also belong to this community. All 12 of the French, all four of the German and eight of ten Canadian firms in the dominant component are members, along with two Australian firms, one Dutch, one Swiss, one American and one Chinese firm, the China Construction Bank. Notably, that bank interlocks with Total, but also with Shell, a member of the UK-centred community with an equally strong presence on the European Continent.

The third community is the most transnationalised. Joining twelve UK-based firms are companies headquartered in ten other countries, most prominently China (four), the Netherlands (three), Russia, Sweden and Australia (two each). Seven of the Top 50 fossil-fuel firms belong to this community, with BP, Shell and PetroChina in central locations. Mining giant Rio Tinto[10] (with head offices both in Melbourne and London) is by far the most central of the 15 non-fossil industrials in this community, interlocking with two major fossils (Shell and PetroChina), four other industrials and four financial institutions. As for the community's eight financial institutions, in addition to London-based HSBC, Prudential and Lloyds Bank, Basel-based UBS and Edinburgh's Royal Bank of Scotland are also centrally placed.

On the margins of the UK-centred community are four China-based and two Russia-based corporations. PetroChina figures importantly as a hub, interlocking on the one hand with Lloyds and Rio Tinto and on the other with two China-based financial institutions as well as China's Daqing Oil and Russia's privately owned Lukoil. Moscow-headquartered Rosneft, which is 50.01 per cent owned by the Russian state but 20 per cent owned by BP, shares a director with BP.

Despite such interlocks, BRICS-based corporations have not become central players in what is still an overwhelmingly Northern formation of fossil capital and neighbouring firms. The six China-based and two Russia-based companies are relatively marginal in the dominant component, and no companies from India, Brazil or South Africa participate. It is also interesting that China's and Russia's elite ties lead not to the US but to the European corporate community, through interlocks with Total, Shell, BP, Lloyds Bank and Rio Tinto.[11]

Figure 2.3 Interlocks among eight major fossils and 23 financial institutions, 2018

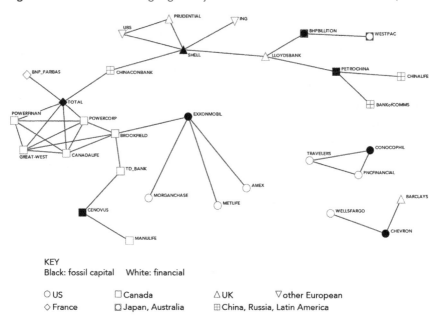

KEY
Black: fossil capital   White: financial

○ US   □ Canada   △ UK   ▽ other European
◇ France   ◌ Japan, Australia   ⊞ China, Russia, Latin America

Source: Author.
Note: See the appendix for explanations of the abbreviations.

Finally, to highlight the key financial-industrial relations in the elite network, figure 2.3 maps, as a subnetwork of the dominant component in figure 2.2, the eight fossils whose boards interlock with multiple financial institutions and the 23 financial institutions with which they interlock. Many of the financial-industrial interlocks link companies based in the same country, as in Total's interlock with BNP Paribas and ConocoPhillips's interlocks with Travelers and PNC Financial. Among the fossil-fuel companies, PetroChina, Shell and Total stand out as particularly transcontinental in their financial interlocks, each linking into both European and Chinese finance. The US firms and Canada's Cenovus are less transnational in their financial interlocking, except for two interlocks to other Anglo-American corporations. ExxonMobil shares a director with Toronto-based asset manager Brookfield Investments while Chevron's board interlocks with that of Barclays.

Our exploration of the neighbourhoods of the world's Top 50 fossil-fuel firms suggests (i) the continuing centrality of the fossil-capital sector within American capitalism, (ii) a weaker positioning of fossil capital on the European continent, and an incipient alignment of European and Chinese capital, both financial and industrial and (iii) the continuing marginality in the global corporate elite (with the partial exception of China) of Southern fossils. As mentioned earlier, this stems in part from the history of oil imperialism. Northern-based capital has been the dominant player, obliging Southern states eventually to launch NOCs which, however, are not immersed in global capital markets, nor in the corporate communities associated with those markets (Stephen 2014).

CONCLUSION

In the decade since De Graaff's study, Southern carbon elites have become only slightly more integrated into the global corporate elite, and most of that involves a single country, China. Now the world's largest economy according to the IMF,[12] China's elite ties lead mainly to European capital, which is not to deny China's co-dependency on the US, both as a market and an outlet for surplus capital. Importantly, the interlocks involve both Chinese fossil capital and Chinese financial capital, the latter being one of the largest funders of fossil capital today, with China Construction Bank (interlocked with both Total and Shell) at the top of the league table, according to research by the Rainforest Action Network.[13] But China's banks are also major funders of China's BRI, and acquisitions by Chinese companies in participating countries are soaring (*China Daily* 2017), while sovereign wealth funds from Kuwait and Qatar invest heavily in the same Chinese banks (Krahl 2013: 57). Intersecting circuits of finance capital (and joint ventures such as the 2011 deal between Shell and China National Petroleum Corporation [CNPC] to develop Qatar's gas fields [*China Daily* 2017]) complement and sometimes underlie elite-level interlocks – all pointing toward closer relations. US-based capital seems somewhat detached from these developments.

The transnational network is regionally clustered and overwhelmingly Northern, actually North-Atlantic, in composition. Its three distinct corporate communities make for an interesting contrast. Oil interests are central within the US corporate elite, but less so on the European continent. The UK-centred community occupies a middle ground in this respect. The network bears traces of geopolitical-economic history – the succession of two Anglophone hegemons in the ages of coal and oil, the Anglo-American legacy of the Seven Sisters, the Lockean heartland of an expanding imperialism. In all this we glimpse a structure of imperialism, into which a few NOCs have tentatively inserted themselves. Transnationalisation of ownership has engendered some North-South interlocks (Lukoil-BP, S-Oil-Saudi Aramco, Cosmo Energy-Cepsa-Abu Dhabi Oil), though these are marginal to the carbon-elite network overall. Still, such relations show that the Saudi and Abu Dhabi ruling classes have been gaining positon in Northern corporations.

The network of fossil capital provides a distinctive view of the shifting shape of imperialism. With De Graaff, we can acknowledge a sea change, as NOCs now control most oil reserves and even account for the lion's share of refining worldwide. Three of the BRICS – each home to three or more of the world's largest fossil firms – are major carbon-energy producers, as is Brazil, via Petrobras. Yet corporations based in other countries of the global South – most notably, in the Middle East – are also key players. The tendency to view BRICS as the main vehicle for Southern contender states may be a mis-specification, when we consider how regionalised global capitalism continues to be. BRICS is a summit-oriented group based on reverse trilateralism (Latin America, Africa, Eurasia), to counter the G7 leaders' summit. With two BRICS leaders now committed to far-right economic nationalism (Modi of India and Bolsonaro of Brazil), the future of this summit-oriented group is unclear (Ebrahim 2018). In contrast, the Shanghai Cooperation Organisation (SCO), formed in 2001, is an actual pact that deepens political and economic relations among its members, which include the three largest BRICS and contiguous states along China's BRI. Compared to the BRICS, SCO may prove to be the more important organisation of contender states. At SCO's June 2018 summit China committed to a US$4.6 billion lending facility to build the SCO as a community 'with a shared future with a view toward an inclusive world that enjoys lasting peace, shared security and common prosperity'.[14] Noting the regional dynamic within globalisation, Chinese Premier Xi stated, 'Economic globalization and regional integration are the compelling trend of our times.'[15]

China's state-capital complex now has both the financial power and industrial clout to lead major regional initiatives that may reshape the geography of accumulation in the next decade. The elite network's structure mapped in this chapter intimates that China may align with continental-European capital, in preference to US-based capital, and only selectively with other BRICS. Rising political-economic tensions between the US and China and the ongoing deployment of the BRI are creating the structural momentum for such realignment. The logic of the situation favours BRICS-minus-2: an alignment of China, Russia and India, within regional agreements such as SCO and the Regional Comprehensive Economic Partnership (RCEP), currently under negotiation.[16]

The situation, however, is highly unstable, and defies any hard-and-fast predictions. According to Morgan Chase's top analyst, Marko Kolanovic, within a year or so the longest bull market in history will crash in a financial meltdown 'likely to result in social tensions similar to those witnessed 50 years ago in 1968' (Sol 2018). Such a meltdown could revive the global crisis management of 2008/9 in a scenario of collective imperialism, but other possibilities can hardly be dismissed. Within the scope of contemporary imperialism, perhaps the most likely alternative, grounded in an economic nationalism that renounces core aspects of neoliberal globalisation, would see an intensification of inter-imperial rivalry (likely centring upon the US versus China rivalry). In either scenario, the two pillars of distinctively American imperial power – military superiority[17] and dollar hegemony – will continue to shape events. However, in the latter case there is reason to doubt continued dollar hegemony, which among other things supports American military dominance by allowing the US to run a permanent budget deficit. The share of dollar-denominated transactions has been falling, and as Matthews and Selden (2018) note, countries aligned with China through the BRI already form a significant monetary bloc, and accept the yuan as means of payment for commodities (particularly oil) supplied to China, and for goods supplied from China. They go on to suggest that

> BRI trade and investment conducted in yuan promises to promote not only Chinese economic growth and financial clout but also its geopolitical influence and soft power while serving as a means for countries to evade US sanctions. Both Russia and Iran are selling oil to China and accepting payment in yuan, as a response to (actual and potential) sanctions imposed on these countries by the US.

These developments in the geopolitical economy of finance capital take place within a deepening climate crisis. As major financial institutions such as BNP Paribas divest from the dirtiest fossil fuels, as European automobile makers commit to exclusively electric vehicles, as the price of renewable energy undercuts carbon, we can expect further shifts and realignments. In March 2018, for instance, Saudi Arabia announced a US$200 billion solar power installation, in partnership with Japan-based venture-capital fund SoftBank, to be paid out of current oil reserves (Wald 2018).

Meanwhile, dismissing climate change as a Chinese hoax, the rogue government of Donald Trump has abdicated America's leadership role on this and other issues. Trump's retrograde embrace of coal and of fossil capital more generally is a rearguard action that exacerbates the climate crisis and may contribute to flagging US competitiveness in the long term, as other countries transition from carbon-based energy thereby relegating fossil-fuel infrastructure to stranded assets. In November 2016 China, responsible for a quarter of global greenhouse gas emissions yet also the world's largest solar energy producer and consumer, responded to Trump's election by announcing a new climate partnership with the European Union at the COP climate summit (Linnitt 2016), which was further cemented in July 2018 (European Commission 2018). China's ascension toward global climate leadership dovetails closely with an accumulation strategy pitched toward the production of renewable energy technology, both for domestic use and export. As Rosalyn Hsueh (2017) has commented, 'With the United States taking a back seat on climate change, if China exerts leadership it would be about enhancing China's global prestige and economic clout – and diversifying energy sources at home, while managing China's energy infrastructure.' Although geopolitical-economic realignments may further weaken US hegemony and open new escape hatches from US domination, the 'climate leadership' on offer is not likely to challenge the capitalist growth imperative at the heart of the climate crisis. Authentic climate leadership is more likely to come from below, in the form of anti-capitalist and anti-imperialist movements and political parties committed to climate justice.

ACKNOWLEDGEMENT

This research was supported by the Social Sciences and Humanities Research Council of Canada (Partnership Grant 895-2015-1021: Mapping the Power of the Carbon-extractive Corporate Resource Sector).

APPENDIX: NAMES OF COMPANIES IN FIGURES 2.1–2.3

3M	3M Company
ABBOTTLABS	Abbott Laboratories
ABBVIE	Abbvie Inc.
ABUDHABI_OIL	Abu Dhabi National Oil Company
ACCENTURE	Accenture plc.
AIRBUS	Airbus SE
AIRFRANCE	Air France - KLM
AIRLIQUID	L'Air Liquide SA
AKZONOBEL	Akzo Nobel NV
ALBERTSONS	Albertsons Co. Inc.
AMEX	American Express Company
AMGEN	Amgen Incorporated
ANDEAVOR	Andeavor
ANGLOAMER	Anglo American plc.
APPLE	Apple Inc.
ARCHERDANIEL	Archer Daniels Midland Company

ASTRAZENECA	AstraZeneca plc.
AVNET	Avnet Inc.
BA_TOBACCO	British American Tobacco plc.
BAE	BAE Systems plc.
BAKERHUGHES	Baker Hughes a GE Company
BANKofCOMMS	Bank of Communications Company Limited
BARCLAYS	Barclays plc.
BHARATPETRO	Bharat Petroleum Corporation Limited
BHPBILLITON	BHP Billiton Limited
BNPPARIBAS	BNP Paribas
BOEING	Boeing Company
BOMBARDIER	Bombardier Inc.
BOUYGUES	Bouygues SA
BP	BP plc.
BROOKFIELD	Brookfield Asset Management Inc.
CANADALIFE	Canada Life Assurance Company
CARNIVAL	Carnival Corporation
CATERPILLAR	Caterpillar Inc.
CENOVUS	Cenovus Energy Inc.
CENTRICA	Centrica plc.
CEPSA	Compania Espanola De Petroleos SAU
CHEVRON	Chevron Corporation
CHINACONBANK	China Construction Bank Corporation Joint Stock Company
CHINAHUADIA	China Huadian Group Company Limited
CHINALIFE	China Life Insurance Company Limited
CHINARAIL	China Railway Group Ltd
CHINASHENHUA	China Shenhua Energy Company Limited
CHINOVERSEAS	China Overseas Land & Investment Limited
CHINSOUTHAIR	China Southern Airlines Company Limited
CNOOC	China National Offshore Oil Corporation
COMPASS	Group Compass Group plc.
CONOCOPHIL	ConocoPhillips
COSMO_ENERGY	Cosmo Energy Holdings Company Limited
CVSHEALTH	CVS Health Corporation
DAQING_OIL	Daqing Oilfield Limited Company
DELTA_AIR	Delta Air Lines Inc.

DEUTSCHEBANK	Deutsche Bank AG
DUKEENERGY	Duke Energy Corporation
EMPRESACOLOM	Empresa Colombiana De Petroleos - Ecopetrol SA
ENGIE	ENGIE
ENI	Eni SpA
EXXONMOBIL	Exxon Mobil Corporation
FAURECIA	Faurecia SA
FEMSA	Fomento Económico Mexicano SAB de CV
FUJIXEROX	Fuji Xerox (Hong Kong) Limited
GE	General Electric Company
GENERALI	Assicurazioni Generali SpA
GLAXO	GlaxoSmithKline plc.
GM	General Motors Company
GREAT-WEST	Great-West Lifeco Inc.
HALLIBURTON	Halliburton Company
HENKEL	Henkel AG & Co. KGaA
HINDUSTANPET	Hindustan Petroleum Corporation Limited
HITACHI	Hitachi Ltd
HONEYWELL	Honeywell International Inc.
HSBC	HSBC Holdings plc.
IDEMITSU	Idemitsu Kosan Company Limited
IMPERIALOIL	Imperial Oil Limited
INDIANOIL	Indian Oil Corporation Limited
ING	ING Groep NV
INNOGY	Innogy SE
INTERNAT_PAP	International Paper Company
ISUZU	Isuzu Motors Limited
JOHNSON&JOHN	Johnson & Johnson
KERING	Kering SA
KOCH	Koch Industries Inc.
LAFARGE	LafargeHolcim Limited
LIBERTYLIFE	Liberty Mutual Holding Company Inc.
LLOYDSBANK	Lloyds Bank plc.
LOWES	Lowe's Companies Inc.
LUKOIL	Public Joint Stock Company Oil Company Lukoil
MACYS	Macy's Inc.

MANULIFE	Manulife Financial Corporation
MARATHON_PET	Marathon Petroleum Corporation
MARRIOTT	Marriott International Inc.
MCDONALDS	Mcdonald's Corporation
MERCK	Merck & Co. Inc.
METLIFE	Metlife Inc.
MITSUBISHI	Mitsubishi Chemical Holdings Corporation
MOLLER	AP Møller – Maersk A/S
MONDELEZ	Mondelez International Inc.
MORGANCHASE	JPMorgan Chase & Company
MORGANSTAN	Morgan Stanley
NESTLE	Nestlé SA
OMV	OMV Aktiengesellschaft
ONGC	Oil & Natural Gas Corporation Limited
ORACLE	Oracle Corporation
ORANGE	Orange SA
PBF_ENERGY	PBF Energy Inc.
PETROBRAS	Petroleo Brasileiro SA
PETROCHINA	PetroChina Company Limited
PEUGEOT	Peugeot SA
PHILIPS	Koninklijke Philips NV
PHILLIPS66	Phillips 66
PNCFINANCIAL	PNC Financial Services Group Inc.
POWERCORP	Power Corporation of Canada
POWERFINAN	Power Financial Corporation
PROCTER&GAMB	Procter & Gamble Company
PRUDENTIAL	Prudential plc.
QANTAS	Qantas Airways Limited
R_BANKofCAN	Royal Bank of Canada
RBANKofSCOTT	Royal Bank of Scotland Group plc. (The)
REPSOL	Repsol SA
RIOTINTO	Rio Tinto Limited
ROLLS-ROYCE	Rolls-Royce Holdings plc.
ROSNEFT	Publichnoe Aktsionernoe Obschestvo Neftyanaya Kompaniya Rosneft
S-OIL	S-Oil Corporation
SAINTGOBAIN	Compagnie de Sain-Gobain SA
SAUDIARAMCO	Saudi Aramco Company

SBERBANK	Sberbank of Russia OAO
SHELL	Royal Dutch Shell plc.
SIEMENS	Siemens AG
SK	SK Innovation Co. Ltd
SK_HYNIX	SK Hynix Inc.
SKANSKA	Skanska AB
STATOIL	Statoil ASA
SUNCOR	Suncor Energy Inc.
TD_BANK	Toronto Dominion Bank
TELEFONICA	Telefonica SA
TOTAL	Total SA
TRAVELERS	Travelers Group
UBS	UBS AG
UNICREDIT	Unicredit SpA
UNILEVER	Unilever plc.
UNIONPACIFIC	Union Pacific Corporation
UNITEDTECH	United Technologies Corporation
VALEO	Valeo SA
VALERO	Valero Energy Corporation
VATTENFALL	Vattenfall AB
VOLVO	AB Volvo
WALMART	Walmart Inc.
WELLSFARGO	Wells Fargo & Company
WESTPAC	Westpac Banking Corporation

NOTES

1. Hydro-generation accounts for only 15.7% of electricity in contemporary Russia. Earth Policy Institute, *Statistical Review of World Energy*, London, June 2012.

2. Richard Heede has calculated that, of the total carbon released into the atmosphere since 1751, 15 per cent was released between 1751 and 1950, 35 per cent was released between 1950 and 1988, and 50 per cent was released between 1988 and 2014. See http://www.climateaccountability.org/pdf/CDIAC1751-2014%20ForUCS%20Dec14.pdf (accessed 13 June 2018).

3. I count firms majority-owned by a state as state-owned. Rome-based Eni SpA, fully state-owned until its privatisation in the 1990s, is categorised as an IOC, although the state of Italy retains a 30 per cent stake. The same goes for Vienna-based OMV (31.5% owned by Austria). On the other hand, Moscow-based Gazprom (50.01% owned by Russia) and Stavanger-based Statoil (67 per cent owned by Norway) are considered NOCs. Most NOCs are wholly owned by their respective states.

4   In Shell's case the base of operations is equally Britain and the Netherlands.

5   Imperial Oil's two-step reach of 16 is generated by its strong interlock with ExxonMobil, the second most central corporation in the network.

6   The former include China Petroleum & Chemical Corporation and Shanxi Yanchang Petroleum (Group) Co. Ltd (based in China), Gazprom (based in Russia), Kuwait Petroleum Corporation, National Iranian Oil Company, Petroleos De Venezuela S.A., Indonesia-based Pertamina, Thailand-based Ptt Public Company Limited, Qatar Petroleum and Petroleos Mexicanos. The latter include PKN Orlen and Jxtg Nippon Oil & Energy Corporation.

7   See https://www.mubadala.com/en/who-we-are/our-history (accessed 5 May 2018). Mubadala also owns 25 per cent of Vienna-based OMV, a fossil whose main minority shareholder is Austria.

8   These communities were identified using the Girvan and Newman (2002) algorithm. The statistical relationship between membership in the three communities and country of domicile is very strong (contingency coefficient = 0.757).

9   FujiXerox, based in Hong Kong, is considered here as domiciled in China.

10   Although Rio Tinto is primarily invested in metal mining, it held significant coal assets, from which it has divested in recent years. Its sale of the Kestrel mine in Australia to a private equity manager in March 2018 completed its divestment from the coal sector. See http://www.mining.com/rio-tinto-fully-coal-sector-2-25bn-kestrel-mine-sale/ (accessed 18 January 2019).

11   The one interlock between US- and China-based companies connects Fuji Xerox of Hong Kong (controlled by FujiFilm of Tokyo) with ExxonMobil and Amex, by virtue of Xerox CEO Ursula Burn's affiliations with all three boards. Fuji Xerox's board is comprised of Japanese capitalists, with the exception of Burns.

12   Calculated in purchasing power parity (PPP), the IMF estimates China's 2018 GDP as US$25.3 trillion and the US's as US$20.5 trillion. From the World Economic Outlook Database, available at https://www.imf.org/external/pubs/ft/weo/2018/02/weodata/weoselgr.aspx (accessed 18 January 2019).

13   See https://www.ran.org/banking_on_climate_change (accessed 25 May 2018).

14   'Xi: China to invest 30 billion RMB to build an SCO community with shared future.' See https://news.cgtn.com/news/3d3d674d7949444d78457a6333566d54/share_p.html, 10 June 2018 (accessed 14 June 2018).

15   'Xi: Broad consensus reached during the 2018 SCO summit.' See https://news.cgtn.com/news/3d3d514e3549444d78457a6333566d54/sharep.html, 10 June 2018 (accessed 14 June 2018).

16   The RCEP includes the ten ASEAN countries of Southeast Asia plus Australia, China, India, Japan, the Republic of Korea and New Zealand.

17   Including more than 3 500 military bases, nearly half of which are ironically threatened by extreme weather linked to climate change (US Department of Defense 2018).

REFERENCES

Angus, I. 2016. *Facing the Anthropocene*. New York: Monthly Review Press.

Bukharin, N. 1973. *Imperialism and World Economy*. New York: Monthly Review Press.

Carroll, W.K. 2003. 'Undoing the end of history'. In Y. Atasoy and W.K. Carroll (eds), *Global Shaping and Its Alternatives*. Toronto: Garamond Press, pp. 33– 56.

Carroll, W.K. 2010. *The Making of a Transnational Capitalist Class*. London: Zed Books.

Carroll, W.K. 2018. 'Rethinking the transnational capitalist class', *Alternate Routes* 29: 188– 206.

Carroll, W.K. (ed.). 2020. *Regime of Obstruction: How Corporate Power Blocks Energy Democracy*. Edmonton: Athabasca University Press.

Chesnais, F. 2016. *Finance Capital Today*. Chicago: Haymarket Books.

China Daily. 2017. 'China's "big four" banks to raise billions for Belt and Road deals'. Accessed 25 May 2018, http://www.chinadaily.com.cn/business/2017-08/23/content_30990300.htm.

ChinaPower. 2018. 'Does China dominate global investment?' Accessed 13 June 2018, https://chinapower.csis.org/china-foreign-direct-investment/.

Cole, M. 2017. 'Neoliberal global capitalism and imperialism in the twenty-first century'. In M. Cole (ed.) *Critical Race Theory and Education: A Marxist Response* (second edition). New York: Palgrave Macmillan, pp. 155–181.

Cox, R. 1987. *Production, Power and World Order*. New York: Columbia University Press.

De Graaff, N. 2013. 'Towards a hybrid global energy order: State-owned oil companies, corporate elite networks and governance', unpublished PhD thesis, Free University of Amsterdam.

Ebrahim, S. 2018. 'Brazil's Jair Bolsonaro creates a dilemma for BRICS', *IOL*, 4 November. Accessed 18 January 2019, https://www.iol.co.za/news/opinion/brazils-jair-bolsonaro-creates-a-dilemma-for-brics-17766249.

European Commission. 2018. 'EU and China step up cooperation on climate change and clean energy'. Accessed 18 January 2019, https://ec.europa.eu/clima/news/eu-and-china-step-cooperation-climate-change-and-clean-energy_en.

Fennema, M. 1982. *International Networks of Banks and Industry*. The Hague: Martinus Nijhoff Publishers.

Girvan, M. and Newman, M.E.J. 2002. 'Community structure in social and biological networks', *Proceedings of the National Academy of Sciences* 99 (12): 7821–7826.

Harvey, D. 2003. *The New Imperialism*. New York: Oxford University Press.

Heemskerk, E.M., Fennema, M. and Carroll, W.K. 2016a. 'The global corporate elite after the financial crisis: Evidence from the transnational network of interlocking directorates', *Global Networks* 16: 68–88.

Heemskerk, E.M., Takes, F.W., Garcia-Bernardo, J. and Huijzer, M.J. 2016b. 'Where is the global corporate elite? A large-scale network study of local and nonlocal interlocking directorates', *Sociologica* 2: 1–31.

Heemskerk, E.M., Young, K., Takes, F.W., Cronin, B., Garcia-Bernardo, J., Popov, V., Winecoff, W.K., Henriksen, L.F. and Laurin-Lamonghe, A. 2017. 'The promise and perils of using big data in the study of corporate networks: Problems, diagnostics and fixes', *Global Networks* 18 (1): 3–32.

Hildyard, N. and Sol, X. 2017. *How infrastructure is shaping the world*. Accessed 12 June 2018, http://www.counter-balance.org/new-study-challenges-the-infrastructure-mega-corridors-agenda/.

Hilferding, R. 1981. *Finance Capital*. London: Routledge.

Hsueh, R. 2017. 'Why is China suddenly leading the climate change effort? It's a business decision', *Washington Post*, 22 June. Accessed 18 January 2019, https://www.washingtonpost.com/news/monkey-cage/wp/2017/06/22/why-is-china-suddenly-leading-the-climate-change-effort-its-a-businessdecision/?utm_term=.ff62687a1496.

Huber, M. 2013. *Lifeblood: Oil, Freedom and the Forces of Capital*. Minneapolis: University of Minnesota Press.

Krahl, D. 2013. 'Springtime on the New Silk Road? China and the Arab world after the revolutions'. In B. Gransow (ed.) *China's South-South Relations*. Zurich: Lit Verlag, pp. 50–62.

Le Billon, P. and Bridge, G. 2017. 'The politics of oil in the Anthropocene'. In B.D. Solomon and K.E. Calvert (eds), *Handbook on the Geographies of Energy*. Cheltenham: Elgar, pp. 38–56.

Lenin, V.I. 1917. *Imperialism, the Highest Stage of Capitalism*. Accessed 14 June 2018, https://www.marxists.org/archive/lenin/works/1916/imp-hsc/index.htm.

Lenin, V.I. 1920. 'Our foreign and domestic position and party tasks'. Speech delivered to the Moscow Gubernia conference of the R.C.P.(B.), 21 November. Accessed 9 May 2018, https://www.marxists.org/archive/lenin/works/1920/nov/21.htm.

Linnitt, C. 2016. 'Earth to America: Trump's not the centre of the universe (or the climate)', *The Narwhal*, 17 November. Accessed 18 January 2019, https://thenarwhal.ca/earth-america-trump-s-not-centre-universe-or-climate.

Malm, A. 2016. 'Who lit this fire? Approaching the history of the fossil economy', *Critical Historical Studies* 3 (2): 215–248.

Mathews, J.A. and Selden, M. 2018. 'China: The emergence of the petroyuan and the challenge to US dollar hegemony', *The Asia-Pacific Journal: Japan Focus* 16 (3). Accessed 18 January 2019, https://apjjf.org/2018/22/Mathews.html.

Mitchell, T. 2011. *Carbon Democracy*. London: Verso.

Pineault, E. 2018. 'The capitalist pressure to extract: An ecological and political economy of extreme oil in Canada', *Studies in Political Economy* 99 (2): 130–150.

Rahnema, S. 2017. 'Neoliberal imperialism, the latest stage of capitalism', *New Politics* 16 (2). Accessed 22 May 2018, http://newpol.org/content/neoliberal-imperialism-latest-stage-capitalism.

Sol, H. 2018. 'JP Morgan's top quant warns next crisis to have flash crashes and social unrest not seen in 50 years', *CNBC*, 4 September. Accessed 18 January 2019, https://www.cnbc.com/2018/09/04/jpmorgan-says-next-crisis-will-feature-flash-crashes-and-social-unrest.html.

Stephen, M.D. 2014. 'Rising powers, global capitalism and liberal global governance: A historical materialist account of the BRICs challenge', *European Journal of International Relations* 20: 912–938.

Trotsky, L. 1936. 'The New Constitution of the USSR'. Accessed 9 May 2018, https://www.marxists.org/archive/trotsky/1936/04/ussrconst.htm.

US Department of Defense. 2018. *Department of Defense Climate-Related Risk to DoD Infrastructure: Initial Vulnerability Assessment Survey(SLVAS) Report*, January. Accessed 18 January 2019, https://climateandsecurity.files.wordpress.com/2018/01/tab-b-slvas-report-1-24-2018.pdf.

Van der Pijl, K. 1984. *The Making of an Atlantic Ruling Class*. London: Verso.

Van der Pijl, K. 1998. *Transnational Class Formation and International Relations*. London: Routledge.

Wald, E.R. 2018. 'Saudi Arabia to build massive solar power installation', *Forbes*, 29 March. Accessed 13 June 2018, https://www.forbes.com/sites/ellenrwald/2018/03/29/saudi-arabia-to-build-massive-solar-power-installation/#3e09d7277a90.

Weeks, J. 1981. 'The differences between materialist theory and dependency theory and why they matter', *Latin American Perspectives* 8 (3-4): 118–123.

World Energy Council. 2016. *World Energy Resources 2016*. London: World Energy Council.

Wright, C. and Nyberg, D. 2015. *Climate Change, Capitalism, and Corporations*. Cambridge: Cambridge University Press.

3

WATER WARS IN THE WORLD AND SOUTH AFRICA

Ferrial Adam

Water is important for all life on earth; however, it is not equally distributed or shared across the globe. Almost one billion people in developing countries lack access to safe, clean potable water.[1] The quantity and quality of our global water resources is further threatened by climate change, which will only worsen the current shortages in basic food supplies, water resources and energy supplies. It is very likely that these shortages will lead to increased unrest, protests and conflicts over resources.

South Africa is a water-scarce country, whose situation is worsened by climate change and by the politics of water. Naturally, South Africa is characterised by low levels of rainfall, with an average annual rainfall of 490 mm, which falls well below the world average of 860 mm a year (CSIR 2010). Climate change is affecting the country's rainfall patterns, causing longer, harsher droughts on the one hand and extreme flooding on the other. Furthermore, the way government is managing its water resources will make these impacts harder for people to overcome. The scarcity is also political as it is impacted by the structure of South Africa's economy (i.e. domination of the minerals-energy complex and extractivist industries), the country's post-1994 political economy (i.e. neoliberal policies and thus exacerbation of developmental deficits) and finally its governance (i.e. corruption, patronage and political deployment) (Fallon 2018; Jankielsohn 2012).

Combined, these factors have become like a powder keg waiting to explode. This chapter argues that in South Africa, service delivery protests related to water, the effects of extreme droughts and floods, industrial pollution, infrastructure failure and lack of access to clean water represent a cumulative instability that could result in water wars being waged at a local level. This chapter explores the state of the world's water, the supposed myth of water wars and the consequent challenges facing South Africa.

THE STATE OF GLOBAL WATER

If at least three quarters of the earth's surface is covered by water, why is there growing concern about the state of global water resources? The simple answer is that there is very little water available for human consumption. More than 96 per cent of all the water on earth is held by the oceans, which is not exactly available for humans to drink. It is estimated that only three per cent of all the water on earth can be regarded as fresh water.[2] Most of this is found in icecaps and glaciers (about 68 per cent), while a further 30 per cent is found in groundwater. That leaves a mere 0.3 per cent of the total fresh water on earth in lakes, rivers and wetlands.[3] Specter (2006) offers a good analogy that provides a vivid picture of the amount of water available for humans: 'If a large bucket were to represent all the seawater on the planet, and a coffee cup the amount of freshwater frozen in glaciers, only a teaspoon would remain for us to drink.' The teaspoon of water that Specter refers to is vital for life. We need it for healthy people, biodiversity and ecosystems. The reality, however, is that the little water that we do have is neither properly cared for nor equally distributed across the planet. This is then subject to considerations of political and economic power that influence who gets access and who does not get access to water.

So for example, globally, the large agricultural sector gets 70 per cent of all the water drawn from aquifers, streams and lakes. Other industries (including mining) get 19 per cent and a mere 11 per cent is allocated for domestic and municipal use (FAO 2011). A recent study on southern Africa by the International Water Management Institute reveals that large-scale commercial farmers, who are predominantly white, were favoured under apartheid and are still benefiting, whereas small-scale farmers face enormous bureaucratic hurdles to obtain water permits (Van Koppen and Schreiner 2018).

Not only are our water resources distributed unequally, they are also subjected to unequal access, pollution, poor management and privatisation. According to the International Water Association, almost 4 billion people lack proper access to water, 4.5 billion do not have access to a proper sewage system and at least 5.5 billion drink untreated water (Cosgrove 2013). The people most affected by all of this are in developing countries.

Furthermore, water supplies are being polluted by heavy industry, agriculture, mining and untreated urban wastewater. Poor management, underinvestment and corruption further exacerbate the situation as local governments are unable to meet infrastructure demands and upkeep. In a developed country like the USA, it is reported that by 2020 there will be an investment deficit of US$84 billion for ageing infrastructure. This could be much worse for developing countries, given that many cities in developing countries do not even have the necessary infrastructure to adequately manage and treat wastewater (FAO 2011; WWAP 2015).

All of these problems – poor access, pollution, mismanagement – have allowed privatisation to gain traction, especially with regard to aspects of local government functions. There is a belief that with privatisation comes improved service. This could not be further from the truth. Privatisation will widen the gap between those who have and those who do not. Private companies will not prioritise the needs of poorer communities. The cost of water could increase beyond their reach and even limited access to water could be denied.

Privatisation is already translating into an ever-expanding bottled water industry. In 2010, it was estimated that six per cent of the world population relied on bottled water for drinking and cooking, a number that is increasing (WHO 2012 report, quoted in WWAP 2015).

The United Nations World Water Development Report of 2015 suggests that given these realities, there is an increasing risk of competition for water – 'between water "uses" and water "users" that could lead to the risk of localized conflicts and continued inequities in access to services, with significant impacts on local economies and human well-being' (WWAP 2015: 2). Adding in the impacts of climate change is like pouring fuel onto the existing fires.

CLIMATE SHOCKS AND WATER SCARCITY

Climate change is one of the biggest challenges facing the world as it threatens all life on earth. It directly affects food systems, global temperatures, rainfall, sea-levels, biodiversity and ecosystems. We are already experiencing global increases in the frequency and intensity of droughts, fires and flooding. For example, it is believed that climate change has intensified the drought and fires in California by at least 15 to 20 per cent, which could get worse in the future (Ebbs 2018; Gillis 2015).

Climate change will also affect the availability and demand for water in an already water-scarce world. There are three main challenges facing global water resources that will be worsened by climate change: (i) the continued demand for more water (in a world where our water supplies are dwindling); (ii) the existing shortages faced by billions of people (where people lack access to clean potable water and live in climate-risk areas that reduce access); and (iii) the pervasive pollution from industries and agriculture (which means that the little water we do have is subject to despoliation). According to the United Nations, at the present rate of water demand versus supply, by 2025 almost 60 per cent of the global population will live in water-stressed areas with poor sanitation. In addition, future water demand is likely to increase by 55 per cent by 2050 – mostly due to industrial and domestic use, as well as electricity generation[4] (FAO 2011; WWAP 2015).

All of this can be directly linked to the increase in incidences of water-related violence around the world at both local and national level (Gleick 2014). A case in point is what has happened in Syria. For many years, the country experienced devastating water and climate conditions that caused massive migration from rural to urban areas and played a role in the weakening of the economy. In turn, this contributed to the 2011 uprisings that soon escalated into a fully fledged civil conflict (Eklund and Thompson 2017). There were other complex factors contributing to this conflict, but the drought and climate conditions cannot be ignored.

The combination of increasing numbers of people facing water scarcity through a lack of access, the growing gap between the rich and poor, higher levels of pollution and poor governance (both political and corporate) all exacerbated by climate change impacts, are likely to give rise to a lot more violence and conflict over this precious resource (*IRIN News* 2014).

It is these conflicts that can be termed the coming 'water wars'.

DEFINING WATER WARS

The phrase 'water wars' conjures up a picture of a post-apocalyptic world such as we see in Hollywood movies like *Waterworld* and *Mad Max*. The common theme here is a fight for survival around the lack of fresh water resources as well as the food and energy needed to sustain a living planet. An important and telling aspect of these movies is the consequent class, racial and gendered character of the conflict over possession and control of those water resources.

Battles over water are not a new phenomenon. The term 'water wars' has historically referred to the conflicts between countries or states over access to fresh water resources. Some scholars point to an ancient Babylonian conflict – 4 500 years ago – as being the only true 'water war' to have ever occurred (*IRIN News* 2014). The Pacific Institute has established a chronology of water conflicts that dates back to 3000 BCE and according to Specter (2006) water has been a principal source of conflict since ancient times. He highlights that the word 'rivals' even has its roots in fights over water, coming from the Latin *rivalis*, for 'one taking from the same stream as another' (Specter 2006).[5]

The Pacific Institute's chronology describes different types of conflict and ways in which water is used in conflict. For example, by polluting or poisoning it, water itself can be used as a weapon. In 1904, German troops poisoned desert wells in Namibia that killed thousands of Herero people.

Water can also be the trigger for a conflict as was the case between South Africa and Lesotho. All evidence points to South Africa's support for the 1986 coup in Lesotho as being driven by the need to access Lesotho's water resources.[6] It is believed that the coup was due to the Lesotho government's delay in signing off on the Lesotho Highlands Water Project (Mills 2015). There are numerous other examples of conflicts, including those between herders and farmers, and between animals and people in drought-affected Kenya.[7]

The term 'water wars' gained prominence only in the late 1990s and is probably linked to Ismail Serageldin, the then vice president of the World Bank, who in 1995 said, 'If the wars of this century were fought over oil, the wars of the next century will be fought over water – unless we change our approach to managing this precious and vital resource' (Cosgrove 2013). At the time, the main focus was on wars between countries. Peter Gleick (1993) predicted that where countries share rivers such as the Nile in North Africa, the Indus in Southeast Asia and the Rio Grande in North America, there is the real potential for serious conflict over the shared water resource.

Despite there being almost two decades of 'water war' threats, there are those who argue that since such wars have not materialised over the last two decades there is no such thing as 'water wars' (*IRIN News* 2014). Furthermore, for some the use of the word 'war' is alarmist and creates unnecessary fear. For example, Paula Hanasz (2014) and Dan Tarlock and Patricia Wouters (2015) argue that focusing on the definition of water wars detracts from finding effective responses to an evolving and complex problem, namely water scarcity and use. Among others, Hanasz (2014) and Gleick and Heberger (2014) have also suggested using the term 'water conflicts', which they view as a more nuanced term that captures complex socio-economic and political issues.

However, the issue is not really about what term is used, but how we define 'water wars'. Conflicts involving water that have occurred over the past few decades are not all being waged between states but have also taken place at a local level. Further, such conflicts have involved 'wars' over various aspects of water provision, access, infrastructure and despoliation as opposed to being mostly militarily driven. A definition of water wars that encapsulates this fact expands the definition and includes local and national water conflicts.

The online Merriam-Webster dictionary defines a war as 'a state of hostility, conflict, or antagonism; a struggle or competition between opposing forces or for a particular end – a class war, a war against disease, etc.'[8] The conflicts presently being waged across the world of water are ones that directly involve people's livelihoods and survival for a very particular end. Ergo, they are at their core, wars!

The environmental activist, Vandana Shiva, agrees. She argues that it is convenient to label water wars as something other – for example as cultural or religious wars – than what they are. Not only does this deflect from the seriousness of the fight for and over water, it also allows for the water crises to continue being seen and treated as an 'invisible dimension of the ecological devastation of the earth' (Shiva 2002: 1).

Shiva even goes as far as describing certain activities and practices around water as acts of terrorism and the perpetrators of such as terrorists:

> Destruction of water resources and of forest catchments and aquifers is a form of terrorism. Denying poor people access to water by privatizing water distribution or polluting wells and rivers is also terrorism. In the ecological context of water wars, terrorists are not just those hiding in the caves of Afghanistan. Some are hiding in corporate boardrooms and behind the free trade rules of the WTO, North American Free Trade Agreement (AFTA), and Free Trade Area of the Americas (FTAA). They are hiding behind the privatization conditionalities of the IMF [International Monetary Fund] and World Bank. (Shiva 2016: xii)

In reality then, there has been an overall increase in water wars over the last two decades, especially at a subnational level, as shown in figure 3.1, which also shows a huge spike in state-to-state conflicts from 2009 to 2011. These are the new water wars and continuing to refer to them as mere conflicts diminishes their systemic causes and frames them as simply local issues to be solved at a local level. Perhaps it is now time to use the term 'water wars' precisely in order to raise the alarm about a situation that is getting worse and has the potential to destabilise all aspects of society. Certainly, we should pay serious attention to the words of a protest placard outside a South African court (by protesters trying to get justice for activist Andries

Figure 3.1 The increasing water conflicts at a subnational level, 1931–2011

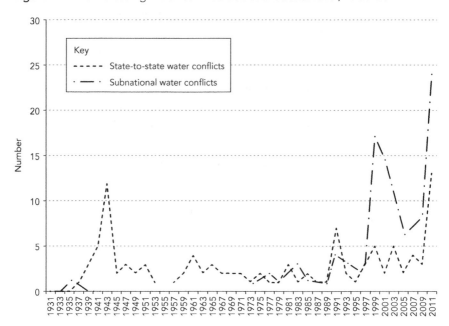

Source: Gleick and Heberger (2014).

Tatane who was killed during a water protest): 'We wanted water, but we got blood'
(De Waal 2014).

WATER WARS: THE REAL STORY

In recent years, there have been some serious tensions and conflicts over water
resources across the world, both between states and within states. We need only
look at the Brazil-Russia-India-China-South Africa (BRICS) network of five countries – whose populations make up almost 50 per cent of the world population and
whose economies account for about 20 per cent of the world's economic pie – to get
a sense of the seriousness and extent of these wars (Khaled 2016).

Case number 1
In 2012, a severe drought in the north-east of Brazil affected 1 100 towns, triggering
violent clashes in rural areas which reportedly resulted in an average of one person
a day being killed. While the government sent in water tankers to supply people
with water, it was reported that the water tanker drivers would make deliveries

only if people promised to vote for certain local political candidates, thus operating like a mafia that holds people to ransom for a basic resource (*Independent Online* 2012).

Case number 2
In 2014, after Crimea broke away from the Ukraine and declared itself part of Russia, the Ukrainian government shut down the North Crimean Canal, the main source of water for the entire area. Russia responded by placing troops in and around Crimea and Ukraine responded in kind. The population of Crimea continue to face water shortages that have affected the agricultural sector in the area (Mirovalev 2017).[9]

Case number 3
The long-standing disputes between India and Pakistan, which go back to the original partition of the subcontinent, have consistently been worsened by water disputes. India's use of much of the shared resource for energy, through the construction of dams along the Indus River Basin, has resulted in clashes with Pakistan. Pakistani farmers – who are dependent on the shared water – have been directly affected by a lack of access to and dwindling supply of water.[10] India also faces internal water wars. Because a third of its potable water is lost to leaks and poor infrastructure, in drought-stricken areas people largely rely on water tankers. However, water is siphoned off by an increasingly brazen water-tanker mafia, which then sells it to people in slums who are supposed to get it for free. As sources dry up and wells are abandoned, farmers have turned on one another and on themselves. Indian newspapers are filled with accounts of often violent fights between Indian states or between neighbours over access to lakes and reservoirs, and of 'suicide farmers', driven to despair by drought-related poverty and debt (Specter 2006).

Case number 4
China has been dubbed the 'hydro-hegemon' of Asia as it controls key water sources on the continent (Moore 2018). Such control has been tightened by the construction of dams that have affected flows to India and Vietnam. This has resulted in increased tensions which have the potential to start wider conflicts between these countries. Internally, China is also experiencing local water conflicts between provinces and prefectures as pollution flows from heavy industrial areas have negatively impacted on water quality and agricultural production (Moore 2018).

In other parts of the world, we see similar tensions – for example, between Kenya and Ethiopia in the Lake Turkana region where the shrinking lake and increased salinity has resulted in a fight not only for water but also for food between local farmers and herders from the two countries.

Water wars do not end here, however.

PRIVATISATION

Water is clearly a stress multiplier and the unequal and discriminatory access to and distribution of water is also a political issue. Issues such as privatisation, corruption, and poor infrastructure can act as tipping points for further socio-political instability and conflict. So for example, a natural disaster such as a drought or a flood can boil over into a water war that can give rise to larger political conflicts resulting in violence and loss of life (*Independent Online* 2012).

A classic example is what has been referred to as the Arab Spring, which has been linked to droughts and resource shortages in the Middle East (McDonnell 2013). Researchers at the Center for Climate and Security in Washington DC convincingly argue that a series of droughts from 2006 to 2010, which displaced poor farmers and increased bread prices, contributed to the tipping point for the Arab Spring uprisings (Cambanis 2015). Climate change, water scarcity and politics thus together all play a role in water wars (Gleick and Heberger 2014).

Another good example is in Ghana, where a civil society campaign has managed to successfully stop the installation of prepaid water meters. In India, there is a 'People's Campaign' to oppose the privatisation of water supplies as well as to re-establish water as a basic human right. In Indonesia, the expanding fights against water privatisation have pushed the Jakarta city government to announce plans to 're-municipalise' Jakarta's water supply (Transnational Institute 2015). The re-municipalising of water, which has increasingly been occurring across the globe, highlights the flawed argument of privatisers who blame poor people/residents as opposed to big industries such as mining and agriculture for water shortages and associated problems.

Institutions such as the African Development Bank worsen the situation by insisting that the only way to tackle the water and sanitation crisis on the continent is through privatising public water entities and resources and making everyone pay the full cost. But putting a price on water has a contentious history (Provost 2018). The Cochabamba water wars were a response to the privatisation of the municipal water supply in Cochabamba, Bolivia. This resulted in months of protests and violent confrontations that forced the government to eventually change their policy (Galvin 2016). South Africa has had its own war against the privatisation of water that saw large-scale protests and a court case to challenge the installation of pre-paid water meters (Dugard 2010; McKinley 2008).

According to Shiva (2016), the pro-privatisation arguments wrongly suggest that privatisation will counter poor performance and corruption in the public sector because there is an incorrect assumption that private companies are more account-able. Shiva (2016) shows that there is no concrete evidence to sustain that argument. The reality is that private companies regularly inflate prices, flout regulations and are prone to corruption. Water, as a basic right, becomes inaccessible and expensive for poor households, resulting in a pushback. Water wars for water justice have seen the defeat of privatisation programmes in Bolivia and Indonesia, among many others (Bond and Dugard 2008; Sultana 2018).

The real war is one for equitable access for all. A leader of the South African Water Crisis Committee puts it succinctly: 'Privatisation is a new kind of apartheid. Apartheid separated whites from blacks. Privatisation separates the rich from the poor' (Provost 2018).

THE SOUTH AFRICAN REALITY

South Africa has fairly good policies on water, but poor implementation is fuelling its water wars. The Constitution and the National Water Act of 1998 are clear when it comes to the duty of government to provide water to people. Policy allows gov-ernment to hold water resources in public trust for the people; legally this means that the water belongs to all South Africans (Feris 2012). There is, furthermore, a national policy that each person should get a basic, and free, allowance of 25 litres per day or 6 000 litres per household per month. This policy was a response to an outbreak of cholera in 2000 that spread from KwaZulu-Natal to five provinces, resulting in 265 deaths (Hemson and Dube 2004; Muller 2008). Its implementation is determined at a local government level. This means that some get it, some don't; some get a bit of it, while others get more. For example, the City of Johannesburg has recently decided to limit free basic water to the indigent; but in order to access that free amount, one must prove indigency.

If one believes the ANC government, then one can be easily convinced that there are no water challenges in the country. The ANC claims that nine out of ten people now have access to water, and that (in 2013) 'more than 92% of our communities have access to safe water' (De Waal 2014). The reality, however, is very different. According to avail-able evidence from 2014, less than half of all South African households obtained their water from a tap inside their home and only 27 per cent had a tap on their property.

Furthermore, approximately six per cent of the population accessed piped water at a distance greater than 200 metres and at least nine per cent of the population had no access to piped water, instead relying on springs, rivers and wetlands (WWF-SA 2016). A 2013 nationwide investigative journalism project undertaken by Eyewitness News found that millions of people don't have any access to drinkable water while others report queuing for almost a day to get a single bucket of water (De Waal 2014).

While South Africa boasts about its rich and diverse natural environment, its own Department of Environmental Affairs describes it as being 'close to the tipping point' in terms of water scarcity, water quality, land degradation, greenhouse gas emissions and its dependence on non-renewable energy resources. Most of the country's key river systems, such as the Vaal, Olifants and Crocodile, are severely affected by salinity, which has been attributed to mining activities. Groundwater is being polluted and over-abstracted with very few checks and balances (DEA 2012; DWA 2012). Government has allowed farmers and private home owners to drill borehole wells, thus creating a borehole bourgeoisie as it is mostly rich land owners who can afford it.[11]

Gauteng, the smallest (but most populous) of the country's provinces, is experiencing ongoing acid mine drainage within the West and East Rand of Johannesburg as well as the immense pollution of the Hartebeespoort Dam and the Vaal River Barrage through sewerage and multiple other pollutants. In addition, to the west of Johannesburg there have been cases of contamination of water by radioactive pollutants.[12]

This then leaves communities, both directly and indirectly, vulnerable to poisoned and polluted water (Munnik 2007). Climate change exacerbates the situation, with the more vulnerable and poor being hardest hit as they lack the resilience to withstand the onslaught of the impacts (Cock 2006). The cumulative result will surely be an increase in the occurrence of water wars in South Africa.

SOUTH AFRICA'S WATER WARS

Water wars in South Africa mostly manifest in what have come to be known as 'service delivery' or 'community' protests. Carin Runciman et al. (2016) suggest that it is better to use the term 'community protests as it encapsulates various types of protests and can be viewed broadly as a "rebellion of the poor"' (Sinwell et al. 2009 cited in Runciman et al. 2016: 13). The character of these protests differ: they can be peaceful or violent depending on the issues, context and level of frustration experienced by affected communities.

According to the Social Change Research Unit at the University of Johannesburg, there were approximately 71 000 police-recorded protests between 1997 and 2013. This equates to about 11 protests a day over a 15-year period. The largest number of these protests were labour related (46 per cent) with community protests being the second most common (22.1 per cent). Motivations behind the protests could be anything from poor working conditions, to a lack of electricity, to lack of access to water and land (Runciman et al. 2016).

With specific regard to water, the Institute for Poverty, Land and Agrarian Studies suggests that water protests are spreading across rural and urban areas and could become more violent and more frequent (Tapela 2013). It is important to note, however, that these wars are not all the same; they have different battlegrounds and enemies. There are water wars against mining that are linked to encroachment on land, water pollution and acid mine drainage. There are water wars related to the struggle for access to clean, piped water. There are water wars directly targeting the privatisation of water utilities and resources. There are water wars revolving around poor governance, failing infrastructure and waste mismanagement. And finally, there are wars in response to climate risks, impacts and pressures.

For example, in Xolobeni along the Eastern Cape Wild Coast, communities in the area are opposed to proposed titanium mining as it has the potential to threaten water resources, wildlife and livelihoods. It has been a more than ten-year struggle for control over their land. In 2016, Sikhosiphi 'Bazooka' Rhadebe, the activist and chairperson of the Amadiba Crisis Committee (a key group fighting the mine) was assassinated. It was clear that this was a response to the group's opposition to the Australian mine developer. The South African government has been accused of being sympathetic to the mine as they believe it will contribute to economic growth in the area (Schneider 2016).

The impacts of mining are well known and can be felt across the country. Civil action groups in various parts of Gauteng and Mpumalanga, and organisations such as the Bench Marks Foundation, Mining Affected Communities United in Action and the Federation for a Sustainable Environment (FSE) are all challenging mining pollution and acid mine drainage. These groups are using a combination of protest, legal action and citizen science to fight their struggles against the impacts of mine pollution on people, land and water resources. FSE have been challenging the acid mine drainage in the west of Johannesburg as well as the radioactive contamination of water by AngloGold Ashanti (Kings 2013).

The Bench Marks Foundation has conducted health studies to show that mine dumps are responsible for the high numbers of young children suffering from cerebral palsy in the south of Johannesburg. The foundation has also trained activists to monitor and keep watch over water resources in their communities (Bench Marks Foundation 2017).

There are many environmental justice organisations that are challenging industrial pollution head on. Groundwork and the South Durban Community Environmental Alliance have challenged climate injustice and industrial pollution for more than two decades. The Vaal Environmental Justice Alliance (Veja) has been challenging industrial air and water pollution for about a decade. They have taken companies like Arcelor Mittal to court and have embarrassed Sasol through using citizen science to prove that Sasol was responsible for air pollution in the Vaal.

Undoubtedly, the largest number of water wars are being waged against municipal failure and corruption that, it is believed, is only going to get worse. In 2014, four people were killed during violent protests in Mothutlung near Brits. The protests were a response to water shortages and maladministration. Added to this is the water tanker mafia, who are destroying pipelines so that they will continue receiving tenders from the municipality (De Waal 2014). Veja has also exposed the Emfuleni local municipality for the infrastructure and municipal failures that have resulted in sewage being pumped into the Vaal River over a period of ten years with no respite in sight (Watson 2018).

South Africa's drought has put a spotlight on the climate challenges facing the country, and Cape Town became the poster child of what to expect in a climate-related war. The provincial and local municipalities had to increase security at many of the water collection points as people were not only fighting among themselves but also turning on the authorities. This also highlighted the class conflict between those who have and those who do not (Chambers 2018).

These are but a few of the examples of the water wars taking place in the country. If we look at each one on its own, then yes, water scarcity is a problem, but a manageable one. But when we take a cumulative view over all of these wars mushrooming across the country, it is easy to see that the more people's access to water as a basic human right fails, the more we are going to witness raging battles for water on the streets. These water wars will affect us all – regardless of race, class and gender.

CONCLUSION

South Africa's water wars are fuelled by a lack of access to water, unequal supply, privatisation of water services and government corruption. These wars are manifested in dispersed local community protests but they are all responses to the same challenges and concerns (access to clean, drinkable water), and more importantly, are proving to be deadly. With the increasing harshness of climate change, it is clear that we have to find ways to overcome the issues underlying these water wars (De Vos 2014).

Governments need to acknowledge the seriousness of poor water governance, increasing corruption and infrastructure failure. They also need to understand that to deal with the effects of climate change, there needs to be a system change related to water; an integrated system of water resource management is needed. In addition, governments must be held accountable for their failures and they must involve people and communities in their planning and decision making around water. This should be the first step in democratising our water.

People's concerns and voices on all aspects of water must be heard. Citizen science or 'street science' can give people power over water resources as it allows them to monitor, protect and influence decisions related to water. Many of the environmental justice organisations in South Africa are using science in one way or another to open a dialogue and to revisit collective control.

It took the recent drought to really make people sit up and take stock of our water resources. Not only did it highlight the fact that we will all be affected by water shortages, it also demonstrated that we all need to be involved in keeping our water resources safe. Further, it created a range of links and networks in civil society, government and the private sector. In particular, civil society organisations, movements and communities must continue to work together to build a strong water justice movement – a movement that can develop a people's water and climate justice charter that gives a voice to the voiceless and strengthens people's democratic water rights. Only then can we prevent further water wars.

NOTES

1   See https://thewaterproject.org/water-scarcity/ (accessed 13 September 2018).
2   See https://water.usgs.gov/edu/earthhowmuch.html (accessed 30 July 2018).
3   See www.nationalgeographic.org/media/earths-fresh-water/ (accessed 30 July 2018).
4   See http://www.un.org/waterforlifedecade/scarcity.shtml (accessed 10 September 2018).
5   See http://www.worldwater.org/conflict/list/ (accessed 31 July 2018).
6   See http://www.worldwater.org/conflict/list/ (accessed 31 July 2018).
7   See http://www.worldwater.org/conflict/list/ (accessed 31 July 2018).
8   See https://www.merriam-webster.com/dictionary/war (accessed 25 June 2018).
9   See also https://www.wateronline.com/doc/ukraine-russia-conflict-results-in-water-war-0001 (accessed 12 September 2018).
10   See https://www.crisisgroup.org/asia/south-asia/pakistan/pakistan-s-relations-india-beyond-kashmir (accessed 12 September 2018).

11   See https://www.property24.com/articles/boreholes-and-all-the-legal-need-to-know/ 25871 (accessed 31 July 2018).

12   See http://www.unisa.ac.za/news/index.php/2014/04/south-africas-water-resources-under-immense-pressure/ (accessed 31 July 2018).

REFERENCES

Bench Marks Foundation. 2017. 'Policy Gap 12 Soweto report "waiting to inhale": A survey of household health in four mine-affected communities'. Accessed 17 September 2018, http://www.bench-marks.org.za/research/policy_gap_12.pdf.

Bond, P. and Dugard, J. 2008. Water, human rights and social conflict: South African experiences, *Law, Social Justice and Global Development Journal* 11. Accessed 12 August 2019, https://warwick.ac.uk/fac/soc/law/elj/lgd/2008_1/bond_dugard/bond_dugard.rtf.

Cambanis, T. 2015. 'The Arab Spring was a revolution of the hungry', *The Boston Globe*, 23 August. Accessed 6 September 2018, https://www.bostonglobe.com/ideas/2015/08/22/ the-arab-spring-was-revolution-hungry/K15S1kGeO5Y6gsJwAYHejI/story.html.

Chambers, D. 2018. 'Fight in water queue forces Cape Town to crack down', *Times Live*, 31 January. Accessed 17 September 2018, https://www.timeslive.co.za/news/south-africa/2018-01-31-fight-in-water-queue-forces-cape-town-to-crack-down/.

Cock, J. 2006. 'Connecting the red, brown and green: The environmental justice movement in South Africa'. In R. Ballard, A. Habib and I. Valodia (eds), *Voices of Protest: Social Movements in Post-Apartheid South Africa*. Pietermaritzburg: University of KwaZulu-Natal Press, pp. 179–201.

Cosgrove, B. 2013. 'Assessing the future of water', *Options Magazine*, 24 June. Accessed 31 July 2018, http://www.iiasa.ac.at/web/home/resources/mediacenter/FeatureArticles/ Water-Meeting-Report.en.html.

CSIR (Council for Scientific and Industrial Research). 2010. 'A CSIR perspective on water in South Africa'. Accessed 17 September 2018, http://www.csir.co.za/nre/docs/CSIR Perspective on Water_2010.PDF.

DEA (Department of Environmental Affairs). 2012. '2nd South Africa environment outlook: A report on the state of the environment. Executive summary'. Accessed 17 September 2018, https://www.environment.gov.za/sites/default/files/reports/environmentoutlook_ executivesummary.pdf.

De Vos, P. 2014. 'Water is life, but the struggle for it is deadly', *Daily Maverick*, 15 January. Accessed 17 September 2018, https://www.dailymaverick.co.za/opinionista/2014-01-15-water-is-life-but-the-struggle-for-it-is-deadly/#.WuiNyYhubIV.

De Waal, M. 2014. 'South Africa's water wars', *GroundUp*, 5 February. Accessed 25 June 2018, https://www.groundup.org.za/article/south-africae28099s-water-wars_1482/.

DWA (Department of Water Affairs). 2012. 'Proposed National Water Resource Strategy 2: Summary'. Accessed 12 August 2019, http://biodiversityadvisor.sanbi.org/wp-content/ uploads/2016/07/Proposed-National-Water-Resource-Strategy-II.pdf.

Dugard, J. 2010. 'Civic action and legal mobilisation: The Phiri water meters case'. In J. Handmaker and R. Berkhout (eds), *Mobilising Social Justice in South Africa: Perspectives from Researchers and Practitioners*. Pretoria: Pretoria University Law Press, pp 71–99.

Ebbs, S. 2018. '"Undeniable link to climate change" in California's fire season, expert says', *ABC News*, 8 August. Accessed 5 September 2018, https://abcnews.go.com/Politics/ climate-change-make-wildfires-spread-factor/story?id=56937704.

Eklund, L. and Thompson, D. 2017. 'Is Syria a climate war?' *The Conversation*. Accessed 5 September 2018, https://theconversation.com/is-syria-really-a-climate-war-we-examined-the-links-between-drought-migration-and-conflict-80110.

Fallon, A. 2018. 'A perfect storm: The hydropolitics of Cape Town's water crisis'. Global Water Forum. Accessed 30 June 2018, http://www.globalwaterforum.org/2018/04/17/the-hydropolitics-of-cape-towns-water-crisis-a-perfect-storm/?pdf=15361.

FAO (Food and Agriculture Organization). 2011. *The State of the World's Land and Water Resources for Food and Agriculture: Managing Systems at Risk*. Rome and London: Food and Agriculture Organization and Earthscan.

Feris, L. 2012. 'The public trust doctrine and liability for historic water pollution in South Africa', *Law Environment and Development Journal* 8 (1): 1–18.

Galvin, M. 2016. 'Leaving boxes behind: Civil society and water sanitation struggles in Durban, South Africa', *Transformation: Critical Perspectives on Southern Africa* 92 (1): 111–134.

Gillis, J. 2015. 'California drought is made worse by global warming, scientists say', *The New York Times*, 20 August. Accessed 5 September 2018, https://www.nytimes.com/2015/08/21/science/climate-change-intensifies-california-drought-scientists-say.html.

Gleick, P.H. 1993. 'Water and conflict: Fresh water resources and international security', *International Security* 18 (1): 79–112.

Gleick, P.H. 2014. 'Water, drought, climate change, and conflict in Syria', *Weather, Climate, and Society* 6 (3): 331–340.

Gleick, P. and Heberger, M. 2014. 'Water and conflict: Events, trends and analysis (2011–2012) (Water Brief 3)'. In *The World's Water (Vol. 8)*. Washington, DC: Island Press. Accessed 1 August 2018, http://worldwater.org/wp-content/uploads/2013/07/www8-water-conflict-events-trends-analysis.pdf.

Hanasz, P. 2014. 'Water war: What is it good for?' Asia and the Pacific Policy Society, Crawford School of Public Policy, Australian National University. Accessed 25 July 2018, https://www.policyforum.net/water-war-what-is-it-good-for/.

Hemson, D. and Dube, B. 2004. 'Water services and public health: The 2000–2001 cholera outbreak in KwaZulu-Natal, South Africa'. Paper presented at the 8th World Congress on Environmental Health, Durban, South Africa, 22–27 February). Accessed 25 July 2018, http://repository.hsrc.ac.za/bitstream/handle/20.500.11910/7937/2696 Hemson Waterservicesandpublichealth.pdf?sequence=1&isAllowed=y.

Independent Online. 2012. 'Brazilian towns suffer amid "water wars"', 14 May. Accessed 25 June 2018, https://www.iol.co.za/news/world/brazilian-towns-suffer-amid-water-wars-1295664.

IRIN News. 2014. 'Water and conflict', 22 April. Accessed 5 September 2018, http://www.irinnews.org/analysis/2014/04/22/water-and-conflict.

Jankielsohn, R. 2012. 'Defining hydropolitics: The politics of water in South Africa', *Journal for Contemporary History* 37 (1): 123–141.

Khaled, S. Md. S. 2016. 'BRICS facing own challenges as their economies slowing', *The Independent*, 2 November. Accessed 12 September 2018, http://www.theindependentbd.com/post/66614.

Kings, S. 2013. 'AngloGold mine charged with radioactive contamination', *Mail & Guardian*, 8 January. Accessed 13 September 2018, https://mg.co.za/article/2013-01-08-mine-charged-with-radioactive-contamination.

McDonnell, T. 2013. 'Climate change: The secret inflamer of the Arab Spring', *CityLab*, 6 March. Accessed 25 June 2018, https://www.citylab.com/equity/2013/03/climate-change-secret-inflamer-arab-spring/4896/.

McKinley, D. 2008. 'Water is life: The anti-privatisation forum and the struggle against water privatisation', *Southern African Regional Poverty Network* 16 (3). Accessed 25 July 2018, http://www.sarpn.org/documents/d0000584/index.php%5Cnhttp://www.waterjustice.org/?mi=16&resid=88.

Mills, G. 2015. '"A fractious lot": Anatomy of (another) coup in Lesotho', *Daily Maverick,* 3 July. Accessed 10 November 2018, https://www.dailymaverick.co.za/article/2015-07-03-a-fractious-lot-anatomy-of-another-coup-in-lesotho/.

Mirovalev, M. 2017. 'Dam leaves Crimea population in chronic water shortage', *Al Jazeera,* 4 January. Accessed 12 September 2018, https://www.aljazeera.com/indepth/features/2016/12/dam-leaves-crimea-population-chronic-water-shortage-161229092648659.html.

Moore, S. 2018. 'China's water wars', *East Asia Forum,* 28 June. Accessed 12 September 2018, http://www.eastasiaforum.org/2018/06/28/chinas-water-wars/.

Muller, M. 2008. 'Free basic water: A sustainable instrument for a sustainable future in South Africa', *Environment and Urbanization* 20 (1): 67–87.

Munnik, V. 2007. 'Solidarity for environmental justice in Southern Africa'. Groundwork special report. Accessed 25 July 2018, http://www.groundwork.org.za/specialreports/Solidarity for EJ in SA.pdf.

Provost, C. 2018. 'Is the stage being set for new water wars in Africa?' *The Guardian,* 26 November. Accessed 25 June 2018, https://www.theguardian.com/global-development/poverty-matters/2010/nov/26/africa-water-privatisation.

Runciman, C., Alexander, P., Rampedi, M., Moloto, B., Maruping, B. and Khumalo, E. 2016. *Counting police-recorded protests: Based on South African Police Service data.* South African Research Chair in Social Change Report No. 2. Social Change Research Unit, University of Johannesburg.

Schneider, K. 2016. 'A murder on wild coast escalates conflict over water, land, mining', *Fin 24,* 1 April. Accessed 17 September 2018, https://www.fin24.com/Companies/Mining/a-murder-on-wild-coast-escalates-conflict-over-water-land-mining-20160401.

Shiva, V. 2002. *Water Wars: Privatization, Pollution and Profit* (first edition). Boston: South End Press.

Shiva, V. 2016. *Water Wars: Privatization, Pollution and Profit* (second edition). Berkeley, California: North Atlantic Press.

Specter, M. 2006. 'The last drop: Confronting the possibility of a global catastrophe', *The New Yorker,* 23 October. Accessed 25 July 2018, https://www.newyorker.com/magazine/2006/10/23/the-last-drop-2.

Sultana, F. 2018. 'Water justice: Why it matters and how to achieve it', *Water International* 43 (4): 483–493.

Tapela, B.N. 2013. 'Social protests and water service delivery in South Africa'. Report to the Water Research Commission. Accessed 12 August 2019, http://www.wrc.org.za/wp-content/uploads/mdocs/TT%20631-15.pdf.

Tarlock, D. and Wouters, P. 2015. 'Reframing the water security dialogue', *The Journal of Water Law* 20 (2/3): 53–60.

Transnational Institute. 2015. 'It's time to end water privatisation', Fact Sheets. January, accessed 9 November 2018, https://www.tni.org/files/download/fact_sheets_1_it_is_time_final.pdf.

Van Koppen, B. and Schreiner, B. 2018. 'A hybrid approach to decolonize formal water law in Africa'. IWMI Research Report No. 173. International Water Management Institute, Colombo.

Watson, A. 2018. 'Emfuleni water stinks to high heaven', *The Citizen*, 17 August. Accessed 13 September 2018, https://citizen.co.za/news/south-africa/1996860/emfuleni-water-stinks-to-high-heaven/.

WWAP (United Nations World Water Assessment Programme). 2015. *The United Nations world water development report 2015: Water for a sustainable world*. Paris: UNESCO.

WWF-SA (World Wildlife Fund-SA). 2016. *Water: Facts and Futures: Rethinking South Africa's Water Future*. Cape Town: WWWF-SA.

4

SUBIMPERIAL BRICS ENTER THE BOLSONARO-PUTIN-MODI-XI-RAMAPHOSA ERA

Patrick Bond

INTRODUCTION: BRICS DIVERGE UPON SHIFTING SUBIMPERIAL SANDS

Renewed political tensions within the Brazil-Russia-India-China-South Africa (BRICS) network of countries were no better reflected than when in March 2019, Brazilian foreign minister Ernesto Araújo announced he would use the bloc – specifically Moscow and Beijing – to help Donald Trump rid neighbouring Venezuela of its president, Nicolás Maduro. As Araújo told the *Wall Street Journal,* 'Brazil has a unique responsibility in foreign affairs. It is a matter of common sense. Nobody wants an ally like Maduro. These countries (Russia and China) have a reputation to preserve' (Trevisani and Pearson 2019). It was not surprising that the reactionary president Jair Bolsonaro – who assumed power in Brazil on 1 January – had chosen Araújo precisely for such aggressive reasons, to become what *Jacobin* magazine recognised as 'the worst diplomat in the world' (Pagliarini 2019).[1]

Even before Bolsonaro came to power, there was growing evidence of extreme internecine intra-BRICS competition – instead of collaboration – at certain times and in places of high stakes. Clashes occurred not just in crisis-ridden economic sectors such as steel, due to Chinese overaccumulation of capital, as discussed below. Tensions also exploded on the China-India-Bhutan border when in mid-2017 fisticuffs broke out between Beijing's and Delhi's troops, nearly scuttling the Xiamen summit a few weeks later. Further west, conflict over Pakistan is increasingly acute, over whether Kashmir – claimed by Indian prime minister Narendra Modi as his country's territory (not yet returned) – will host Beijing's most crucial 'Belt and Road Initiative' transport and pipeline corridor: from the Arabian Sea's Gwadar port to Western China. The BRICS' assimilation into global governance has not eased these internal tensions, and when the Bretton Woods Institutions were not sufficiently malleable to support the desired scope of Belt and Road financing, Beijing developed its own Asia Infrastructure Investment Bank, a source of yet more strife. Modi's boycott of the Belt and Road Forum for International Cooperation in both 2017 and 2019 clarifies how far and deep the ripples of discordant geopolitics continue to be felt.

Is there anything comprehensible in this set of divisions, in addition to which conflicts over Syria and Palestine, Poland and Ukraine, Yemen and the Horn of Africa, Iran, and the South China Sea would likewise fracture the world? Sam Moyo and Paris Yeros (2011: 19) long ago anticipated the BRICS' internecine political chaos, given their very diverse material realities, stating that 'the degree of participation in the Western military project is also different from one case to the next although, one might say, there is a "schizophrenia" to all this, typical of "subimperialism"'. For Bob Jessop (2018), the BRICS are too differentiated, economically, to establish unity: 'the distinctive crisis tendencies of their respective varieties of capitalism and the constraints associated with their differential insertion into the variegated world market has meant that only China has fulfilled the expectations hyped in the BRICS'.

In contrast, writing in the *Financial Times,* Wang Wen and Guan Zhaoyu (2017) dispute the 'myth of BRICS schizophrenia' that follows from their dispersed and often divergent interests:

> BRICS countries share the common values of reform and development. Reform is meant to improve global economic governance; to reform the unfair, unreasonable, and imperfect aspects of the old governance systems. Development is to promote developing countries in the global agenda, and establish a sustainable path so that economic globalisation can evolve in a more balanced way.

This more 'balanced way' resembled, rhetorically, what in 2015 at the BRICS Ufa Summit, Xi Jinping (2015) reflected as 'the *centripetal* force of BRICS nations', permitting the five members to 'tap their respective advantages and potentials and carry out cooperation in innovation and production capacity'. In fact, upon closer examination, the BRICS were part of a *centrifugal* process: worsening disruptions based on deep-rooted, underlying economic contradictions (Bond 2017, 2018b; Garcia and Bond 2018), in a context in which the world often appeared to be spinning out of control, sometimes falling apart at the seams. Therefore, it is best to consider the Moyo-Yeros description of the BRICS' political allegiances not *metaphorically* (in terms of mental health), but instead *methodologically*: as a challenge for analytical generalisation. If so, it soon becomes clear that *it is impossible to predict what kind of reaction these middle-income countries will exhibit at any given opportunity.*

Nevertheless, in some crucial respects, there are theoretical *necessities* behind how the BRICS will play their diverse roles at a time of brewing economic-ecological crises, as noted below. The surface-level geopolitical rivalries and shifting alliances noted above suggest not only 'logics of capital' and also logics of state territorial expansion that follow universal 'laws of motion' with respect to global uneven and combined development – but also the opposite: *contingencies* associated with leadership choices and political foibles that often reflect the host country's prerogative of setting the agenda at each annual meeting. (One example was on display at the 2016 Goa summit: Modi's US-style fetish with the critique of terrorism, as an ultimately futile way to divide Pakistan from China and Russia.[2])

So we may superficially *describe* the conjuncture based on the contingencies of the moment. But if instead we want to *theorise* these political-economic processes, we need a more powerful conceptual apparatus that cuts across politics, economics, ecology and the internal social conditions of very different places. Such a theory should also explain how the incorporation of BRICS within the imperial project displaces underlying economic tensions –the centrifugal processes of capitalist crisis formation – into the realms of geopolitical and 'global governance' rivalries. (Recall the hostility of Barack Obama's regime to both the Asian Infrastructure Investment Bank and the Belt and Road Initiative, as well as Chinese capital's penetration into Africa, which has motivated the Trump regime's rediscovery of the continent since 2018.) Instead of muting these rivalries, the assimilation of BRICS displaces them onto terrains that are more liable to disintegrate; at the time of writing, both the world's trade and climate policy-making bodies are subject to collapse, mainly due to Trump's sabotage, defunding and ultimately withdrawal.

That conceptual apparatus is the theory of subimperialism. But it is controversial, so after clarifying its meaning, we then turn to recent leftist and Third Worldist critiques of this idea, and offer rebuttals. Then we move to interrogate one particularly vivid illustration in the contemporary period: malgovernance of global finance, in which the BRICS are increasingly implicated. We conclude by considering the geopolitical fracturing, economic chaos and ecological catastrophe which in turn, as the analysis of subimperialism confirms, are the logical results of the BRICS' amplification of global crisis tendencies – even as they appear to have offered an illusory 'fix' and maintain rhetorical innocence in the crimes of Western imperialism.

A CONCEPTUAL APPARATUS FOR
CENTRIFUGAL, SUBIMPERIAL TIMES

The term subimperialism was first coined by Brazilian political economist Ruy Mauro Marini (1932–1997), and will be referred to periodically, below, where it is useful to indicate the overlapping interests of Western and BRICS powers, or ways that BRICS-based firms (including state-owned capital) penetrate their societies and hinterlands in a manner comparable to Western multinational corporations. This threatens world stability largely because of China's contribution to capital over-accumulation, a process which is the most rigorous basis for the Marxist theory of economic crisis (Harvey 1999). The BRICS not only seek to shore up global economic governance under such conditions, they also play a role as 'deputy sheriffs' in their respective hinterlands, since the political-economic domination of regions surrounding each of the BRICS are important to enhancing their power.[3]

As a bloc, BRICS issues periodic communiques and occasionally acts in concert, and as a result, regularly resorts to using *anti-imperial* rhetoric. One example was the successful lobbying by BRICS foreign ministers against the proposed expulsion of Russia from the 2014 G20 Brisbane summit, following sanctions the West imposed on Moscow after the March 2014 transfer of power in Crimea. In another example, at the St Petersburg G20 summit in 2013, Washington's plan to bomb the Syrian leadership (following a reported nerve gas attack on dissidents) was vetoed by not only Russian leader Vladimir Putin but also South African president Jacob Zuma.

At that point, BRICS was considered a coherent 'bloc' in the making, and indeed during its first decade, from 2009 to 2018, it increasingly asserted an 'alternative' strategy against the most notable features of the Western-dominated power structure. These included multilateral political conflicts over finance, trade, climate policy and even soccer (through a controversial, corruption-riddled Swiss agency, FIFA, which granted World Cup hosting rights to three BRICS countries between 2010 and 2018). Much of the rhetoric restates the BRICS' opposition to 'unfair, unreasonable, and imperfect aspects of the old governance systems' (Wang and

Guan 2017). But in reality, the BRICS had fitted fairly tightly within imperialism during the pre-Trump era. This fit worked through an amplification of neoliberal multilateralism by the likes of Obama in the US, Angela Merkel in Germany and most of the global-scale institutions' leadership.

Global financial, trade and climate policies are, thanks to the G7–BRICS alliance, disastrous for the world's poor people and for planetary survival. The policies reflected how capitalist crisis tendencies are amplified through neoliberal multilateralism, as corporations utilise the global governance regime to aid in displacing overaccumulated capital, financialisation, natural resource extraction and persistent super-exploitative social relations. The BRICS emerged immediately after the 2008/09 world financial meltdown, where China's turn to (high-carbon) infrastructure investments – such as ghost cities and massive highway expansion (along with lower-carbon high-speed trains, to be sure) – allowed world capitalism to continue stumbling forward, in classical Keynesian mode, displacing but not resolving the crisis tendencies. Although in 2014/15, the overaccumulation crisis discussed below had become evident, the next effort by Beijing along these lines – the Belt and Road Initiative – was similarly oriented to infrastructure construction, but now much further afield, stretching even to Africa's east coast.

How are we to explain this, in theoretical terms? Earlier, in his 2003 *The New Imperialism,* Marxist geographer David Harvey (2003: 185–186) observed:

> The opening up of global markets in both commodities and capital created openings for other states to insert themselves into the global economy, first as absorbers but then as producers of surplus capitals. They then became competitors on the world stage. What might be called 'subimperialisms' arose . . . Each developing centre of capital accumulation sought out systematic spatio-temporal fixes for its own surplus capital by defining territorial spheres of influence.

The existence of surplus capital caused falling rates of profit in the productive sectors of the BRICS as well as the Western powers. What Harvey (2003) terms 'spatio-temporal fixes' and 'accumulation by dispossession' then helped to displace the surpluses elsewhere, and thus partially restored profits. But instead of resolving the crisis symptoms, the BRICS now play a role in amplifying the underlying contradictions. These start with overaccumulation and then move to globalisation (the spatial fix), financialisation (the temporal fix), and imperialist super-exploitation (accumulation by dispossession). The strategies of 'shifting, stalling and stealing' succumb to various internal contradictions, however, and so subimperial collaboration is both integral to and undermining of (due to amplified crisis tendencies) the broader imperial agenda, in a way that we have never witnessed before with semi-peripheral states in the world-system.

Nevertheless, this is not an easy segue way from one hegemon (the US) to the next (China), but instead happens in terms of uneven and combined development: overaccumulation of capital, the spatial fix and financialisation occur at different tempos across different spaces, with centrifugal divergences quite apparent within the BRICS (hence meriting the description 'schizophrenic'). To illustrate, given that three of the BRICS – Brazil, Russia and South Africa – had de-industrialised during the 1990s and mainly become exporters of raw materials, the 2014/15 commodity price crash hit them particularly hard. China and India maintained steady demand for the three others' fossil fuels and minerals during the high-growth era. So by 2019, two of the five BRICS' currency values – as a proxy for economic health – soared to levels between 25 and 55 per cent greater than in 2010 against the dollar (the rupee and the renmimbi), while the other three (the real, the ruble and the rand) each lost 15 per cent.

The main problem below these shifting economic sands, though, was that Chinese state capitalists were engaged in such massive overproduction during their Keynesian inward-oriented infrastructure boom in the early 2010s that their own capacity to produce steel, cement, coal and other raw and semi-beneficiated products suddenly outran their internal demand. That, in turn, led to such high levels of global overcapacity – the 'overaccumulation of capital' – that the subsequent export of the surplus at often subsidised rates wiped out other countries' industries. In 2015, mining industry shares fell precipitously, with the two leading mining and commodity firms, BHP Billiton and Glencore, respectively, dropping more than 85 per cent of their stock market share value. China's artificially low currency valuation, especially in the 2015–2019 years of declining yuan strength against the dollar, resulted in a steady competitive attack on even BRICS partners (notwithstanding a brief dip in Chinese output in 2015, when its main producers first became extremely overexposed).

To illustrate using the case of the steel industry, South Africa today produces around 6 million tons annually, after having peaked at over 9 million tons in the 1990s – a puny figure compared to China's output of more than 820 million tons (figure 4.1). The world's largest manufacturer, Arcelor Mittal (with output of 96 million tons annually), is owned by Lakshmi Mittal, an Indian based in Luxembourg. He shuttered several of his South African foundries in 2015–2016, just as an apparently impotent Minister of Trade and Industry documented how Mittal had engaged in overpricing and disinvestment (Davies 2015). The Russian – London-based Roman

Figure 4.1 Steel overaccumulation driven by China

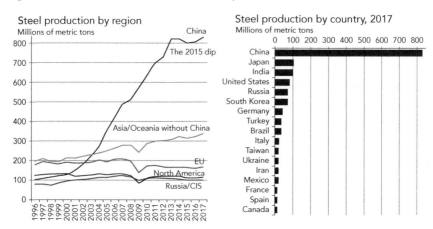

Source: World Steel Association, in Richter (2018).

Abramovich – who owned South Africa's second steel company, Evraz Highveld, took the company into formal bankruptcy in 2015, costing 1 700 well-paid jobs. He too was suspected of milking that firm in order to pay higher salaries to his best Chelsea soccer players (Crowley 2015).

Wild swings in the world price were also evident (figure 4.2). From an index level ranging between 100 and 110 during the period 1982–2002 (i.e., relatively unchanging), the subsequent hike in steel prices reflected fast-rising Chinese demand. As the commodity super-cycle unfolded, the price rose to an index level of 294 in mid-2008. The Great Recession caused an index-level crash to 169 a year later, but Beijing's rapid Keynesian interventions allowed a recovery to 258. However, after a brief plateau, overcapacity became acute, causing the price to fall to 172 by late 2015. There was sufficient shake-out that year, thanks to a dip in Chinese production and the collapse of other countries' industries, for the price to recover to 245 by late 2018. But another serious fall in prices during 2019 reduced the index to 210 by September 2019. From the standpoint of the BRICS bloc, the catalytic Chinese overproduction accompanied substantial declines in all the other BRICS countries. Hence, instead of a centripetal, collaborative relationship, the experience of BRICS steel-industry corporations was one of centrifugal, ultra-competitive cannibalism.

Nevertheless, in spite of the underlying tendencies to overaccumulation and subsequent devaluations that sometimes tear the BRICS asunder, a universal dynamic had, until 2019, usually reasserted itself: imperial powers used subimperial allies to

Figure 4.2 Producer price index for iron and steel, 2002–2019

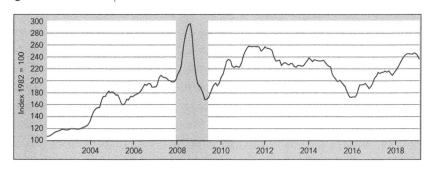

Source: Federal Reserve Bank of St Louis.[4]

strengthen global governance. This may well have ended with the Bolsonaro-Trump project of selective multilateralism, as we will conclude below. Regardless, the general thesis of subimperialism remains hotly contested within both the political scene and in geopolitical relations, so it is important to review the current debate.

CONTESTED BRICS NARRATIVES: ANTI-IMPERIAL, SUBIMPERIAL OR IN-BETWEEN?

The very word subimperialism raises hackles, especially in cities like Pretoria where a 'talk left, walk right' stance prevails (Bond 2006, 2019a). As the BRICS emerged and visited South Africa, host foreign minister Maite Nkoana-Mashabane (2013) expressed this frustration:

> To see BRICS countries as 'subimperialists' is the result of a dogmatic application of classical notions of imperialism and Immanuel Wallerstein's centre-periphery model to a situation that is fundamentally different from what these theories were trying to comprehend and explain. Our scholars have to be innovative and courageous enough to develop new tools of analysis and theoretical models when history challenges us to do so.

However, Nkoana-Mashabane neglected to engage the actual argument about subimperialism. Indeed, the anti-imperial refrain is typically heard in African National Congress (ANC) circuitries, for as Zuma (2016) explained the BRICS to grassroots activists, 'It is a small group but very powerful. [The West] did not like BRICS. China is going to be number one economy leader . . . [Western countries] want to dismantle this BRICS. We have had seven votes of no confidence in South Africa. In Brazil, the president was removed' (referring to what was essentially an *internal* parliamentary coup against Dilma Rousseff). Zuma (2017) reiterated the same point at his party's mid-2017 policy conference: 'The ANC is part of the global anti-imperialist movement. We are historically connected with the countries of the South and therefore South–South cooperation such as BRICS is primary for our movement.' During 2016 and 2017, Zuma repeatedly claimed that because he brought South Africa into the BRICS, the West wanted him out of power, even murdered.[5] There was a certain pride that in the 2017–2018 United Nations General Assembly, South Africa's representative voted with the United States just over ten per cent of the time, leading to opprobrium by Washington's then ambassador, Nikki Haley.

Much anti-imperialist rhetoric has focused on the injustice of Western control of global financial circuits. At the 2015 Ufa summit, Zuma expressed the need for an alternative to the Bretton Woods Institutions in a *Russia Today* interview: 'They want to dictate what you should do. You can't utilise that kind of assistance the way you want. So, in a sense, it has conditions that will keep you dependent all the time. That's what we're trying to take ourselves out of' (Ebrahim 2015).

His successor Cyril Ramaphosa (2018) told the United Nations annual leaders' summit in 2018 that the International Monetary Fund (IMF) and other multilateral institutions 'need to be reshaped and enhanced so that they may more effectively meet the challenges of the contemporary world and better serve the interests of the poor and marginalised'. In early 2019, Ramaphosa went further: 'We are not going to be a puppet of the West. We are a proud nation and can never subject ourselves to that after going through what we went through . . . We are trying to do everything we can to not fall into the hands of the IMF' (Malope 2019).

In December 2018, similar language was heard in Russian Communist Party chairperson Gennady Zyuganov's speech to the Johannesburg meeting of the BRICS 'Political Parties Plus Dialogue':

> For the first time in history a powerful group of countries representing three continents has emerged to protect the interests, not only of their population but of many other countries not prepared at this stage to challenge the global rule of the West . . . New forces emerging in Africa, Asia, Latin America and the Middle East are increasingly challenging the global domination of the old colonial powers, which are determined to retain control over the world by economic blackmail, information genocide and military interventions . . . The results of this important forum will be a major step in the liberation of

mankind of the last vestiges of neocolonialism – a guiding star on the road to universal peace and prosperity. (Sokutu 2018)

For such reasons, one of Africa's leading Third-World-nationalist political strategists, Yash Tandon (2018), does not agree that we should consider the BRICS to be subimperial:

Imperialism is a historical phenomenon created during the rise of capitalism and its by-product, colonialism. China and India traded with Africa for a thousand years but never colonised Africa. There are undoubtedly asymmetrical power relations between China and African countries, just as there are asymmetrical power relations between the US and Europe. But in terms of their relationship, *the US does not have imperial relations with, for example, the United Kingdom. In the same vein, Chinese (and Russian and Indian) relations with Africa are not imperial, nor subimperial.* (original emphasis)

Tandon (2018) doesn't see this as permanent, however:

Africa's principal contradiction is with the Anglo-American Empire. Russia and China might become 'imperialist' in relation to Africa. They might, but for now they are 'tactical' allies of Africa. In this struggle – for some 30 years, and in the case of South Africa, nearly 50 years – the Soviet Union and China were 'tactical' allies. They provided diplomatic as well as military support to Africa . . . For Africa and the global South, BRICS offers a promising tangible alternative to the declining Western powers and their institutions of global economic and political governance. These have lost their credibility and legitimacy. As for the 'Ultra-Left' comrades, you may throw bricks at BRICS but these will land, surely, on your own feet.

Like the politicians quoted above, Tandon (2014, 2018) has not yet openly conceded the malevolent roles of BRICS countries in institutions such as the IMF and the World Bank, the World Trade Organization (WTO), United Nations Framework Convention on Climate Change (UNFCCC) and G20, nor the often predatory roles of the BRICS' firms in Africa. So although Tandon (2017) termed South Africa a 'neo-colony' when Zuma played a subservient role in the 2018 G20 summit, it was as if the political problem remains one of neocolonial power relations, instead of the global imposition of neoliberal capitalism, *against which Tandon himself was long on the frontlines of struggle.*[6] The BRICS' role within the broader operation of an imperialism that is not merely a colonial legacy, but instead an ongoing system of multinational corporate extraction, is not – perhaps for tactical reasons related to alliances – up for discussion in his otherwise prolific geopolitical commentary.

Tandon's (2014) main confusion concerns which countries qualify as subimperialist, a conundrum repeated by the lead scholar of transnational capitalist class formation, William Robinson (2015: 9). Tandon (2014) insinuates that those of us who deploy the idea of subimperialism in turn imply that

> every country that follows the neoliberal economic paradigm, and seeks market or an avenue for capital export to a neighbouring country [is] a subimperialist. Thus, in their lexicon, Kenya becomes a subimperialist country in the East African region – it exports both goods and capital within the region. But then what about Uganda? It exports Chinese-made 'subimperialist' goods to Rwanda and the DRC, as well as acting as conduit for Chinese capital in the region. Does that make Uganda also 'subimperialist'?

Tandon's questions can be readily answered with another: to what extent can these particular states exercise power in the world economy? Kenya and Uganda are somewhat trivial, and South Africa is less so. To provide one indicator, surplus flows between the corporations of various countries reveal a clear hierarchy: first, a group of imperialist countries whose firms draw in above 100 per cent of dividends from other countries, net of payments of dividends to others; second, a group which draws net dividends in the 20–60 per cent range; and third, a group of peripheral countries below 20 per cent (figure 4.3).[7]

Similarly, leading world-systems scholar William Martin (2013, 2019) reaffirms his opposition to the term subimperial. The problem he sees in relation to South Africa – which before apartheid ended in 1994, was the West's main African ally – is the evolution of international power over the past quarter century. Martin (2019: 54) argues: 'Subimperial relationships created by white-settler rule have been rent asunder by two forces: one, the slow demise of US hegemony and its neoliberal counter-revolution; and two and most disruptively for current theoretical schemas, the displacement of North–South relationships with East–South engagements.'

Yet the 'old' apartheid-corporate relationships of white South Africa backed by the West got a new, relegitimised lease on life after Nelson Mandela (1994–1999) and Thabo Mbeki (1999–2008) repeatedly reinserted South Africa into global neoliberal management, to the benefit partly of those very white elites who liberalised their wealth out of South Africa and restructured the local economy to become

Figure 4.3 Profit flows, 2015–2017 (average dividend receipts as a per cent of dividend payments)

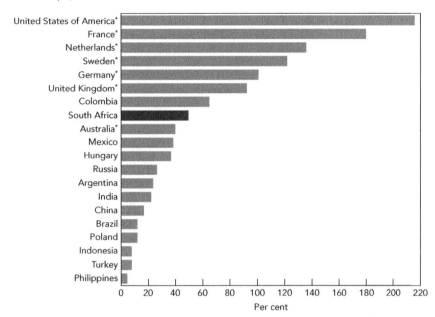

Source: SA Reserve Bank (personal correspondence, 1 October 2019). Reproduced with permission.
Note: * Advanced economies

even more unequal and poverty-stricken than before (Bond 2005, 2006, 2014). The demise of Washington's hegemony may continue apace as the US loses world economic market share, but parts of it – such as in global finance, trade and climate policy – remain formidable. The 'displacement' of North–South with East–West lines of power is hotly debated, for example, by John Smith (2018) and David Harvey (2018).[8] Martin's deeper critique, however, is that the very framing of imperialism in terms of the capitalist versus the non-capitalist spheres, following Rosa Luxemburg, causes 'a major difficulty':

> The concept inevitably traces downward from crises of accumulation in advanced capitalist states (via overproduction, underconsumption, falling rate of profit, etc.), to their resolution by a new burst of forcing open and exploiting poorer, so-called 'pre-' or 'non-' capitalist areas, states and peoples . . . Contemporary discussions of 'accumulation by dispossession' by following this path often construct a relatively homogeneous, residual and objectified Global South that is operated upon from above. In a common

scenario: an accumulation crisis in the North is resolved by Northern states and capital opening up 'non-capitalist' areas in the South. (Martin 2013: 166–167)

One part of Martin's concern is correct: the argument stretching back to Luxemburg (1913) that the overaccumulation crisis is often behind the metabolism of capital penetrating the non-capitalist spheres – whether in the 'South' considered geographically, or instead, as does Vijay Prashad (2014), with respect to class power, including within the North. (There, urban ghettoes are better considered to be 'global South' than my neighbourhood and office in central Johannesburg.) But Martin (2019: 55) incorrectly smears this argument as a 'reductive, Euro-American conception', neglecting that the leading *dependencias* also focused on super-exploitative relationships associated with multinational corporate exploitation. Critics from Latin America (e.g. Marini 1972) and especially Africa – for example, Samir Amin (1990), Dani Nabudere (2009), AnnMarie Wolpe (with Annette Kuhn 1978) and Harold Wolpe (1980) – were acutely aware of this superexploitation. Indeed, the 'scramble for Africa' in 1885 (Phimister 1992) and subsequent twists and turns in the colonial and apartheid systems ravaging Africa reflected bouts of overaccumulation crisis in the North (Bond 2003). (For example, South Africa's most rapid historical growth spurt, especially in manufacturing, occurred during the 1930s–1940s, demonstrating the economy's ability to 'delink' from the then-collapsing northern capitalist circuits.)

This misreading leads to another of Martin's concerns, regarding agency:

In these formulations, the South and its peoples play little role, if any, in the crisis and its resolution through a geographical 'spatial fix' that provides new markets and new sources of cheap labour and raw materials . . . This is particularly problematic for eminently capitalist areas as illustrated by Lenin's short, ambiguous references to 'semi-colonies' and 'semi-independent countries', or today's uncertain formulations surrounding the so-called BRICS, Newly Industrialising Countries (NICs), Turkey, Venezuela and similarly strong ex-colonial and ex-imperial states. (Martin 2019: 54)[9]

Again, Martin misses a most crucial point stemming from the *anti-subimperial* literature, which is that if 'the South' is now led by the BRICS, it is *mainly* their state and corporate elites' compradorism on the one hand, and progressive movements' agency on the other, that are under our 'brics-from-below' microscopes (e.g. Bond 2018a; Bond and Garcia 2015; Garcia and Bond 2018).[10] Still, Martin concludes his most recent argument with the allegation that 'China, and the BRICS more generally, are not, of course, an anti-capitalist initiative. But neither are they handmaidens of US neoliberalism' (2019: 69). On the contrary, in January 2017 at the World Economic Forum, Xi was – for all effective purposes – handed the baton of world neoliberal leader (formerly held by Obama), as Donald Trump prepared to enter the White House. Xi had become a Davos Man:

> Economic globalisation resulted from growing social productivity, and is a natural outcome of scientific and technological progress, not something created by any individuals or any countries. Economic globalisation has powered global growth and facilitated movement of goods and capital, advances in science, technology and civilisation, and interactions among peoples . . . Whether you like it or not, the global economy is the big ocean that you cannot escape from. Any attempt to cut off the flow of capital, technologies, products, industries and people between economies, and channel the waters in the ocean back into isolated lakes and creeks is simply not possible. (Xi 2017)

In this context, in which the BRICS fit within – not against – the global corporate system of accumulation, Martin's (2019: 68) view of South–South elite relationships is disappointingly uncritical, since, for example, all the South Africa–China deals of which he approves – dating to the 2015 peak period of Zuma-era larceny – were actually duds: unworkable, extremely corrupt and notably carbon-intensive.[11]

WESTERN–BRICS POWER RELATIONS DURING WORLD BANK AND IMF 'REFORM'

One way to assess current imperial-subimperial relations is the debate over global policy reform, especially in contested sites such as the IMF and the World Bank, the WTO, UNFCCC and the G20 and the G8 (until 2014, and now G7 without Vladimir Putin's Russia). In practically all of these, the BRICS are in diverse ways implicated in nurturing imperial power relations. Consider first, trade, then climate and then an in-depth view of global financial power relations.

First, trade: in 2015, the Nairobi summit of the WTO brought agricultural subsidies and hence food sovereignty to an end, once US and European negotiators drew support from Brazilian agribusiness (as expected) and even Modi's Indian delegation. The Chinese, South African and Russian delegations did not object, although this was a major attack on the ability of poor countries to feed their populations (Raghavan 2015). The objective, Xi (2017) made clear in Davos, was to prohibit 'any attempt to cut off the flow of capital, technologies, products, industries . . .', even if that included the kinds of protection required to ensure food sovereignty, or safeguard organic agriculture, or establish infant industries.

Second, the 2015 UNFCCC Paris Climate Agreement reflected a deal between four of the BRICS (minus Russia) with Obama in Copenhagen six years earlier. The result is that commitments to emissions cuts are too small and in any case non-binding. There continues to be unending extraction of fossil fuels, with no UNFCCC regulation. Nor are emissions caused by military, maritime and air transport covered. The return of carbon trading is endorsed. The main beneficiaries of the inevitable increase in emissions in the wake of Paris are corporations and wealthy residents of carbon-intensive, rich and middle-income countries, especially the BRICS (Bond 2016).

Third, since the financial meltdown of 2008/09 – the world's worst since the Great Depression – financial power has been hotly contested. The initial Western response was a massive artificial boost to financial liquidity (mainly through 'quantitative easing' by central banks in the US, Britain, Europe and Japan), the IMF's special drawing rights quotas (its underlying capitalisation) and other financing powers were raised by members to US$1 trillion. As a result, its conditionality capacity grew dramatically (Varoufakis 2017). A further 2012 recapitalisation – mainly used in southern European countries – included US$75 billion more in donations from the BRICS countries, but with distortions in voting power that mainly hurt poorer countries. In both the 2009 and 2012 recapitalisations, South African finance ministers Trevor Manuel and Pravin Gordhan were instrumental in Bretton Woods Institution relegitimisation. Manuel was the main IMF ally during Dominique Strauss-Kahn's successful attempt at recapitalising, between the IMF annual meeting in October 2008, all the way through his May 2011 resignation-in-disgrace. Gordhan regularly supported the World Bank and IMF in ideology and concrete machinations, even at the trough of its legitimacy.[12]

But it was telling that finally, the 2010–2015 negotiations over 'quota reform' – that is, a less unfair distribution of power within the IMF – ended when the US Congress agreed to shift most countries' voting weight, some quite significantly. Washington agreed to drop its share by two per cent and Tokyo agreed to shrink by one per cent, while the main European powers each declined by between five and nine per cent. That, in turn, allowed the share controlled by four of the BRICS (all except South Africa) to rise substantially: China by 37 per cent, Brazil by 23 per cent, India by 11 per cent and Russia by 8 per cent (see table 4.1).

However, to round out the changes to the voting shares, not only did the BRIC countries become the main gainers (with these four states among the top ten IMF

Table 4.1 Changes in the IMF top ten owner-countries' voting shares, 2010–2019

Country	2010	2019	Per cent change
United States	16.7	16.5	−2
Japan	6.2	6.1	−1
China	3.8	6.1	37
Germany	5.8	5.3	−9
France	4.3	4.0	−7
United Kingdom	4.3	4.0	−7
Italy	3.2	3.0	−5
India	2.3	2.6	11
Russian Federation	2.4	2.6	8
Brazil	1.7	2.2	23

Source: International Monetary Fund 2019.

owners), some of the poorest countries were, in the process, dramatically disempowered at the IMF. Nigeria lost 40 per cent of its votes and South Africa lost 21 per cent, with weaker African countries losing shares between those two: Libya (−39 per cent), Morocco (−27 per cent), and Gabon, Algeria and Namibia (all −26 per cent). Many Latin American and Asian countries also lost substantial amounts of IMF voting shares. In short, the BRIC countries gained power and a seat at the IMF high table, mainly by standing on poorer countries' heads, pushing them down. This is one basis for the label coined by Marini (1972), to describe the role of nations that 'actively collaborate' in the extension of imperial power: subimperial.

Moreover, after 2009, the IMF came to rule over not just impoverished but also so-called emerging economies (the recipient of its largest-ever loan, for example, was Argentina following its 2017/18 meltdown) – just as during the 1980s and 1990s – and even began imposing austerity on poor residents of the southern European countries that had fallen into crisis.[13] Unfortunately, the BRICS offered no alternative to this power, for in 2014, at the Fortaleza BRICS summit, the original Articles of Agreement of the Contingent Reserve Arrangement (CRA) (signed by Gordhan) actually strengthened the IMF, against the expectations of many observers.[14] Due to Chinese pressure, the CRA founding agreement required that after 30 per cent of a country's quota was borrowed (e.g. US$3 billion for South Africa), the debtor would then need to access an IMF structural adjustment programme to receive the next 70 per cent.[15]

Meanwhile, across 18th Street in Washington, the World Bank turned even more decisively to serving private-sector interests during the BRICS' ascent, culminating in 2018 when, according to *The New York Times,* its president Jim Yong Kim became intent on the Bank 'remaking itself as a creature of Wall Street . . . Kim has tried to present the bank as a tool to enhance the [Trump] administration's "America First" policy'. As he told *The Times,* 'Ivanka, Jared, Gary Cohn, Dina Powell – they all know our business model very well' (Thomas 2018). In his final lecture as Bank president, at the University of the Witwatersrand in Johannesburg in December 2018, Kim (2018) announced, 'The ten things that are included in the Washington Consensus, most of them are really good. Most of them are things like central banks should be independent from state government. Most of those ideas are really good.' Kim had co-edited a 2000 book, *Dying for Growth* (Kim et al. 2000), which was extremely critical of neoliberalism as practised at the Bank, but he was wrong on this elementary point. Of the ten commandments associated with the Washington Consensus (Williamson 2004), an independent Reserve Bank was not included.

Assimilation of critics is an old, effective strategy, including the likes of Kim, his replacement David Malpass and the BRICS leadership. To illustrate, in 2008 the G20 was created by expanding the traditional G7, which generally coordinated geopolitical and economic strategy for global capitalism. As the global financial meltdown began, the new grouping incorporated all the BRICS and several other middle-income regimes (which were especially vital for fund-raising during the world financial bailouts). It is apparent that the IMF and World Bank simply co-opted the BRICS elites by adding them to the power structure, for example, granting second-tier leader roles for several bureaucrats from the BRICS. In the case of the WTO, the director-general during the 2010s was a Brazilian, Roberto Azevêdo, a man described by Tandon (2015) as 'not neutral – a free market fundamentalist [who] works for the Empire'.

Reflecting how such assimilation can prevent collective action for genuine reform, the BRICS directors at the Bretton Woods Institutions were divided about suggesting non-Western leaders when the opportunities arose, especially, first, during the 2011 replacement of the IMF managing director, a position which went from the neo-Keynesian Dominique Strauss-Kahn to the neoliberal Christine Lagarde. She was also reappointed with BRICS directors' support in 2015 and reaffirmed unanimously even after her 2016 Paris court conviction on corruption charges (for 'negligence' in giving a French Conservative Party donor US$430 million) (Thomas et al. 2016). Second, a split emerged, as well, during the 2012 replacement of the World Bank president, from neoconservative Robert Zoellick during the Bush administration to the neoliberal Kim during the Obama administration (Bond 2012).

In February 2019, Trump announced Kim's replacement by Malpass, a China-basher of note who, as Bear Stearns chief economist in mid-2007, notoriously predicted that 'the housing- and debt-market corrections will probably add to the length of the US economic expansion' (Malpass 2007). Instead, his own institution went bankrupt in March 2008 and within months, the world financial meltdown was underway. In spite of that exceptional display of incompetence, Malpass offered at least one useful insight about World Bank staff when testifying a decade later to the US House Committee on Financial Services (2017):

> Malpass: They're often corrupt in their lending practices, and they don't get the benefit to the actual people in the countries. They get the benefit to the people who fly in on a first-class airplane ticket to give advice to the government officials in the country – that flow of money is large – but not so much the actual benefit to normal people within poor countries, and that's what I'd like to see change.

> Representative Maxine Waters: Do you have an example of that?

> Malpass: Well, for example, we have countries such as South Africa that are deteriorating rapidly as their government is unable to provide efficiency and effectiveness . . . South Africa is heavily indebted and not making progress and is not being well served by its relationships with international financial institutions.

If he had been pushed for a more detailed reply, Malpass could have referred to the World Bank's largest-ever project loan (US$3.75 billion): the Medupi coal-fired power plant, a project rife with not only extreme incompetence (in 2019 half the plant was still under construction, seven years behind schedule, but suffering debilitating design flaws that reduced its generation capacity to half-power), and corruption (involving the ruling ANC and Hitachi, which was prosecuted successfully in Washington under the US Foreign Corrupt Practices Act, although South Africans received none of the proceeds from the US$19 million fine). Indeed, the outstanding debt should simply be cancelled on grounds of lender co-liability (Bond 2012). But most remarkably, in spite of a blunt corruption allegation of this sort – bound to sting South African elites like Gordhan, who in 2010 lobbied hard for the Bank loan to Medupi – none of the BRICS leadership publicly opposed Malpass's appointment or suggested their own replacement.

Instead, the overarching sentiment was one of despondent resignation, for example in Beijing's *Global Times* (usually a reliable indicator of elite opinion) where Export-Import Bank chief risk analyst Zhao Changhui (2019) looked ahead:

> When the world needs the World Bank most in order to maintain, defend and lead multilateralism, Malpass is about to assume the leadership of the organisation, which is not a good sign. Under these circumstances, China must recognise the devastating consequences of the US containment to the nation and must implement the Chinese solution wisely and with strategic initiative. In other words, we must keep an objective and realistic attitude. The World Bank should no longer be the main battleground for China's efforts. While it may receive loans as a recipient country, it is in fact facing increasingly harsh pressure.

As for more general prospects that the Bank's perspective could shift, said Zhao (2019):

> From the perspective of governance structure, as long as the US still wants to maintain its grip on the World Bank, it would be hard to see any actual reform progress, with major shareholders, other than the US, unlikely to push for any new changes. There is no need for China to rush to spend too much time, efforts and resources on this issue, unless a new opportunity presents itself for World Bank reforms.

However, well before the Malpass appointment, reform had failed. Judging by how little had changed at the Bretton Woods Institutions since the advent of the BRICS – notwithstanding the replacement of a sex pest (indeed, alleged rapist) with a woman to lead the IMF, and the appointment of a former leftist NGO activist as World Bank president – the Bretton Woods Institutions were impervious to the kinds of pressure these countries' leaders attempted to apply. Notwithstanding all the hype, the BRICS' multilateral financial strategy appears to have derailed. Moreover, the Malpass era will likely witness the end of World Bank support to Chinese projects.

In short, power structures can readily integrate not only the appointment of unusual personnel (a woman lawyer – then, in 2011, already facing corruption charges – to lead the world's main financial institution and a radical intellectual at the Bank), but also an unusual power bloc of aspiring capitalist states (the BRICS). Zhao (2019) is correct that no further gestures towards changing Western-dominated multilateral finance are likely to come from China, or indeed from the BRICS.

CONCLUSION

The argument presented above suggests that instead of declining US hegemony and the assimilation of a united, reform-oriented BRICS within global economic governance, as would follow logically from 'middle power' rhetoric (whether from politicians or sympathetic analysts), a more nuanced approach to subimperial analysis is required. That nuance starts with the difference between necessary and contingent processes, and moves through the kinds of overaccumulation crises and reactions in capital's shifting, stalling and stealing processes described above. The rise of the subimperial powers is logical, as the hegemonic power goes into decline and geopolitical multipolarity emerges. At this point, the BRICS (especially China) are implicated in catalysing the overaccumulation and in arranging new spatio-temporal fixes and amplified processes of accumulation by dispossession. As an ersatz bloc, the BRICS' participation in world financial (mis)management is just one example (see Bond 2018a and Garcia and Bond 2018 for many others).

No matter how schizophrenically their geopolitical behaviour appears, the BRICS are, evidently, consistent in one process: amplifying world capitalism's centrifugal self-destruction. Historically, the only solution to the global-scale overaccumulation crisis has been 'devaluation,' which took the forms of world-wide depressions and wars in prior epochs. Both types of devaluation destroy productive capital, and thus clear the way for a new round of accumulation (Bond 2019b; Harvey 1999). Today, partial devaluation is so difficult to control, strategically, that even as centralised a capitalist state as Beijing finds it impossible to manage the promised industrial capacity cuts. The most exposed, least competitive economic units – such as South Africa's steel plants, not to mention vastly over-indebted corporations and countries – will continue to go bankrupt at an increasing pace, into the next world recession and perhaps depression.

Such devaluation could, in theory, contribute to the emergence of a 'degrowth' political economy, in which a globally planned Just Transition away from fossil-intensive energy, transport, agriculture, urbanisation, production, consumption and disposal systems occurs, a '*This Changes Everything*' opportunity (Bond 2019b; Klein 2014). But it is far more likely, given the balance of forces, that the centrifugal pressures will take the form of much more uncreative destruction of overaccumulation, including mass economic misery and heightened geopolitical rivalries, probably leading to renewed war.

It is already obvious how such contemporary centrifugal tensions can be felt, politically, in catastrophic forms, and it is here that we might better understand the

BRICS' own fracturing due to the Bolsonaro wedge. One aspect of the current crisis was discussed in Houston, Texas, after nearly two years of the Trump presidency, in November 2018. At Rice University's James Baker Center, Obama openly confessed to Baker – formerly a Reagan-Bush era foreign and finance minister – how neoliberalism dating to the early 1980s bred a right-wing backlash: 'You have this period of great smugness on the part of America and American elites, thinking, "We got this all figured out." Remember there were books coming out that it's the end of history.' Baker replied, 'Yeah, *The End of History*, Francis Fukuyama.' Concluded Obama, 'Yeah, that came back to bite us' (Norton 2018).

That 'bite' was from the right; it may well signal Washington's 'retreat' from multilateralism (e.g. in the UNFCCC and WTO); or on the other hand, if Trump continues with the sort of strategy unveiled in early 2019 with the World Bank presidency, it may simply be a case of more bullying to get his way. But there are also left-wing reactions to the imperial-subimperial relationship, and particularly to the way the BRICS damage their own people, their environment and their hinterland neighbours. To address the potential for resisting subimperialism first requires that the underlying characterisation of the phenomenon is addressed (including persistent denialism in use of the term, as shown above). That, in turn, allows for greater clarity about who allies are – in contrast to the denialism of Tandon (2018) who, for all his superb contributions to weakening global neoliberalism, bizarrely considers the Moscow and Beijing regimes as Africa's allies.

Turning finally to the weakest link in the BRICS from the standpoint of bottom-up resistance – Pretoria – the history of anti-imperialist activism in South Africa is impressive. It ranges from anti-apartheid/colonial movements up to 1994; to ongoing Cuba, Palestine and Burma solidarity and regional campaigning for freedom in Zimbabwe and eSwatini (Swaziland), to the fight against Big Pharma over AIDS medicines from 1999–2005, to 'Jubilee 2000' debt cancellation and reparations advocacy, to early 2000s integrated global struggles against French and British water privatisers, to critiques of specific firms including Lonmin (UK), BASF (Germany) and MRC (Australia), to building a climate-justice movement (especially when Durban hosted the UNFCCC in 2011), to internal anti-xenophobia activism. Some internationalism is self-interested and not 'progressive', but is still useful: for example when white capital, led by Johann Rupert, helped liberals and a few radical activists drive the London public relations firm Bell Pottinger to bankruptcy in 2017, as part of the overall critique of the 'Zupta' (Zuma-Gupta) power structure. That process continued with the delegitimation and corporate boycott of KPMG, McKinsey, SAP, Bain and several other multinational corporations, for their role in covering up Gupta corruption (Bond 2019a).

The fragmented, disconnected character of these sorts of anti-imperial and anti-subimperial politics also requires more attention. More coordination will be necessary if activists and the allies in society aim to be increasingly effective in the period ahead, given that the targets for critics of subimperial capital accumulation are so diverse. It was relatively easy for South African activists to push back Rosatom's 2015–2018 US$100 billion nuclear energy deal signed with Zuma at the 2015 Ufa summit. Resisting the largest shareholder in the Anglo American Corporation – India's notorious Anil Agarwal[16] – will be harder. Chinese state capital's incursions into South Africa, including financial relations through the China Development Bank, were rife with corruption, a problem that continues with the BRICS New Development Bank's 2016–2019 loans to Eskom, Transnet, the Development Bank of Southern Africa, the South African Roads Agency and the Trans-Caledon Tunnel Authority (Bond forthcoming).

Perhaps the greatest challenge of all in coming years, aside from climate change, will be the so-called Fourth Industrial Revolution. After all, the vast majority of South African investors (including those workers with pension funds) have unwittingly acquired a material interest in Chinese state surveillance of their Facebook/Twitter-equivalent customers, and in the 'social credit' manipulation and repression of 1.4 billion people. This is because Beijing's primary corporate agent, Tencent, is 30 per cent owned by Naspers (a formerly pro-apartheid media house), which accounts for 22 per cent of the Johannesburg Stock Exchange share value. In 2018, Tencent assisted in prohibiting 23 million people from travelling on Chinese planes and trains, because of those citizens' personal social-credit ratings by the Beijing regime as 'anti-social'. The same term will readily fit those progressive Chinese activists organising trade unions, fighting pollution, trying to halt rural land-grabs, or even convening Marxist reading groups.

These are the contradictions now surfacing in South African, BRICS and global politics, representing the most sophisticated top-down attack on the rights of the masses ever witnessed in human history. Bottom-up resistance – which we might term 'brics from below' – has enormous potential, as a result of so many different kinds of targets.[17] It does probably help to name the broader problem 'imperialism', no matter its Trumpian 'anti-globalist' deviations, and also name the BRICS (not just Bolsonaro) as 'subimperial' accomplices, for these labels represent the first analytical steps that must be taken to confront the world's contradictions and power relations with the clarity required. Still, while theory is vital to work out – so as to assess opportunities for appropriate principles, analyses, strategies, tactics and alliances – the semantic disputes reviewed above do appear relatively trivial, compared to the concrete struggles for humanity's and the planet's survival that appear on the immediate horizon.

NOTES

1 In 2018, according to Pagliarini (2019), 'Araújo ingratiated himself to the United States by proposing an alliance between the world's three largest Christian countries – Brazil, the United States, and Russia – to counter what he called "the globalist axis" made up of China, Europe, and the US left. Other symbolically important gestures include Brazil's withdrawal from the UN Compact on Migration; equivocation over whether it will abandon the Paris climate accord; its stated intention to move its embassy in Israel from Tel Aviv to Jerusalem, irking important trading partners in the Arab world; and its participation in the aggressive international campaign to isolate and ultimately remove Venezuela's Nicolás Maduro. Brazil's new willingness to cede its hemispheric leadership is linked to a desire to defer to a Trump-led United States.'

2 The first formal BRIC gathering was in 2006 when foreign ministers met at the United Nations, followed by heads-of-state summits at Yekaterinburg hosted by Vladimir Putin in 2009, by Lula da Silva at Brasilia in 2010, Wen Jia Bao at Sanya in 2011, Manmohan Singh at New Delhi in 2012, Jacob Zuma at Durban in 2013, Dilma Rousseff at Fortaleza in 2014, Putin at Ufa in 2015, Narendra Modi at Goa in 2016, Xi Jinping at Xiamen in 2017, Cyril Ramaphosa in Johannesburg in 2018, and Jair Bolsonaro in Brasilia in 2019.

3 Since 2013, leaders from neighbouring states and regional blocs have also been invited to spend time with the BRICS leaders (usually a half-day after the members' meeting closes). In Johannesburg in 2018, in addition to select African heads of state, the main guests were regional leaders who were also heads of state of: Egypt (as Chair of the G77+China), Argentina (Chair of the G20 and a Southern Common Market [MERCOSUR] member), Indonesia (Co-chair with South Africa of the New Africa-Asia Strategic Partnership and an Association of Southeast Asian Nations [ASEAN] member), Jamaica (incoming Chair of the Caribbean Community [CARICOM]), and Turkey (as Chair of the Organisation of Islamic Cooperation [OIC]). In Xiamen in 2017, the BRICS-Plus group was initiated to include Egypt, Guinea, Mexico, Tajikistan and Thailand. In Goa in 2016, notably, regional collaboration did *not* include Pakistan, but did include India's Bay of Bengal Initiative for Multi-Sectoral Technical and Economic Cooperation neighbours: Bangladesh, Myanmar, Sri Lanka, Thailand, Bhutan and Nepal. In Ufa in 2015, the BRICS overlapped with the Shanghai Cooperation Organisation, which includes Kazakhstan, Tajikistan, Kyrgyzstan and Uzbekistan along with the observer states Afghanistan, India, Iran, Mongolia and Pakistan. In Brasilia just after the 2014 Fortaleza meeting, the Brazilian hosts invited leaders from the Union of South American Nations, including Argentina, Bolivia, Chile, Colombia, Ecuador, Guyana, Paraguay, Peru, Suriname, Uruguay and Venezuela. The tradition of drawing in the host's friendly neighbours was begun in Durban in 2013, when more than a dozen African leaders (never formally named) joined the summit at Zimbali Lodge.

4 See https://fred.stlouisfed.org/series/WPU101 (accessed 16 August 2019).

5 In mid-2017, Zuma announced to grassroots supporters, 'I was poisoned and almost died just because South Africa joined BRICS under my leadership' (Matiwane 2017). His mid-2014 poisoning was actually carried out by his fourth wife, whom Zuma's confidant Gayton McKenzie (2017) claimed was operating in league with the US Central Intelligence Agency, to halt the progress of the BRICS. However, no one has produced any proof and state investigations mysteriously ground to a halt in 2016.

6 Among Tandon's heroic roles were leading insider African critiques of the 1999 WTO – which put an end to the West's Seattle 'Millennial Round' ambitions – and directing the South Centre in the 2010s.

7   Data in figure 4.3 from the South African Reserve Bank (supplied to this author) provide the most up-to-date snapshot of net profit flows that I have found. Prior to the data's availability, Robinson's (2015: 7) critique was that, 'Bond seems to see the world economy as boxed into national economies and capitals, yet the extent of global economic integration and the transnationalisation of capital in the twenty-first century undermines any significant analytical purchase to dividing the world's economies into imperialist, subimperialist and imperialised.'

With the 2015 data suggesting a clear division in surplus flows, assuming their country headquarters are valid units of analysis, Robinson nevertheless offered this reply, in correspondence with the author in 2019: 'I would not change my critique of the subimperialist thesis. Specifically, I understand the surplus flows you are documenting and they are highly relevant, but my critique in terms of who (what capitalist groups) control and appropriate these flows has not changed, in so far as the transnational and interpenetrated structure of global capital and the global financial infrastructure renders an analysis that takes nation-states as a stand-in for global capital clusters is misleading, i.e., the imperialist extraction is not by nation-states but by transnational capital. This does not at all render irrelevant your data but means we need to interpret it in terms other than the subimperialist frame.'

My rebuttal is that naturally, the extraction is by corporations, not 'nation-states' – but these national units, their currency valuations – as above – and their leaders' capacity to marshal their capital-fractional elites' interests as a national project are all quite evident within the BRICS. What geographers often describe as a *nested hierarchy* of bounded spaces of differing size (Delaney and Leitner 1997: 93) still corresponds to these capitals' interests and their national projects.

8   See Bond 2018b for the argument that neither is correct, having neglected subimperial powers and resource extraction from their recent polemics. Smith (2019) later acknowledges that subimperialism occurs 'when the capitalist rulers of a subject nation in turn subject other, even weaker, nations and peoples to their political and economic domination' but neglects to develop the theme notwithstanding its importance to the current conjuncture.

9   Martin (2019) worries that my using an 'anti-imperialist' framing to describe BRICS elite rhetoric (as above) – particularly the anti-imperialist fantasies of supporters such as the eloquent commentator Pepe Escobar (2013) – is to make 'analytical and political missteps'. But in claiming that 'BRICS go over the wall', Escobar (2013) certainly does at least try to posit anti-imperialist if not inter-imperialist possibilities: 'When Putin stressed that he does not see the BRICS as a "geopolitical competitor" to the West, it was the clincher; the official denial that confirms it's true. Durban may be solidifying just the beginning of such a competition. It goes without saying that Western elites – even mired in stagnation and bankruptcy – won't let any of their privileges go without a fierce fight.'

10 See also http://www.bricsfrombelow.org (accessed 13 August 2019).

11 Martin (2019: 68) first approvingly cites a '$2.5 billion credit line to South African rail and transport operator Transnet' – one which by 2017 was revealed to be rife with corruption associated with the Gupta immigrants' role in Transnet's purchase of 1 000 locomotives from China South Rail, especially for coal exports, but with such a large share going to dubious middle men that by 2018 Transnet's chief executive was fired and in early 2019, the new chair had to beseech China South Rail to repay some of the funds.

Second was 'a $500 million China Development Bank loan to electricity utility Eskom for badly needed power plant construction', but instead of financing renewables, it went to two coal-fired power plants, Medupi and Kusile (at 4 800 MW, the largest being built on the planet at the time), whose procurement system was so corrupt that the US Securities and Exchange Commission successfully prosecuted the Japanese firm Hitachi in 2015 for bribing the ANC through its investment arm.

Third, Martin notes China's 'plans for the country's largest automobile plant', which was in reality only a US$760 million investment by Beijing Auto Investment Company for a project that should have been completed in 2017 but was interminably delayed, at least until late 2019. Moreover, confessed even the pro-Chinese Independent chain of newspapers, the cars emerged from semi-knock-down kits, hence 'serious doubts have been expressed in motor industry circles about the claims that the vehicle was manufactured in South Africa ... the local media reported that the construction had been moving at a snail's pace and all small, medium and micro enterprises had vacated the premises due to non-payment' (Cokayne 2019).

Another high-profile Chinese investment promise, a Hebei Iron and Steel plant able to produce five million ton/year (i.e. raising local output by 80 per cent) promised for 2017, never materialised. The 2018 Chinese pledge to Ramaphosa that a 4 600 MW coal-fired power plant would be built near the South Africa-Zimbabwe border to power a massive new metallurgical complex immediately went quiet after the high-profile announcement. In sum, all such promises by multinational corporations should be taken with a grain of salt, in a neoliberal era in which attracting foreign direct investment often appears as the main role for jejune political leaders.

12   Reflecting only a brief moment of rebelliousness, in 2012 Gordhan proposed an alternative World Bank presidential candidate who was not a US citizen, and hence lost. Nigerian Finance Minister Ngozi Okonjo-Iweala had performed well within the institutional boundaries when she served for 21 years at the Bank, including as a managing director. In January 2012, just before Gordhan's nomination, she nearly caused her own government in Abuja (led by Goodluck Jonathan) to fall, as a result of mass national protests which began when she unquestioningly took IMF advice to end retail petrol subsidies. She then left the Nigerian government to join international bankers Lazard (New York) and Standard Chartered (London).

13   Gordhan favoured applying what he termed 'nasty' austerity policies to these northern countries, as he remarked in a 2011 radio interview (Moneyweb 2011), the effect of which was to line up the South African government and its taxpayers with the IMF and European Union leadership and allied state leadership against poor and working-class people of the peripheral European states, just as he had lined up a similar configuration in the emerging and poorest economies (Bond 2013). While it is true that a British Labour government required an IMF bailout loan and early structural adjustment in 1976, this degree of IMF invasiveness within the EU was unprecedented, because it occurred in combination with the European Central Bank and the European Union (the 'troika') (Varoufakis 2017).

14   There are a dozen cases of leftist political economists misinterpreting the power relations (Bond 2016). One important politically liberal reform-oriented academic, Stephanie Griffith-Jones (2014: 3), who had been sympathetic to the BRICS, argued that the New Development Bank is 'a dream coming true', for she predicted the opposite, namely that 'the BRICS CRA will not include a link to the IMF, which brings about policy conditionality in the event of crisis'.

15   In South Africa's case, this would allow an immediate US$3 billion CRA balance-of-payments loan, but to get the next $7 billion would require IMF intervention. The

US$170+ billion foreign debt South Africa has accumulated will require tranche repayments of such magnitude in coming years, with world financial turbulence growing, that the danger of IMF intervention continually rises.

16   See http://www.foilvedanta.org/ (accessed 13 August 2019).

17   See http://www.bricsfrombelow.org (accessed 13 August 2019).

REFERENCES

Amin, S. 1990. *Delinking*. London: Zed Books.

Bond, P. 2003. *Against Global Apartheid*. London: Zed Books.

Bond, P. (ed.) 2005. *Fanon's Warning*. Trenton: Africa World Press.

Bond, P. 2006. *Looting Africa*. London: Zed Books.

Bond, P. 2012. *Politics of Climate Justice*. Pietermaritzburg: University of KwaZulu-Natal Press.

Bond, P. 2013. 'Sub-imperialism as lubricant of neoliberalism', *Third World Quarterly* 34 (2): 251–270.

Bond, P. 2014. *Elite Transition*. London: Pluto Press.

Bond, P. 2016. 'Who wins from "climate apartheid"?', *New Politics* 15 (4): 122–129. Accessed 14 August 2019, https://newpol.org/issues/new-politics-vol-xv-no-4-whole-number-60/.

Bond, P. 2017. 'BRICS Xiamen summit doomed by centrifugal economics', *Pambazuka* 31 August. Accessed 14 August 2019, https://www.pambazuka.org/global-south/brics-xiamen-summit-doomed-centrifugal-economics.

Bond, P. (ed.). 2018a. *BRICS Politricks*. Johannesburg: bricsfrombelow.org. Accessed 26 March 2019, https://peoplesbrics.files.wordpress.com/2018/07/brics-politricks-for-july-2018-johannesburg-teach-in.pdf.

Bond, P. 2018b. 'East-West/North-South – or Imperial-Subimperial? The BRICS, global governance and capital accumulation', *Human Geography* 18 (2): 1–18. Accessed 14 August 2019, https://hugeog.com/east-west-north-south-or-imperial-subimperial-the-brics-global-governance-and-capital-accumulation/.

Bond, P. 2019a. 'Citizens, states, corporations, and nature', *Dialogues of Civilisation Research Institute Blog*, 29 March. Accessed 14 August 2019, https://doc-research.org/2019/03/citizens-states-corporations-and-nature-eu-south-africa-conflicts-flare/.

Bond, P. 2019b. 'Degrowth, devaluation and uneven development from North to South'. In E. Chertkovskaya, A. Paulsson and S. Barca (eds), *Towards a Political Economy of Degrowth*. London: Rowman and Littlefield, https://www.rowmaninternational.com/book/towards_a_political_economy_of_degrowth/3-156-2c50d07e-66fe-4355-af91-d7966546dfea.

Bond, P. forthcoming. 'The BRICS New Development Bank's false dawn'. In A. Shaw and R. Bhattacharya (eds), *Urban Housing, Livelihoods and Environmental Challenges in Emerging Market Economies*. Delhi: Orient Blackswan.

Bond, P. and Garcia, A. (eds). 2015. *BRICS*. London: Pluto Press.

Cokayne, R. 2019. 'BAIC sets new timelines for projected SA vehicle plant', *Independent Online*, 26 February. Accessed 26 March 2019, https://www.iol.co.za/business-report/companies/baic-sets-new-timelines-for-projected-sa-vehicle-plant-19504827.

Crowley, K. 2015. 'Evraz opposes Highveld Steel rescue through court application', *Reuters*, 23 October. Accessed 26 March 2019, https://www.moneyweb.co.za/news/companies-and-deals/evraz-opposes-highveld-steel-rescue-through-court-application.

Davies, R. 2015. 'The steel industry in crisis', *Politicsweb*, 29 August. Accessed 26 March 2019, http://www.politicsweb.co.za/news-and-analysis/the-steel-industry-in-crisis--rob-davies.

Delaney, D. and Leitner, H. 1997. 'The political construction of scale', *Political Geography* 16 (2): 93– 97.

Ebrahim, S. 2015. 'BRICS bank a move in right direction', *The Star*, 10 July. Accessed 26 March 2019, https://www.iol.co.za/the-star/brics-bank-a-move-in-right-direction-1883626.

Escobar, P. 2013. 'BRICS go over the wall', *Global Research*, 27 March. Accessed 26 March 2019, https://www.globalresearch.ca/brics-go-over-the-wall/5328662.

Garcia, A. and Bond, P. 2018. 'Amplifying the contradictions'. In L. Panitch and G. Albo (eds), *The World Turned Upside Down*. London: Merlin Press, pp. 223–246.

Griffith-Jones, S. 2014. *A BRICS development bank: A dream coming true?* United Nations Conference on Trade and Development Discussion Paper No. 215. Accessed 26 March 2019, https://unctad.org/en/PublicationsLibrary/osgdp20141_en.pdf.

Harvey, D. 1999. *The Limits to Capital*. London: Verso.

Harvey, D. 2003. *The New Imperialism*. New York: Oxford University Press.

Harvey, D. 2018. 'Realities on the ground', *Roape.net*, 2 February. Accessed 26 March 2019, http://roape.net/2018/02/05/realities-ground-david-harvey-replies-john-smith/.

International Monetary Fund. 2019. 'IMF members' quotas and voting power', Washington DC, 19 September. Accessed 20 September 2019, https://www.imf.org/external/np/sec/memdir/members.aspx.

Jessop, B. 2018. 'The world market, "North–South" relations, and neoliberalism', *MROnline*, 8 March. Accessed 26 March 2019, https://mronline.org/2018/03/08/the-world-market-north-south-relations-and-neoliberalism/.

Kim, J.Y. 2018. 'The human capital crisis'. Speech delivered at Wits School of Governance, Johannesburg, 3 December. Accessed 26 March 2019, https://live.worldbank.org/human-capital-crisis.

Kim, J.Y., Millen, J., Irwin, A. and Gershman, J. (eds). 2000. *Dying for Growth*. Boston: Common Courage Press.

Klein, N. 2014. *This Changes Everything*. Toronto: Knopf.

Kuhn, A. and Wolpe, A. 1978. *Feminism and Materialism*. London: Routledge Kegan Paul.

Luxemburg, R. 1913. *The Accumulation of Capital*. Marxist Internet Archives. Accessed 26 March 2019, https://www.marxists.org/archive/luxemburg/1913/accumulation-capital/.

Malope, L. 2019. 'Ramaphosa spurs on entrepreneurs, says SA will not be "puppet of the West"', *CityPress*, 10 March. Accessed 26 March 2019, https://city-press.news24.com/News/ramaphosa-spurs-on-entrepreneurs-says-sa-will-not-be-puppet-of-the-west-20190310.

Malpass, D. 2007. 'Don't panic about the credit market', *Wall Street Journal*, 7 August. Accessed 26 March 2019, https://www.wsj.com/articles/SB118645120890190059.

Marini, R.M. 1972. 'Brazil subimperialism', *Monthly Review* 23 (9). Accessed 16 August 2019, https://monthlyreviewarchives.org/index.php/mr/article/view/MR-023-09-1972-022/0.

Martin, W. 2013. 'South Africa and the "new scramble for Africa": Imperialist, sub-imperialist, or victim?', *Agrarian South* 2 (2):161–188.

Martin, W. 2019. 'South Africa and the new scramble: The demise of sub-imperialism and the rise of the East'. In S. Moyo, P. Jha and P. Yeros (eds), *Reclaiming Africa*. London: Springer, pp. 51–72.

Matiwane, Z. 2017. 'I was poisoned and almost died when SA joined BRICS, says Zuma', *Independent Online*, 14 August. Accessed 26 March 2019, https://www.iol.co.za/news/politics/i-was-poisoned-and-almost-died-when-sa-joined-brics-says-zuma-10782354.

McKenzie, G. 2017. *Kill Zuma by Any Means Necessary*. Johannesburg: ZAR Empire Holdings.

Moneyweb. 2011. 'Special report podcast: Pravin Gordhan, Minister of Finance', Johannesburg, 29 September. Accessed 26 March 2019, https://www.moneyweb.co.za/archive/special-report-podcast-pravin-gordhan-minister-of/.

Moyo, S. and Yeros, P. 2011. 'Rethinking the theory of primitive accumulation'. Paper presented to the 2nd IIPPE Conference, 20–22 May 2011, Istanbul, Turkey. Accessed 26 March 2019, ccs.ukzn.ac.za/files/Yeros%20Moyo%20sub%20imperialism.pdf.

Nabudere, D. 2009. *The Crash of International Finance Capital and Its Implications for the Third World*. Oxford: Fahamu Books.

Nkoana-Mashabane, M. 2013. Speech delivered at the BRICS Academic Forum welcome dinner, Durban, 10 March. Accessed 26 March 2019, https://www.gov.za/speech-ms-maite-nkoana-mashabane-minister-international-relations-and-cooperation-brics-academic.

Norton, B. 2018. 'Obama admits bipartisan capitalist "Washington Consensus" fuelled far-right and multiplied inequality', *TheRealNews*, 21 December. Accessed 26 March 2019, https://therealnews.com/stories/obama-admits-bipartisan-capitalist-washington-consensus-fueled-far-right-multiplied-inequality.

Pagliarini, A. 2019. 'The worst diplomat in the world', *Jacobin*, 26 February. Accessed 26 March 2019, https://jacobinmag.com/2019/02/ernesto-araujo-jair-bolsonaro-brazil.

Phimister, I. 1992. 'Unscrambling the scramble: Africa's partition reconsidered'. Wits Social History Seminar, Johannesburg, 17 August. Accessed 26 March 2019, http://hdl.handle.net/10539/9599.

Prashad, V. 2014. *The Poorer Nations*. London: Verso.

Raghavan, C. 2015. 'Doha SU diminished, not dead, and retrievable', *Third World Network*, 23 December. Accessed 26 March 2019, https://www.twn.my/title2/wto.info/2015/ti151222.htm.

Ramaphosa, C. 2018. Address to the UN General Assembly, United Nations, New York, 25 September. Accessed 26 March 2019, http://www.thepresidency.gov.za/speeches/address-president-south-africa%2C-h.e.-mr-cyril-ramaphosa%2C-un-general-assembly%2C-united.

Richter, W. 2018. 'Who dominates the steel trade that Trump just hit with tariffs?' *Wolfstreet.com*, 1 June. Accessed 26 March 2019, https://wolfstreet.com/2018/06/01/who-dominates-the-steel-trade-that-trump-just-hit-with-tariffs/

Robinson, W. 2015. 'The transnational state and the BRICS', *Third World Quarterly* 36 (1): 1–21.

Smith, J. 2018. 'David Harvey denies imperialism', *Roape.net*, 10 January. Accessed 26 March 2019, http://roape.net/2018/01/10/david-harvey-denies-imperialism/.

Smith, J. 2019. 'Dispossessed workers, farmers, small producers still await their day of liberation', *MROnline*, 19 March. Accessed 26 March 2019, https://mronline.org/2019/03/19/john-smith-on-imperialism-part-1/.

Sokuto, B. 2018. 'BRICS must "fight global domination by old colonial powers"', *Citizen*, 4 December. Accessed 26 March 2019, https://citizen.co.za/news/south-africa/2045719/brics-must-fight-global-domination-by-old-colonial-powers/.

Tandon, Y. 2014. 'On subimperialism and BRICS bashing', *Pambazuka*, 21 May. Accessed 26 March 2019, https://www.pambazuka.org/governance/sub-imperialism-and-brics-bashing.

Tandon, Y. 2015. 'Resisting WTO's culture of terror and impunity', *Pambazuka*, 16 December. Accessed 26 March 2019, https://www.pambazuka.org/global-south/resisting-wto%E2%80%99s-culture-terror-and-impunity.

Tandon, Y. 2017. 'G20: The second Berlin war against Africa', *Pambazuka*, 20 July. Accessed 26 March 2019, https://www.pambazuka.org/economics/g20-second-berlin-war-against-africa.

Tandon, Y. 2018. 'The ultra-left's confusion about the BRICS', *Pambazuka*, 10 August. Accessed 26 March 2019, https://www.pambazuka.org/emerging-powers/ultra-left%E2%80%99s-confusion-about-brics.

Thomas, L. 2018. 'The World Bank is remaking itself as a creature of Wall Street', *The New York Times*, 25 January. Accessed 26 March 2019, https://www.nytimes.com/2018/01/25/business/world-bank-jim-yong-kim.html.

Thomas, L., Alderman, L. and Breeden, A. 2016. 'I.M.F. stands by Christine Lagarde, convicted of negligence', *The New York Times*, 19 December. Accessed 26 March 2019, https://www.nytimes.com/2016/12/19/business/imf-trial-christine-lagarde-france-verdict.html

Trevisani, P. and Pearson, S. 2019. 'Brazil Foreign Minister calls on Russia, China to oppose Venezuela's Maduro', *Wall Street Journal*, 7 March. Accessed 26 March 2019, https://www.wsj.com/articles/brazil-foreign-minister-calls-on-russia-china-to-oppose-venezuelas-maduro-11551995278.

US House Committee on Financial Services. 2017. 'Administration priorities for the International Financial Institutions', Washington, 8 November. Webcast. Accessed 26 March 2019, https://financialservices.house.gov/calendar/eventsingle.aspx?EventID=400919

Varoufakis, Y. 2017. *Adults in the Room*. New York: Vintage.

Wang, W. and Guan, Z. 2017. '10 myths about BRICS debunked', *Financial Times*, 1 September. Accessed 26 March 2019, https://www.ft.com/content/50fe74e6-8f0a-11e7-a352-e46f43c5825d.

Williamson, J. 2004. 'The Washington Consensus as policy prescription for development'. Lecture in the Practitioners of Development series, World Bank, Washington, DC, 13 January. Accessed 26 March 2019, https://piie.com/publications/papers/williamson0204.pdf.

Wolpe, H. 1980. *The Articulations of Modes of Production*. London: Routledge Kegan Paul.

Xi, J. 2015. 'Jointly build partnership for bright future'. Speech delivered to the 7th BRICS Heads-of-State Summit, Ufa, Russia, 9 July. Accessed 26 March 2019, https://brics2017.org/English/Headlines/201701/t20170125_1402.html.

Xi, J. 2017. Opening plenary address to the World Economic Forum, Davos, 17 January. Accessed 26 March 2019, https://www.weforum.org/events/world-economic-forum-annual-meeting-2017/sessions/opening-plenary-davos-2017.

Zhao, C. 2019. 'What are the implications for China resulting from Trump's World Bank presidential nominee?', *Global Times*, 13 February. Accessed 26 March 2019, http://www.globaltimes.cn/content/1138783.shtml.

Zuma, J. 2016. 'I know who are the witches at work'. Speech delivered at the Pietermaritzburg African National Congress Meeting, 19 November. Accessed 26 March 2019, https://www.politicsweb.co.za/news-and-analysis/i-know-who-are-the-witches-at-work--jacob-zuma.

Zuma, J. 2017. 'The ANC must and will emerge from this policy conference stronger', *Daily Maverick*, 30 June. Accessed 26 March 2019, https://www.dailymaverick.co.za/article/2017-06-30-op-ed-the-anc-must-and-will-emerge-from-this-policy-conference-stronger/.

5

A ROAD TO DEVELOPMENT? THE NACALA CORRIDOR AT THE INTERSECTION BETWEEN BRAZILIAN AND GLOBAL INVESTMENTS

Ana Garcia and Karina Kato

Brazil's relations with countries in Africa gained importance at the beginning of the twenty-first century. In that period, trade between Brazil and Africa rose from US$4.9 billion in 2002 to US$26.5 billion in 2012 (BNDES 2013).[1] Brazilian multinational corporations from the extractive and construction industries present in Africa since the 1970s have made their most significant advances in the first decade of 2000. This expansion has been driven largely by public policies, specifically the new lines of credit offered by the Banco Nacional de Desenvolvimento Economico e Social (BNDES, or the Brazilian Economic and Social Development Bank) and the government's proactive foreign policy that has 'cooperation for development' as one of its main pillars.

When international cooperation and private investment arrive in recipient countries, they tend to mix and blend together. The Nacala Development Corridor in Mozambique is illustrative of this process, as it reveals the leading role of corporations on the one hand, and, on the other, the complementarity between cooperation policies and private investment. Infrastructure and logistics are gaining prominence on the agendas of international financial institutions (such as the World Bank), intergovernmental forums and bodies (namely the G8 and the BRICS) and international organisations (including the World Economic Forum and the African Union). This greater emphasis coincides with changes in the rationale behind Brazil's cooperation efforts, which seek to build closer ties with private investors through public-private partnerships (Ikegami 2015). Therefore, the Nacala Corridor is a case that – due to the complexity of the projects involved and its importance to the global market – allows us to understand the political economy of development corridors and their role in connecting territories to global value chains.

In 2019, 100 years since Rosa Luxemburg was brutally murdered, we recover some of the arguments of Luxemburg and David Harvey (2005, 2007). The latter engagement remembers and renews some of Rosa Luxemburg's main ideas, especially the reflection on the central role played by non-capitalist spheres in the dynamics of deepening capitalist accumulation, operating as a source of supply for raw materials and a reservoir of labour power. Harvey points out that investments in infrastructure promote temporal and spatial displacements to temporarily resolve crises of overaccumulation and, at the same time, incorporate new areas into the capitalist accumulation in a process in which force and violence complement the expanded reproduction of capital in advanced economies. Saskia Sassen (2016) also highlights the discussion over infrastructure and changes in territories, as she points to a new 'geography of extraction' led by transnational corporations seeking to incorporate territories into global corporate circuits. Using these lines of theory as a basis, we sought to further our understanding of the relation between Brazilian foreign direct investments and cooperation in Mozambique. This revealed a complex relationship between the state, public policies and corporations that are driving Brazil's international relations. The Nacala Corridor is key for ensuring the feasibility of Brazil's main cooperation project in the area of agriculture, the ProSavana programme, and is a prime location for the implementation of the Vale mining corporation and Mitsui's business strategies. All along the corridor, investments and cooperation projects contribute to the consolidation of global value chains linked to international markets. Thus, we argue that Brazil's actions (as a BRICS country) in Mozambique obey the logic of the dispute for natural resources and market access, in a competition that is imperialist in nature and that has turned its focus once again on Africa.

PUBLIC POLICIES, PRIVATE INTERESTS: BRAZILIAN INVESTMENTS AND COOPERATION IN MOZAMBIQUE

In the transition from a socialist to a capitalist economy in Mozambique, the state actively pursued economic growth by seeking to increase foreign investments and exports, with the support of international aid. Its consolidation as a natural resource and commodity-exporting economy was the result of the actions of agencies and donors who, since the 1990s, have implemented a policy of adjusting Mozambique's economic policy. This opened the door to foreign intervention and led to the convergence of the interests of Mozambican elites with neoliberal values and the global corporate agenda. In Mozambique, there are over 30 credit and donor agencies, notably the International Monetary Fund and the World Bank, which impose conditions and contribute to the national budget with donations. Donors have close relations with the government, participate in internal discussions and intervene in national policy (Hanlon 2017; Macamo 2003; Sombra Saraiva 2012).[2]

In the 2000s, the rediscovery of abundant reserves of natural and energy resources in Mozambique reinforced the central role of foreign investments in the country's economy (Mosca and Selemane 2013). It was in this economic and political context that Brazil sought to tighten its relations with Mozambique again in the twenty-first century, while fostering the internationalisation of Brazilian companies by offering considerable government support. According to Jimene Duran and Sergio Chichava (2013), Brazil, now an 'emerging power', had apparently discovered a 'new Mozambique'. Earlier on in Lula's first presidential mandate, in 2004, Brazil signed an agreement with Mozambique (US$315 million) on the restructuring of the debt that it had incurred in 1978 during the military dictatorship, to make it feasible for Mozambique to purchase Brazilian goods and services for coal exploration back home.[3]

Vale mining corporation is the biggest Brazilian investor in the country (see figure 5.1). It was drawn to the country in 2007 by the quality of the coal deposits in Tete (Vale 2013). The installation (and later the duplication) of the mine was the result of a joint venture between Vale (95 per cent) and Empresa Moçambicana de Exploração Mineral (5 per cent). Brazilian construction companies Odebrecht, Camargo Correa and Andrade Gutierrez were also involved in the operations. In 2012, the company announced US$6.4 billion in investments in the expansion of the Moatize mine (*O País* 2012). In 2014, however, due to the economic crisis and the fall in coal prices, Vale reduced its share in the venture to 81 per cent, after selling 15 per cent to Japan-based Mitsui Group (Vale 2014). In 2018, with the commodities market on a decline, Vale continued to pursue a policy of reducing its leverage in and its dependence on iron ore. Even so, in Mozambique, the mine-railway-port complex still has significant weight in the corporation's portfolio.

Due to the nature of its operations, logistics is central to Vale's activities in Brazil and abroad. In the twenty-first century, the corporation has placed its bets on logistics and invested in the mine-railway-port cycle.[4] In Mozambique, the corporation reproduced 'the success model adopted in Brazil', which seeks to integrate all phases of

Figure 5.1 Vale's business units in Mozambique

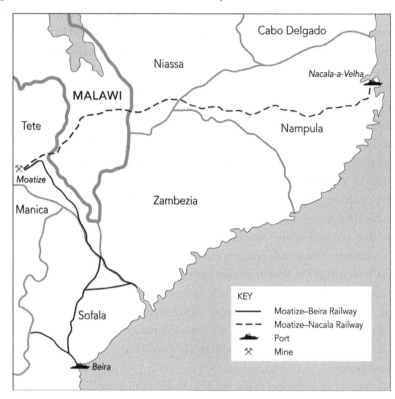

Source: Vale (2013). Redrawn by Janet Alexander.

production vertically into its operations in order to increase its margins by reducing costs (Vale 2011). With the goal of creating an alternative route for getting its coal to markets in Asia, Vale restored (and built parts of) a railway line that connects Tete to Nacala, where it also built an export terminal. This was done in partnership with the state railway company, Caminhos de Ferro de Moçambique (CFM), which owned 30 per cent of the venture. In 2014, Vale kept 35 per cent of its share in the venture and handed over 30 per cent to Mitsui (Durao and Ciarelli 2014; Vale 2014). According to Vale, in addition to being a linchpin in its business portfolio (the Moatize mine produces 57 per cent of all of Vale's coal), the Nacala Corridor has the potential to support the development of agriculture, to transport commercial cargo in Mozambique and Malawi and to operate as a 'connector of remote locations' (Vale 2014).

A complex institutional arrangement, involving several concessionaries and companies, was established. This gives an indication of the difficulties we faced in tracing the ownership and control of value chains at a time when markets are becoming increasingly financialised. The concessionaire Corredor Logístico Integrado do Norte (CLIN), a joint venture between Vale (which owns 80 per cent) and CFM, was in charge of the stretches of the railway track that were still to be built. For the restoration of the existing railway line, the concessionaire was Corredor de Desenvolvimento do Norte (CDN, 51 per cent of which is controlled by the Sociedade de Desenvolvimento do Corredor do Norte, SDCN, which belongs to Vale) and CFM. In Nacala, Vale owns the Nacala-a-Velha port. In Malawi, there are two concessionaires: Vale Logistics Limited (VLL) (owned 100 per cent by Vale), which is building a new stretch of the railway (with MotaEngil from Portugal), and the Central East African Railway Company (CEAR), which is rebuilding part of the existing railway (51 per cent is owned by SDCN and 49 per cent by CFM).[5] In all of these companies, Brazilian-based Vale plays a fundamental role.

The financial architecture of the Nacala Corridor is also highly complex. For the railway line and the coal export terminal in Nacala-a-Velha, the Japanese Mizuho Bank, the African Development Bank (AfDB) and other private institutions[6] signed a funding agreement for the amount of US$2.73 billion in 2017. The funds were handed over to the four companies created by Vale and Mitsui. The corridor had the support of other international financial institutions as well, such as the Japan Bank for International Cooperation (JBIC, US$1 billion) (AfDB 2015; Mizuho Bank 2017). As for railway infrastructure, AfDB is funding a project that seeks to connect Malawi, Mozambique and Zambia (AfDB 2009, 2015). In addition, the BNDES granted a loan of US$125 million to finance the construction of the Nacala airport by Odebrecht. Due to the economic crisis affecting Mozambique since 2016, the country has stopped making its loan payments to the BNDES.[7]

Conflicts related to Vale's operations in Mozambique have been reported by international organisations[8] and in our previous work (Garcia and Kato 2015; Garcia et al. 2013). These conflicts are linked to the opening of the mines (the problem with the resettlement of residents in particular), the treatment of workers and, more recently, the operation of the railway line. Regarding the resettlements, there was a lack of transparency on the part of the company during the negotiations about the conditions of relocation for the families, who suffered from several problems. For one, the areas they were moved to are not suited to agriculture, as there is limited access to water and nearby markets. The way in which the value of the families' farms and homes was calculated resulted in compensation that was too low. Furthermore, there were several problems with the houses in the resettlement areas: not only did they not respect the local culture, it also did not take long for cracks to appear due to the poor quality of the construction work, as well as leakages and security flaws.[9] As for the workers, in addition to the differences in wages and treatment received by Brazilian and by Mozambican workers, there were reports of a lack of security systems and equipment in the workplace, and hence the occurrence of many accidents. The company's actions generated discontent and numerous protests and strikes (Garcia and Kato 2015). It's worth noting that, as the biggest iron ore company in the world, Vale has faced many kinds of social, environmental and labour conflicts, not only in Mozambique – to name just a few; in Canada, the steelworkers' strike against cuts in their pensions and deteriorating work conditions lasted for 11 months; in the north of Brazil, Vale's biggest mine, Carajas, is located in the middle of the Amazon forest, arousing the ire of environmentalists, and in the state of Minas Gerais, the failure of Vale's tailing dams in Mariana (in 2015) and Brumadinho (in 2019) has caused immeasurable damage to the environment and to people living in the surrounding communities (Marshall 2015; *The New York Times* 2019).

The company's strategy in response to the growing number of complaints has been to advance its social responsibility programme. In relation to the resettlement sites created by Vale, the company sought to compensate through measures such as paving the road that linked the Cateme resettlement to the district, donating animals to farming initiatives, building water tanks and so on.[10] Even so, the living conditions in these communities continues to be highly precarious and many of the projects have recently been discontinued. With regard to the railway line, the CDN has been conducting training sessions in schools with the goal of reducing the number of train accidents, which has become a problem in recent years, especially those involving children and animals.

In addition to Vale, we observed the expansion of the operations of Brazilian construction corporations – Odebrecht, OAS and Andrade Gutierrez – in Mozambique, with financing from the BNDES. The BNDES was the main instrument of state support for the internationalisation of Brazilian multinationals during the Lula da Silva (2003–2010) and Dilma Rousseff (2010–2016) administrations. Not only did the development bank provide credit directly to Brazilian companies for their projects in foreign countries, the bank itself internationalised its operations by opening subsidiaries in London (2009), Montevideo (2009) and Johannesburg (2013). The BNDES Exim line of credit has been key in this process. It offers financing for the export of products and services or trade activities abroad. Between 2007 and 2015, 542 projects received funds from BNDES Exim, which lent a total of approximately US$12 billion to construction corporations for the engineering services they offered to construction projects in Latin America and Africa. Odebrecht alone presented 414 projects, the value of which totalled approximately US$7.5 billion.[11]

In Mozambique, the BNDES financed the construction of the Nacala airport; the contracts for this project totalled US$175 million.[12] One of the main investors in Angola (since the 1980s), Odebrecht entered Mozambique only in the 2000s to do work on Vale's coal mine. The company is also involved in the Bus Rapid Transport project in Maputo (with US$180 million in credit from the BNDES) and the industrial free trade zone (US$40 million from the BNDES).[13] As for Andrade Gutierrez, the corporation is involved in the construction of the Moamba-Major dam in the Incomati River Basin, with US$350 million in resources from the BNDES (Goes 2014).

Mozambique has also been the main recipient of Brazilian development cooperation, receiving 15 per cent of the total amount spent between 2003 and 2010 (MRE 2010). The efforts to build closer ties began with the Lula government, which had a policy of diversifying relations at the international level in general, and strengthening those with the African continent in particular. This process was accompanied by broader changes in the area of international aid, as certain interests managed to shift the emphasis of programmes towards the importance of agriculture as a driver of economic growth in Africa. This happened in a context where the actors involved were attaching increasing importance to global value chains and private investments (Ikegami 2015; Smalley 2017).

The primary intervention areas of Brazilian cooperation policies are agriculture, education and health.[14] In the field of agriculture, the cooperation policy legitimises its discourse by pointing to the similarities between the climate of the savannah in Mozambique and the Cerrado biome in Brazil, as well as the Brazilian experience in implementing public policies to support agribusiness and family farming. Thus, the main idea behind cooperation in agriculture is to apply some 'lessons' that Brazil learned 'at home' to the reality in Mozambique (IPEA and World Bank 2011).

One of the main bilateral programmes was the Programa Mais Alimentos África (More Food for Africa[15]), which created a special line of credit for machinery and equipment for family farmers. Approximately 100 Brazilian companies have been involved in the programme, supported by credit from the BNDES. Another initiative launched in partnership with the Food and Agriculture Organization (FAO) and the World Food Programme was the Purchase from Africans for Africa programme,[16] whose purpose is to contribute to food security by setting up systems for the purchase of food from local farmers to supply schools. Despite the important bilateral projects, it should be noted that, in agriculture, one feature of Brazilian cooperation efforts has been the implementation of trilateral initiatives – the third party being either powerhouses from the North (such as the US, Japan and others) or international organisations (such as the FAO and the World Bank). This brings into question the principle of 'horizontality' in South–South relations.

The largest and most visible Brazilian triangular cooperation project in agriculture is the ProSavana programme. Conceived by the heads of state of Brazil and Japan, it was launched in 2009 (Mosca 2014; Schlesinger 2013). The initial plans were to execute the project in the provinces of Niassa, Zambezia and Nampula – an area through which Vale's railway line runs. Inspired by Prodecer, the 1970s Japan–Brazil cooperation programme that fostered the expansion of large-scale export-oriented agriculture into the Brazilian Cerrado biome, ProSavana is a response to the growing interest of the Japanese government and investors in African agriculture (Ikegami 2015). This initiative has three main lines of action: measures to increase productivity and diversify agriculture, the implementation of pilot projects for small and commercial producers, and the construction of infrastructure to support the development of markets and large-scale agricultural production (ProSavana 2015).

However, the programme has run into many operational problems. These range from increasing criticism and resistance from organised civil society in all three countries (due to the lack of transparency about planned programme activities and their potential impact on Mozambican peasant farming) to delays and revisions of timelines by partners (due primarily to the fragility of Brazilian cooperation programmes) (Wise 2015).

In view of the numerous criticisms and controversies, the programme creators attempted to change their discourse by launching the 'zero draft' of the master plan for the Development of the Nacala Corridor in 2015 (MESA 2015). While the new version reaffirms the commitment to sustainable development and the centrality of family farming, its analysis of the situation associates traditional agriculture (subsistence farming and fallow systems) with low productivity levels and defends the introduction of new planting systems focused on raising production and productivity levels (MESA 2015: 3). One of the new document's concerns is to promote public-private partnerships that seek to consolidate competitive and market-oriented agriculture (Aguiar and Pacheco 2016). João Mosca (2014) warned that changes in discourse would not necessarily bring the real change needed if ProSavana were to become a driving force for agricultural and rural development in Mozambique.

As the ProSavana programme continues to inch ahead,[17] the framework for Brazilian cooperation policies has radically changed. Brazil's relations with African countries had already ceased to be a priority under the Dilma Rousseff administration due to the economic and political crisis affecting the country, thus revealing how fragile its ties of cooperation with Africa were.[18] The Rousseff impeachment, the establishment of the Michel Temer administration and, recently, the victory of the far-right candidate Jair Bolsonaro in the 2018 election further weakened these relations. Brazil's cooperation efforts lost the 'solidarity' label and began to focus on the commercial purposes of investments, while Brazilian foreign policy started to prioritise relations with the world superpowers – primarily the US, the European Union and China.

Despite this, one important innovation in the relations between Brazil and Africa is the new Agreement on Cooperation and Facilitation of Investment (ACFI). Launched in 2015 by the Rousseff administration, this agreement model was continued throughout the years of the Michel Temer administration (when the agreement with Angola was ratified) and is likely to continue under the new Bolsonaro government.[19] What is striking is that this 2015 legal framework to protect Brazilian investments and investors was elaborated after broad consultation with the private sector and that Brazil inaugurated this instrument precisely with those three African countries – Angola, Malawi and Mozambique – where the Vale mining corporation, the ProSavana programme and construction conglomerates such as Odebrecht have invested heavily. The fact that these agreements do not provide for the possibility of a company suing a state differentiates them from traditional bilateral investment treaties. Yet, in the case of the ACFIs, when conflicts involving Brazilian multinational corporations in African countries arise, it is the Brazilian state – and not the corporation responsible for the problem – that is to negotiate a solution with the host state. We have argued in other works (Garcia 2017) that this arrangement risks relieving the corporations of any responsibility, as it will be the state that bears the political and economic liability in the dispute. Therefore, the ACFIs consolidate the tendency to mix public policies with private interests. The Brazilian government ends up representing the interests of Brazilian multinationals abroad as 'national interests', and any disputes and conflicts between the corporations and the host state are extended to the Brazilian state. This is evident in the case of the ACFI with Malawi, as the only Brazilian investments in this country are the ones Vale has made in the Nacala Corridor railway line.[20]

THE NACALA CORRIDOR AS AN AXIS FOR THE COORDINATION OF BRAZILIAN AND GLOBAL INTERESTS

The development of the Nacala logistics corridor has drawn the attention of several actors, investors and funding agencies (national, international and multilateral) interested in building infrastructure to export coal and in expanding the agricultural frontier to the north of Mozambique. The development of agriculture in Africa, especially along the Nacala Corridor, is on the agenda of the G8 and the World Economic Forum. It is also an area of priority for international institutions such as the AfDB (which runs the Programme for Infrastructure Development in

Africa), the World Bank, Japan Bank for International Cooperation and the African Union. This web of the interests of multilateral actors (global and regional) is the backdrop for the Brazil–Japan–Mozambique triangular cooperation policy, which was conceived and structured in close alignment with the logistics plans for Vale's and Mitsui's operations in northern Mozambique. At the same time, these interests have certain affinities with plans at the national level: interfaces can be found between them and the *Plano Estratégico para o Desenvolvimento do Setor Agrário* (the Strategic Plan for Agricultural Development) and the *Plano de Investimento Nacional do Setor Agrário* (the National Investment Plan for the Agrarian Sector in Mozambique). The plans are organised around the establishment of logistic corridors and identify the Nacala Corridor as a priority.

The installation and recuperation of the logistics corridor in the north of the country are key for investments in the region and will trigger a process that will reconfigure the territory. While it will be consolidated around coal mining, one of the main motives for creating it is to boost the agrarian and agricultural sectors and connect them to global value chains. Running from Tete to Nacala, the Nacala Corridor is currently the principal project promising to bring development to the north of Mozambique. The Nacala-a-Velha port has become the 'departure gate for coal from Moatize' thanks to the construction of a terminal exclusively for coal exports (Vale and OAS) with funding from the AfDB, the installation of a special economic zone in Nacala, and the Nacala airport, which was built by Odebrecht with BNDES funding (Coutinho 2013; Rossi 2017). The Nacala Corridor brings to light the complementarity and the convergence of initiatives led by public and private actors.

It is known that the plans to transform northern Mozambique into a logistics corridor are not new; they date back to the time of the colonisation of the region by Portugal. In 1996, the Spatial Development Initiative (SDI) programme was launched and Nacala was identified as one of the primary development corridors. In 2001, the African Union created the New Partnership for Africa's Development (NEPAD) and in 2007, it adopted the development corridors as key tools for planning business investments in the African continent. Ikegami (2015) highlights that NEPAD revealed the new approach adopted by African governments, as they went from seeking foreign aid to promoting initiatives for self-development and to attracting investors.

In 2010, the World Bank began to advocate development strategies centred on growth poles and the selection of subregions within the corridors that would be the stage for pilot economic development projects. Tete and Nampula were the main pilot projects in Mozambique, and a special economic zone was to be established in the area (figure 5.2). The plans were to invest US$1.2 billion in close to 53 agro-processing projects (World Bank 2010).

Figure 5.2 World Bank's spatial development initiatives and growth poles

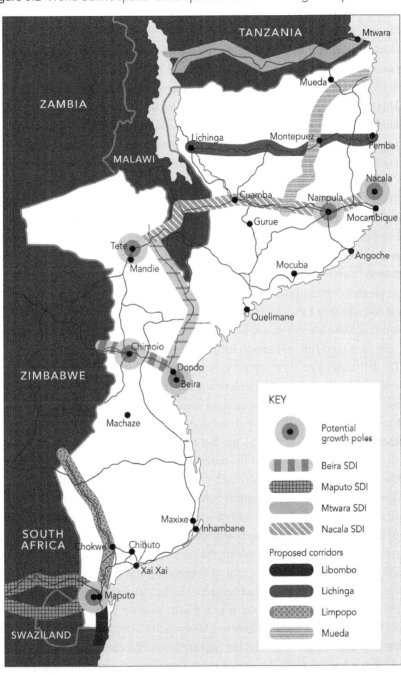

Source: World Bank (2010). Redrawn by Janet Alexander.

Following the same logic, and because of the delays in the implementation of the ProSavana programme, the Japan International Cooperation Agency (JICA) elaborated the Project for Nacala Corridor Economic Development Strategies (PEDEC). The project lists three driving forces for the development of the region: coal mining and coal transport for export, natural gas exploitation and production for export, and investments in the Nacala special economic zone near the Nacala port (MPD and JICA 2014).

This has major consequences for communities, as it changes land use, impacting on local production, rights to land and people's quality of life. Interviews conducted during fieldwork in the region revealed that transportation is one of the key elements of impact.[21] In the absence of public transportation alternatives, trains along the Nacala railway were widely used by peasants, and train stations served as spaces for the exchange of local produce and small markets. The prioritisation of cargo transport over passenger transport and the imperative to reduce travel time from one end of the line to the other (from 11 to seven hours) has led to the closure of several railway stations, leaving the majority of the local population without transportation.[22] Over 20 communities along the Nacala Corridor have been forced to move to other communities to gain access to transport by train. This generates additional costs, as they have to pay for transport to the new community and often also accommodation. Moreover, as places with a high concentration of people, railway stations were (and still are) important points of sale for local farmers.

The territories and their infrastructure began to function according to a new rationale as they became integrated into the dynamics of global markets and agricultural and mining megaprojects, significantly different from the rhythm of life and production methods of the communities that live along the railway line in northern Mozambique.[23] This has sparked numerous protests.

The diversity of actors in and the multiple programmes and initiatives designed for the Nacala Corridor region, driven by the opportunities that the economic corridor has created, are punching massive holes into the structural fabric of the national territory. The land acquisitions and concessions turn the territories into commodities that are geared towards and connected to the dynamics of the global market (Sassen 2013: 26). Along the corridor, the control of land and its conversion from traditional uses to more commercial or speculative ones has proven to be central to this process. Even though land continues to be state property in Mozambique, loopholes in the legislation make it possible to valorise and commercialise land titles (DUATs) and to create an informal land market. Furthermore, with the establishment of the Nacala Corridor, the government of Mozambique has altered the legislation: it has begun to demand that 50-metre partial protection zones be created on each side of the railway line.[24] This has generated more displacements and more pressure on local communities, who depend on the land for their livelihood. Negotiations on the payment of compensation in the form of improvements are conducted by the government and the corporations, especially Vale, and have been the object of many complaints about lack of transparency.

FINAL CONSIDERATIONS

In this chapter, we've explored the relationship between private investments and Brazilian cooperation programmes in Mozambique (specifically along the Nacala Development Corridor) at the beginning of the twenty-first century. During the first decade of 2000, Brazil was recognised as an 'emerging power' and was instrumental in establishing the BRICS group, since when it has worked to become a leader of the global South in different international negotiations. The case studied here demonstrates that the largest Brazilian cooperation initiative is being implemented in the same territories where Brazil's major economic groups (such as the Vale mining corporation and the construction companies), global corporations (such as Mitsui), cooperation agencies from the North (such as JICA) and multilateral financial institutions, such as the World Bank and the AfDB, all have interests. Therefore, we can confirm that there is a convergence of actors and initiatives in the mineral and agricultural commodities production chain, which are essential elements of global capitalist accumulation. The Nacala Corridor suggests that the cooperation efforts and investments of emerging economies of the BRICS, such as Brazil, are not an alternative for development; instead, they participate in the expropriation and pillaging of territories on a global level. The dispossession of peasants and communities caused by changes in the use of land and transportation along the corridor and in territories now destined for agribusiness and mining, as we have shown in the previous section, reinforce Rosa Luxemburg's and Harvey's approach to imperialism.

During Lula da Silva's administration, Brazil sought to gain visibility and weight in multilateral negotiation and dialogue spaces. Boosted by the commodities boom and sustained by changes in their political systems, many Portuguese-speaking African countries became the focus of international investments, which led to the increasing 'foreignisation' of land. In this context, Lusophone Africa has become a region rich in both economic and political opportunities for Brazil. Yet, Brazil's actions (and those of other BRICS countries) are part of the imperialist race among the leading world powerhouses in which it holds a position of regional power. This position is anchored primarily in the relations of exploitation and power that it maintains with its peripheries. Contradictorily, while Brazil has historically

117

defended its sovereignty over its natural and energy resources, it now advances to exploit the natural goods and resources of other populations and regions. These advances can also be seen in the field of ideas, as more and more Brazilian public policies and their concepts are transferred to the African context.

Recently, Brazil has gone through major political and economic changes. Since 2016, with the impeachment of president Dilma Rousseff, to the election of the extreme right-wing government of Jair Bolsonaro in 2018, Brazil has been losing international prominence as it no longer plays a leading role in the global South, and prioritises alliances with the traditional powers, particularly the US. Internally, Bolsonaro has sought to accelerate the process of privatising public companies and services and to promote restructuring environmental agencies and loosening environmental legislation, resulting in increased deforestation and an expansion of mining and agribusiness activities in indigenous territories. Consequently, relations with Africa are off the agenda. However, it is likely that Brazil will keep its interests in the Nacala Corridor, as the project remains strategic for the mining company Vale.

In this context, transnational struggles and alliances between different actors and social movements gain even more importance. An international coalition of the struggles against the violations of human, labour and environmental rights caused by Vale's operations all around the world has been formed.[25] Although it appeared that the ProSavana programme would inevitably succeed, it has been unable to advance due to the formation of a broad resistance struggle. Despite the weaknesses and the fragmentation of international coalitions (such as the 'People Affected by Vale' or the tri-national campaign network 'No to ProSavana'[26]), they are an important example of another form of South–South cooperation – one between the peoples, or the 'BRICS from below' (Bond and Garcia 2015). Recent analysis of the Nacala Corridor, then, reveals that while the consolidation of infrastructure can be an important factor in driving agribusiness due to the effect of investment anticipation and changes in land use, it can potentially unify various struggles against the project and even alter the course of its implementation. The 'No to ProSavana' Campaign is a good example of this.

ACKNOWLEDGEMENT

An earlier version of this article was published as: Ana Garcia and Karina Kato (2016) 'Políticas públicas e interesses privados: uma análise a partir do Corredor de Nacala'. *Caderno CRH*, Salvador, v. 29, n. 76, p.69–86, Jan./Apr. We thank Thomas Selemane for comments and critique on this earlier version.

NOTES

1   This is unlikely to continue, as the new scenario under the far-right president Bolsonaro shows a direct alignment with US president Trump, and the prioritisation of commercial partners such as the European Union and (ambiguously) China.

2   In 2016, a secret debt of US$2.2 billion was revealed. The debt was related to loans used to import arms and fishing boats. The revelation led the International Monetary Fund to cut its loans to the country and 14 donors stopped providing government support, which caused a major crisis in Mozambique's economy (Hanlon 2017).

3   See http://www.fazenda.gov.br/noticias/2004/r010904 (accessed 19 August 2019). According to the Finance Ministry, 'forgiving' debt was part of Brazil's policy of 'solidarity' with African countries. However, it was commonplace for former president Lula to announce the government's intention to increase the exports of Brazilian corporations' goods and services in return for this gesture. This was the case in the cancelling of Congo's debt. See 'Brasil estuda perdoar dívida do Congo', *Valor Econômico*, 17 October 2007, accessed 19 August 2019, https://oglobo.globo.com/economia/brasil-estuda-perdoar-divida-do-congo-4147313.

4   In 2013, however, changes in the international mineral commodities market led Vale to alter its business strategy. It adopted a divestment policy (*Estado de São Paulo* 2014) in order to reduce its shares in logistics while increasing its partnerships in this phase at the same time.

5   Information obtained in an interview with an employee of Portos do Norte, the administrator of the Nacala Port, during our field research in 2014.

6   The resources offered by commercial banks will be covered by insurance policies with Nippon Export and Investment Insurance and Export Credit Corporation of South Africa.

7   See http://www.bbc.com/portuguese/brasil-42074053 (accessed 19 August 2019).

8   International Alliance of People Affected by Vale.The Vale 2012 Unsustainability Report, https://atingidospelavale.files.wordpress.com/2012/06/relatorio-insustentabilidade-vale-2012_en1.pdf and Human Rights Watch, 'What is a house without food?', https://www.hrw.org/report/2013/05/23/what-house-without-food/mozambiques-coal-mining-boom-and-resettlements (both accessed 19 August 2019).

9   Reports obtained during interviews with residents of the Cateme and 25 de Setembro resettled communities in August 2014.

10   Information provided from the interviews and findings of the field visits to the Cateme and 25 de Setembro resettled communities in August 2014.

11   See http://www.bndes.gov.br/SiteBNDES/bndes/bndes_pt/Institucional/BNDES_Transparente/consulta_as_operacoes_exportacao/planilhas_exportacao_pos_embarque.html (accessed 19 August 2019).

12   See https://www.bndes.gov.br/wps/portal/site/home/imprensa/noticias/conteudo/bndes-aciona-seguro-de-credito-para-operacoes-com-mocambique (accessed 19 August 2019).

13   See https://www.odebrecht.com/pt-br/comunicacao/noticias/aeroporto-internacional-de-nacala-e-inaugurado-em-mocambique (accessed 19 August 2019).

14   In the area of health, the primary executing agency is the Oswaldo Cruz Foundation (FIOCRUZ). Its main projects were the construction and implementation of a factory producing anti-retroviral drugs; the provision of training for and institutional strengthening of the regulatory agency for the pharmaceutical sector; the creation of the popular pharmacies programme; and the establishment of the Instituto Nacional Politécnico de

Saúde (National Polytechnic Institute on Health). In education, the majority of technical cooperation activities developed are related to training employees on public management and professional education.

15 See http://www.mda.gov.br/sitemda/noticias/mais-desenvolvimento-para-moçambique (accessed 4 September 2019).

16 See http://www.csa-be.org/IMG/pdf/rapport_fafo-paa_side_event-2.pdf (accessed 9 September 2019).

17 In the first half of 2015, public hearings on the new version of the ProSavana master plan were held in all 19 districts involved in the programme. The meetings were dominated by the voices of civil society organisations and social movements, who complained about lack of transparency and irregularities (Monjane 2015).

18 Brazil's cooperation budget for Africa reached its peak in 2010, the last year of the Lula da Silva government, with a value of approximately R$20 million. Under the Dilma Rousseff administration, resources for cooperation with Africa fell drastically, to R$5 million in 2014. See http://www.abc.gov.br/Content/ABC/imagens/africa_financeiro.png (accessed 20 August 2019).

19 The new far-right government of Jair Bolsonaro has not cancelled ACFI agreements already signed with Latin American and African countries, has even expanded agreements to include the United Arab States, and has started discussing an agreement with the US. See http://www.itamaraty.gov.br/pt-BR/notas-a-imprensa/20160-visita-do-ministro-dos-negocios-estrangeiros-e-cooperacao-internacional-dos-e mirados-arabes-unidos-xeique-abdullah-bin-zayed-al-nahyan-ao-brasil-brasilia-15-de-marco-de-2019 and https://www.valor.com.br/brasil/6169831/investimento-ter a-acordo-de-protecao (both accessed 20 August 2019).

20 See http://www.mdic.gov.br/arquivos/Cooperacao-e-facilitacao-de-investimentos-EN-ASSINADO-(002).pdf (accessed 20 August 2019).

21 The authors conducted two field studies in Mozambique: one from 16 to 30 August 2014 and another in October 2017. In the first field study, 15 interviews were conducted with peasants, government actors, traditional leaders, representatives of social movements, railway workers, port employees, public managers, researchers and academics, among others. The research covered the Nacala Corridor and made stops for interviews in the Moatize district of Tete Province (Cateme and 25 de Setembro and Cambulatsitsi); on the banks of Lake Niassa in Malawi (Balaka and N'Kaia station); Mandimba (Mozambique); Cuamba (where we visited a train station); Mutuali; Ribáuè; Nampula (visit and interview with a professor at the University of Lúrio and an interview with Combonians); Nacala (interview with Justice and Peace, a civil society organisation, a visit to the Port of Nacala, Nacala-a-Velha, and interviews with port employees; a visit to the airport built by Odebrecht and an interview with GAZEDA); and Maputo (interview with the Ministry of Finance, the National Farmer's Union, UNAC, the Academic Action for the Development of Rural Communities, ADECRU, and academics). In the second field study, interviews were carried out in Maputo and Nampula under the umbrella of the Study Group on Social Changes, Agribusiness and Public Policies (GEMAP-UFRRJ).

22 According to interviews held at the Cuamba train station and in Mutuali during the field research in 2014, after the change in the railway concession, the number of passenger trains was cut by half.

23 During the field visits to two communities (Mutuali and Cuamba) in August 2014 in particular, we were able to observe how they were affected by the changes resulting from the decision to prioritise the transportation of goods instead of passengers.

24   Regulation of the Land Law – Decree 66/1998.
25   International Alliance of People Affected by Vale: see https://atingidospelavale.
        wordpress.com/ (accessed 22 August 2019).
26   The campaign was launched at a meeting of social organisations and movements
        from Brazil, Mozambique and Japan in Maputo in 2012. See http://www.unac.org.mz/
        index.php/artigos/nacional/94-campanha-nao-ao-prosavana-mocambicanos-pedem-
        solidariedade-regional (accessed 22 August 2019).

REFERENCES

AfDB (African Development Bank Group). 2009. 'Multinational-Nacala road corridor:
    Phase I (Mozambique/Malawi/Zambia)'. Accessed 2 August 2018, https://www.afdb.
    org/fileadmin/uploads/afdb/Documents/Project-and-Operations/Mozambique_-_
    Malawi_-_Zambia_-_Nacala_Road_Corridor_-_Phase_I_-_Appraisal_Report.pdf.
AfDB. 2015. 'Nacala Corridor resettlements report for lender'. Accessed 2 August 2018,
    https://www.afdb.org/fileadmin/uploads/afdb/Documents/Environmental-and-Social-
    Assessments/Mozambique_-_NACALA_RAIL___PORT_PROJECT_-_Summary_
    RAP_%E2%80%93_10_2015.pdf.
Aguiar, D. and Pacheco, M.E. 2016. *Cooperação Sul Sul dos Povos do Brasil e de Moçambique:
    Memória da resistência ao ProSavana e Análise Crítica de seu Plano Diretor.* Rio de
    Janeiro: FASE.
BNDES (Banco Nacional de Desenvolvimento Economico e Social). 2013. 'BNDES inau-
    gura escritório de representação na África'. Accessed 2 August 2018, http://www.bndes.
    gov.br/SiteBNDES/bndes/bndes_pt/Institucional/Sala_de_Imprensa/Noticias/2013/
    Todas/20131206_africa.html.
Bond, P. and Garcia, A. (eds). 2015. *BRICS: An Anti-Capitalist Critique.* Johannesburg: Jacana
    Media.
Coutinho, L. 2013. 'Investimento, financiamento e o BNDES'. Power Point Presentation.
    Accessed 2 August 2018, http://www.bndes.gov.br/SiteBNDES/export/sites/default/
    bndes_pt/Institucional/Sala_de_Imprensa/Galeria_Arquivos/CAE_FINAL.pdf.
Duran, J. and Chichava, S. 2013. 'O Brasil na Agricultura Moçambicana: Parceiro de
    desenvolvimento ou usurpador de terra?' *Desafios para Moçambique 2013.* Accessed
    2 August 2018, http://www.iese.ac.mz/lib/publication/livros/des2013/IESE_Des2013_
    15.BrasAgrMoc.pdf.
Durao, M. and Ciarelli, M. 2014. 'Vale vende à japonesa Mitsui fatia de ativos de carvãoem-
    Moçambique', *Estado de São Paulo,* 10 December.
Estado de São Paulo. 2014. 'Ordem na Vale é desinvestir', 10 December.
Garcia, A. 2017. 'BRICS investment agreements in Africa: More of the same?'*Studies in
    Political Economy,* 98 (1): 24–47.
Garcia, A. and Kato, K. 2015. 'The story of the hunter or the hunted? Brazil's role in Angola
    and Mozambique'. In P. Bond and A. Garcia (eds), *BRICS: An Anti-Capitalist Critique.*
    Johannesburg: Jacana Media, pp. 117–134.
Garcia, A., Kato, K. and Fontes, C. 2013. *A história contada pela caça ou pelo caçador?
    Perspectivos do Brasil em Angola e Moçambique.* Rio de Janeiro: PACS.
Goes, F. 2014. 'Andrade Gutierrez vai fazer barragem para Maputo'. *Valor Econômico*
    23 June.
Hanlon, J. 2017. 'Following the donor-designed path to Mozambique's $2.2 billion secret debt
    deal', *Third World Quarterly* 38 (3): 753–770.

Harvey, D. 2005. 'O "Novo Imperialismo": Ajustes espaço-temporais e acumulação por desapossamento', *LutasSociais* No. 13/14. São Paulo, Neils.

Harvey, D. 2007. 'In what ways is the "new imperialism" really new?' *Historical Materialism* 15: 57–70.

Ikegami, K. 2015. 'Corridor development and foreign investment in agriculture: Implications of the ProSavana programme in northern Mozambique'. Conference Paper No. 30, International Conference on Land Grabbing, Conflict and Agrarian-Environmental Transformations – Perspectives from East and Southeast Asia, 5–6 June 2015, Chiang Mai University, Thailand.

IPEA (Institute of Applied Economic Research) and World Bank. 2011. 'Bridging the Atlantic – Brazil and Sub-Saharan Africa: South-South partnering for Growth'. Accessed 2 August 2018, http://www.ipea.gov.br/portal/images/stories/PDFs/livros/livros/livro_pontesobreoatlanticoing.pdf.

Macamo, E. 2003. 'Da disciplinarização de Moçambique: Ajustamento estrutural e as estratégias neoliberais de risco', *Africana Studia* 6: 231–255.

Marshall, J. 2015. 'Behind the image of South-South solidarity in Brazil's Vale'. In P. Bond and A. Garcia (eds), *BRICS: An Anti-capitalist Critique*. Johannesburg: Jacana Media, pp. 162–181.

MESA (Ministério da Agricultura e Segurança Alimentar). 2015. 'Plano Diretor para o Desenvolvimento Agrário do Corredor de Nacala em Moçambique'. Maputo: MESA.

Mizuho Bank. 2017. 'Project financing for the Nacala Corridor railway and port project in the Republic of Mozambique'. Japan: Mizuho Bank. Accessed 2 August 2018, https://www.mizuhobank.com/company/release/pdf/20171128release_eng.pdf.

Monjane, B. 2015. 'Auscultação pública sobre ProSavana: Ministro exige intervenções patrióticas e ativistasabandonam a sala'. Accessed 2 August 2018, https://adecru.wordpress.com/2015/06/15/auscultacao-publica-sobre-o-prosavana-ministro-exige-intervencoes-patrioticas-e-activistas-abandonam-a-sala/.

Mosca, J. 2014. 'ProSavana'. Observatório do Meio Rural, *Destaque Rural* No. 5. Accessed 20 August 2019, https://omrmz.org/omrweb/wp-content/uploads/Destaque-Rural-05.pdf.

Mosca, J. and Selemane, T. 2013.'Grandes projetos e segurança alimentar em Moçambique', *Revista Internacional em Língua Portuguesa: Segurança Alimentar* 3 (25): 141–185.

MPD and JICA (Ministry of Planning and Development and Japan International Cooperation Agency). 2014. 'O projeto das estratégias de desenvolvimento econômico do Corredor de Nacala na República de Moçambique (PEDEC-NACALA)'. Volumes 1 and 2. Accessed 2 August 2018, http://farmlandgrab.org/uploads/attachment/Corredor_de_nacala_vol1.1.pdf.

MRE (Ministério das Relações Exteriores). 2010. 'Balanço da política externa 2003–2010'. Accessed 2 August 2018, http://www.itamaraty.gov.br.

O País. 2012. 'Vale quer investir 6,4 bilhões USD na expansão da mina de Moatize', 6 July. Accessed 1 November 2015, http://opais.sapo.mz/index.php/economia/38-economia/21021-vale-quer-investir-64-bilioes-usd-na-expansao-da-mina-de-moatize.html.

ProSavana. 2015. 'Reuniões Distritais de Auscultação sobre a versão zero (Draft Zero) do ProSavana', *ProSavana*, 7 May. Accessed 2 August 2018, http://www.prosavana.gov.mz/pt-pt/reunioes-distritais-de-auscultacao-sobre-a-versao-zero-draft-zero-do-plano-director-do-prosavana/.

Rossi, A. 2017. 'O areoporto fantasma feito pela Odebrecht em Moçambique, que o BNDES financiou e tomou calote'. BBC, 27th November 2017. Accessed 2 August 2018, https://www.bbc.com/portuguese/brasil-42074053.

Sassen, S. 2013. 'Land grabs today: Feeding the disassembling of national territory', *Globalizations* 10 (25): 25–46.

Sassen, S. 2016. *Expulsões: Brutalidade e Complexidade na Economia Global*. São Paulo: Paz e Terra.

Schlesinger, S. 2013. *Cooperação e Investimentos do Brasil na África: O Caso do ProSavana em Moçambique*. Maputo: FASE.

Smalley, R. 2017. *Agricultural growth corridors on the eastern seaboard of Africa: An overview*. Working Paper No. 1. Agricultural Policy Research in Africa, Institute of Development Studies, University of Sussex.

Sombra Saraiva, J.F. 2012. *África parceiro do Brasil Atlântico: Relações Internacionais do Brasil e da África no Início do Século XXI*. Belo Horizonte: Editora Fino Traço.

The New York Times. 2019. 'A tidal wave of mud', 9 February. Accessed 19 August 2019, https://www.nytimes.com/interactive/2019/02/09/world/americas/brazil-dam-coll apse.html.

Vale. 2011. 'Investimento da Vale em Logística nos últimos 6 anos é de US$ 9 bi'. *Especial Logística*, February.

Vale. 2013. 'Sustentabilidade Moçambique 2013'. Accessed 2 August 2018, http://www.vale. com/mozambique/pt/documents/vale_sustentabilidade_mocambique_2013.pdf.

Vale. 2014. 'Relatório de Sustentabilidade 2014'. Accessed 2 August 2018, http://www.vale. com/PT/aboutvale/sustainability/links/LinksDownloadsDocuments/relatorio-d e-sustentabilidade-2014.pdf.

Wise, T.A. 2015. 'Grande concessão de terras em Moçambique'. ADECRU. Accessed 2 August 2018, https://adecru.wordpress.com/2015/05/20/a-grande-concessao-de-terras-em-mocambique/.

World Bank. 2010. 'Prospects for growth poles in Mozambique: Summary report'. Accessed 2 August 2018, http://www.iese.ac.mz/lib/PPI/IESE-PPI/pastas/governacao/geral/ legislativo_documentos_oficiais/Growth_Poles.pdf.

GLOBAL RESISTANCE

6

THE VESSEL: AN ALTERNATIVE STRATEGY FOR THE GLOBAL LEFT

Chris Chase-Dunn

Social movements both reproduce social structures and change them, and they have been important drivers of social change in human societies for thousands of years. The comparative evolutionary world-systems perspective studies the ways that waves of social movements (world revolutions[1]) have driven the rise of more complex and more hierarchical human societies over the past millennia. A long-run historical perspective on these processes is helpful for comprehending the current moment and for devising political strategies that can help mitigate the problems that must be addressed in the twenty-first century so that humanity can move toward a more just, peaceful and sustainable global commonwealth. The contemporary world-system is entering another interregnum and a Malthusian correction similar to, but also different from, the 'age of extremes' that occurred in the first half of the twentieth century (Hobsbawm 1994). Devising a helpful political strategy for the global Left requires understanding the similarities and differences between the current period and the first half of the twentieth century. And it requires a clear comprehension of the cultures of the movements and counter-movements that have emerged in the last few decades. The current period is daunting and dangerous, but it is also a period of great opportunity for moving humanity toward a qualitatively different and improved world society.

THE GLOBAL JUSTICE MOVEMENT AND
THE SOCIAL FORUM PROCESS

The global justice movement that emerged in the 1990s with the rise of the Zapatistas in Southern Mexico was a response to the neoliberal globalisation project. The Latin American 'Pink Tide' was composed of leftist-populist political regimes in most of the Latin American countries, based on movements against the neoliberal structural adjustment programmes promoted by the International Monetary Fund (IMF) (Chase-Dunn et al. 2015). The World Social Forum (WSF) emerged in 2001 in reaction to the exclusivity of the neoliberal World Economic Forum, providing a venue for popular progressive movements to protect politically excluded people from neoliberalism.

The social forum process spread to most of the regions of the world. The charter of the WSF did not permit participation by those who wanted to attend as representatives of organisations that were engaged in, or that advocated, armed struggle. Nor were governments or political parties supposed to send representatives to the WSF (see WSF 2001). There was a great emphasis on diversity and on horizontal, as opposed to hierarchical, forms of organisation. The use of the internet for communication and mobilisation made it possible for broad coalitions and loosely knit networks to engage in collective action projects. The 'movement of movements' at the WSF engaged in a manifesto/charter writing frenzy as those who sought a more organised approach to confronting global capitalism and neoliberalism attempted to formulate consensual goals and to put workable coalitions together (Wallerstein 2007).

One issue was whether the WSF should itself formulate a political programme and take formal stances on issues. The WSF Charter explicitly forbade this, and a significant group of participants strongly supported maintaining the WSF as an 'open space' for debate and organising. A survey of 625 attendees at the WSF meeting in Porto Alegre in 2005 asked whether the forum should remain an open space or should take political stances. Almost exactly half favoured the open space idea (Chase-Dunn et al. 2008). Trying to change the WSF Charter to allow for a formal political programme would have been very divisive.

But this was deemed not to be necessary. The WSF Charter also encouraged the formation of new political organisations. Those participants who wanted to form new coalitions and organisations were free to act, as long as they did not do so in the name of the WSF as a whole. In Social Forum meetings at the global and national levels the Assembly of Social Movements and other groups issued calls for global action and political manifestoes. At the 2006 'polycentric' meeting in Bamako, Mali, a group issued a manifesto entitled 'the Bamako Appeal' at the beginning of the meeting. The Bamako Appeal was a call for a global united front against neoliberalism and United States neo-imperialism (see Sen et al. 2007). And Samir Amin, the famous Marxist economist and co-founder of the world-system perspective, wrote a short paper entitled 'Toward a fifth international?' in which he outlined the history of the first four internationals (Amin 2008). Peter Waterman (2006) proposed a 'global labor charter'. A coalition of women's groups produced a global feminist manifesto that tried to overcome divisive North/South issues (Moghadam 2005).

There was an impasse in the global justice movement between those who wanted to move toward a global united front that could mobilise a strong coalition against the powers-that-be, and those who preferred local, prefigurative actions and horizontalist network forms of organisation that abjure organisational hierarchy and refuse to participate in 'normal' political activities such as elections. Prefigurationism is the idea that small groups can intentionally organise their social relations in ways that will sow the seeds of transformation to a more desirable form of future human society. Utopian socialism and intentional anarchist communities have a long history, during which they have demonstrated that egalitarian intentional communities are possible, and that they have had some consequences for the political evolution of global capitalism and have affected competing social movements attempting to change the central structures and institutions of the capitalist world-system. Most utopian communities have eventually become reintegrated into 'business as usual' but the urge to engage in prefiguration has not gone away.

Horizontalism abjures hierarchy in organisations and promotes egalitarian networks of formally equal members. Modern organisational egalitarianism has been inspired by Roberto Michels's ([1915] 1968) analysis of the oligarchical tendencies of political parties, but Michels's model of the life cycle of an organisation can be extended to apply to all organisations. They become conservative because the leadership ends up defending mainly its own interests and the survival of the organisation. Revolutionary intentions are abandoned, and the organisation eventually becomes a functional part of the larger institutional structure. Political parties and labour unions are usually given as examples of this 'sclerosis issue'.[2] Anarchist political theory has a deep history and anarchist ideas have a wide resonance within the new global Left, even though only 15 per cent of the attendees at WSF meetings describe themselves as strongly identified anarchists (Aldecoa et al. 2019: Table 1).

These political stances had been inherited from the anti-authoritarian and anti-bureaucratic new left movements of the world revolution of 1968. The New Left of 1968 embraced direct democracy, attacked bureaucratic organisations and was resistant to the building of new formal organisations that could act as instruments of revolution (Arrighi et al. 1989: 37–38; SDS 1962). Organisations that had been founded as instruments of revolutionary change and challenges to the existing power structures were thought to have become sclerotic defenders of the status quo in their old age. This was understood as an important lesson of the waves of class struggle and decolonisation that had occurred in the nineteenth and twentieth centuries. Arrighi et al (1989: 64) said:

> The class struggle 'flows out' into a competitive struggle for state power. As this occurs, the political elites that provide social classes with leadership and organization (even if they sincerely consider themselves 'instruments' of the class struggle) usually find that they have to play by the rules of that competition and therefore must attempt to subordinate the class struggle to those rules in order to survive as competitors for state power.

This resistance to institutionalised politics and abandonment of contention for state power has also been a salient feature of the world revolution of 20xx. It is based on a critique of the practices of earlier world revolutions in which labour unions and political parties became bogged down in short-term and self-interested struggles that then reinforced and reproduced the global capitalist system and the system of national states. This abjuration of formal organisation is reflected in the charter of the WSF, as discussed above. And these same political beliefs were strongly present in the Occupy movement, the popular revolts of the Arab Spring (Mason 2013) and in the recent *Gilets Jaunes* (Yellow Vests) demonstrations in France.

Paul Mason's (2013) analysis contended that beyond disappointment with the outcomes of the struggles carried out by the Old Left, the social structural basis for horizontalism and anti-formal organisation was due to the presence of many middle-class students as activists in the movements.[3] The world revolution of 1968 was led mainly by college students who had emerged on the world stage with the global expansion of higher education after World War II. John W. Meyer (2009) explained the student revolt and the subsequent lowering of the voting age as another extension of citizenship to new and politically unincorporated groups demanding to be included, analogous to the earlier revolts and incorporations of men of no property and women.

Mason (2013) pointed out the similarities (and differences) with the world revolution of 1848, in which many of the activists were educated but underemployed students. He also argued that the activists and participants in the current world revolution (here called world revolution 20xx) have mainly been highly educated young people who are facing the strong likelihood that they will not be able to find jobs commensurate with their skills and certification levels (see also Milkman et al. 2013). Many of these 'graduates with no future' have gone into debt to finance their education, and they are alienated from institutional politics and enraged by the failure of global capitalism to continue the expansion of middle-class jobs. These graduates can be considered part of Guy Standing's (2014) 'precariat', as they are increasingly forced to participate in the gig economy with little hope of future stability. In this aspect, highly educated young people share an uncertain economic future with poor workers across the globe, posing the possibility of national and transnational alliances among these different sectors of the precariat. Mason (2013) also pointed out that the urban poor, especially in the global South, and workers whose livelihoods have been attacked by the neoliberal globalisation project were important elements in the revolts that occurred in the Middle East, Spain, Greece and Turkey. He also stressed the importance of the internet and social media in allowing disaffected young people to organise and coordinate large protests. He sees the 'freedom to tweet' as an important element in a new level of individual freedom that has been an important driver of those middle-class graduates who enjoy confronting the powers-that-be in mass demonstrations.[4] The celebration of individual freedom by the educated precariat is cited by Mason as another reason why the movements have been reticent to develop their own hierarchical organisations and to participate in traditional political activities.

Mason and other participants and observers of the global justice movement may have somewhat overemphasised the extent to which the movement of movements has been incoherent regarding goals ('one no, many yeses') and shared perspectives. Based on the reported identification of activists with movements, surveys of attendees at both world-level and national-level social forums have found a relatively stable multicentric network of movement themes in which a set of more central movements serves as a link to all the movements (Chase-Dunn and Kaneshiro 2009). All the 27 movement themes used in the surveys were connected to the larger network by means of co-activism, so it was a single, linked network without subcliques. This multicentric network was quite stable across venues.[5] This suggests that there has been a fairly similar structure of network connections among movements that are global in scope and that the global-level network is also very similar to the network that exists among social-forum activists from grassroots movements within the US (Chase-Dunn and Kaneshiro 2009). The central cluster of movement themes to which all the other movements were linked included human rights, anti-racism, environmentalism, feminism, peace/anti-war, anti-corporate and alternative globalisation.

JUSTICE GLOBALISM AS A DISCOURSE

An organisational structure that can gain the allegiance of large numbers of activists, especially young ones, will need to consider the culture of the global Left that has emerged since the world revolution of 1968. Two important studies that have empirically studied this culture are reviewed here.

Manfred Steger, James Goodman and Erin K. Wilson (2013) presented the results of a systematic study of the political ideas employed by 45 NGOs and social movement organisations associated with the International Council of the WSF. Using a modified form of morphological discourse analysis developed by Michael Freeden (2003) for studying political ideologies, Steger et al. (2013) analysed texts (websites, press releases and declarations) and conducted interviews to examine the key concepts, secondary concepts and overall coherence of the political ideas expressed by these organisations as proponents of 'justice globalism'.

The key concepts of justice globalism extracted by Steger et al. (2013: 28–29, Table 2.1) are

- participatory democracy,
- transformative change,
- equality of access to resources and opportunities,
- social justice,
- universal rights,
- global solidarity and
- sustainability.

The meanings of each of these concepts have emerged in an ongoing struggle against the neoliberal globalisation project. Steger et al. discuss each of these and evaluate how much consensus exists across the 45 movement organisations they studied. They found a relatively impressive degree of consensus, but their results also reveal a lot of ongoing contestation. For example, though most of the organisations seem to favour one or another form of participatory democracy, there is also awareness of some of the limitations of participatory democracy, and different attitudes toward participation in representative democracy. The important notion of 'horizontality' was not examined in detail, but networks of equal and leaderless individuals were preferred to formal hierarchies within movements and organisations.

Some of the organisations studied by Steger et al. (2013) eschewed participation in established electoral processes, while others did not. Steger et al. (2013)

highlighted the importance of 'multiplicity' as an approach that values diversity rather than trying to find 'one size fits all' solutions. They noted that the WSF Charter values inclusivity and the welcoming of marginalised groups. They also document the important efforts that have been made to link groups that operate at both local and global levels of contention.

The Steger et al. (2013) study did not give much attention to the issue of prefiguration – 'building the new society inside the shell of the old', though prefiguration has found wide support from many global justice social movement organisations. The Zapatistas, the Occupy activists and many in the environmental movement are engaged in efforts to construct sustainable, egalitarian, alternative communities rather than organisations that are meant to challenge existing institutions in order to change the whole system. In addition, the study attended neither to alternative versions of the human rights discourse such as the notion of community rights, nor to the idea that nature ('Mother Earth') has rights, as proposed by the World People's Conference on Climate Change and the Rights of Mother Earth held in Cochabamba, Bolivia in 2010. The discussion of global solidarity in the Steger et al. study emphasises the centrality of what Ruth Reitan (2007) has called 'altruistic solidarity' – concern for the plight of poor and marginalised peoples – without much attention to solidarity based on common circumstances or identities.

Reitan (2007) addresses the issue of types of solidarity among global activists. Conscience constituents are direct supporters of a social movement organisation who do not stand to benefit directly from the accomplishment of that organisation's goals (McCarthy and Zald 1977). According to Reitan, two forms of solidarity emerge from activists who are distant from the immediate consequences that are the focus of the movement: altruistic solidarity and reciprocal solidarity. Altruistic solidarity occurs when '*sympathy* with the suffering of others who are deemed worthy of one's support seems to be the prevailing affective response among those who choose to act' (Reitan 2007: 51). Altruistic solidarity is characterised by low-risk activism that may be largely apolitical, suppress contentious action, and even reproduce inequality. On the other hand, 'reciprocal solidarity' emerges when 'a perceived connection between one's own problems or struggle and that of others tends to lead to empathy with another's suffering and a sense that its source is at least *remotely threatening* to oneself' (Reitan 2007: 51). Reciprocal solidarity is characterised by pluralism and cooperation between conscience constituents and beneficiary constituents in pursuit of structural change. Conscience constituents engaged in reciprocal solidarity may attempt to unpack privilege in order to understand their position(s) in larger systems of power that tend to recreate themselves in social movements. These stark distinctions, however, are largely analytical, as 'movements today are comprised of identity, reciprocal, and altruistic solidarities alike, in different mixes towards different outcomes' (Reitan 2007: 56).

Reitan recognises the importance and validity of both altruistic and reciprocal solidarity, but also considers their limitations. She tells the story of Jubilee 2000, a coalition of churches in the global North, who began a campaign of debt relief for countries in the global South that had become hugely indebted to banks in the global North during the last decades of the twentieth century. Jubilee 2000 was based mainly on altruistic solidarity with somewhat weak participation from the global South. But, when the campaign succeeded in bringing banks to the table for negotiations about debt relief, the leadership of Jubilee 2000 made compromises that were seen as betrayal by the activists from the global South, who then formed their own organisation, Jubilee South. This story is meant to show the limitations of altruistic solidarity and the necessity for activists from the global South to have their own autonomous organisations. A related issue is the sometimes contentious relationship between NGOs (organisations with budgets and paid staff) and social movement organisations that rely on mass memberships and volunteer (unpaid) leadership. Reitan (2007) tells the story of Via Campesina, a global union of small farmers, that rejected participation by NGOs after these were seen as attempting to steer the organisation. Via Campesina opted to restrict membership to farmers only, even excluding friendly participant-observing sociologists as well as the NGOs.

Steger et al. (2013) also designate five central ideological claims that find great consensus among the global justice activists:

- Neoliberalism produces global crisis;
- Market-driven globalisation has increased worldwide disparities in wealth and well-being;
- Democratic participation is essential for solving global problems;
- Another world is possible and urgently needed;
- People power is wanted, not corporate power.

These assertions shape the policy alternatives proposed by global justice activists. The Steger et al. study and the movement network results summarised above imply that the global New Left does have a degree of coherence that could be the basis of much greater articulation.

William Carroll's thorough study of progressive global think tanks (transnational alternative policy groups) is intended to provide suggestions for how to build a transnational progressive counter-hegemonic bloc of social forces (Carroll 2016: 23). Carroll agrees with the results of the Steger et al. study regarding the discursive content of the global justice movement and notes that the progressive counter-hegemonic think tanks he studied are trying to produce knowledge that is useful for prefigurative social change, and democratic forms of globalisation that are intentional alternatives to the neoliberal globalisation project. Carroll critiques anarchist anti-hierarchy and localism and proposes a process of *counter-hegemonic globalisation*: 'a globally organized project of transformation aimed at replacing the dominant global regime with one that maximizes democratic political control and makes the equitable development of human capabilities and environmental stewardship its priorities' (Carroll 2016: 30).

The Steger et al. and Carroll studies and the research done on the social forum process are not the last word on the culture of the contemporary global Left, but they are solid beginnings.

THE CURRENT WORLD REVOLUTION

The global political, economic and demographic situation has evolved in ways that challenge many of the assumptions that were made during the rise of the global justice movement and that require adjustments of the analyses, strategies and tactics of progressive social movements. The Arab Spring, the Latin American Pink Tide,[6] the Indignados in Spain, the Occupy movement, the rise of progressive, social-media-based parties in Spain (Podemos) and in Greece and the spike in mass protests in 2011 and 2012 inspired some activists to label the contemporary world revolution that emerged in the last decade of the twentieth century 'the world revolution of 2011'. But the left-wing Syriza Party, elected in Greece in 2015, was a debacle that was crushed by the European banks and the EU. They doubled down on austerity, threatening to bankrupt the pensioners of Greece unless the Syriza regime agreed to new structural adjustment policies, which it did. This was a case in which another world was possible, but it did not happen. This outcome was a slam on the other new leftist social-media parties in Italy and Spain as well as on the global justice movement.

The huge spike in global protests in 2011–2012 was followed by a lull and then a renewed intensification of citizen revolts from 2015–2016 (Youngs 2017). The Black Lives Matter movement, the Dakota Access Pipeline protest, the Me-Too movement, the anti-Trump Women's Marches and the Antifa rising against neo-fascism and the somewhat ambiguous rise of popular protests that have been sparked by rising fuel costs (the Yellow Vests in France and many similar demonstrations elsewhere) suggest that the world revolution of 20xx is still happening. But the setbacks and the rise of populist nationalism, anti-immigrant movements and neo-fascist regimes that play to these movements, along with defeats of progressive movements and the demise of the Pink Tide in Latin America, require a reassessment of the context and strategies of the progressive movement of movements.

The mainly tragic outcomes of the Arab Spring and the decline of the Pink Tide progressive populist regimes in Latin America have been bad hits for the global Left. The social forum process and progressive mass demonstrations in favor of democracy were late in coming to the Middle East and North Africa, but they eventually did arrive in the form of the Arab Spring. The demonstrations were mainly rebellions of progressive students using social media to mobilise mass protests against old authoritarian regimes (Korotayev and Zinkina 2011). The outcome in Tunisia, where the sequence of protests started, has been fairly good. But the outcomes in Egypt, Syria, Turkey, Iran and Bahrain were disasters (Moghadam 2017, 2018).[7] Repression by the old regimes, by Islamist movements that were better organised (Egypt) and by outside intervention (Syria) defeated these popular democratic movements. In Syria the movement was able to organise an armed struggle, but this was defeated by the old regime with Russian help. Extremist Muslim fundamentalists took over the fight from progressive students. The Syrian civil war produced a huge wave of refugees who, together with economic migrants from Africa, crossed the Mediterranean Sea to Europe. This added fuel to the already existing populist nationalist movements and political parties in Europe, propelling electoral victories inspired by xenophobic and racist anti-immigrant sentiment. In Iran, the green movement was repressed. In Turkey, Erdogan has prevailed, repressing the popular movement and continuing to fight the Kurds. All these developments, except those in Tunisia, have been setbacks for the global Left.

The Pink Tide in Latin America emerged in the last decade of the twentieth century and the first decade of the twenty-first century when progressive populist politicians were able to mobilise the urban poor to support expanded welfare states based on the export of raw materials. These regimes did not much challenge the global power structure and did not try to dispossess their domestic elites, but they did provide services and encouragement to traditionally marginal groups and support for the social forum process despite its formal refusal to allow participation by elected political authorities. These regimes emerged in reaction to crackdowns on state subsidies and labour unions that were supported by domestic neoliberals and by the early structural adjustment programmes imposed by the IMF.

The replacement of most of the Pink Tide progressive regimes in Latin America by reinvented local neoliberals has largely been a consequence of falling prices for agricultural and mineral exports because Chinese demand has slackened. The social programmes of the leftist populist movements were dependent on their ability to tax and redistribute returns from these exports. But both the rise of the Pink Tide and its demise may be an improved new normal for Latin America because almost all earlier transitions involved military coups and violent repression, whereas the rise of the Pink Tide and most of the more recent rightward regime transitions have been relatively peaceful and have not involved takeovers by the military or much real violent repression. The legal shenanigans in Brazil are not pretty, and the threat of a military coup continues to play a role in politics, but, at least so far, the right-ward shift has been less violent than earlier regime transitions. Stable parliamentary democracy may have finally arrived in most of Latin America. This is not utopia, but it is progress. Leftists can contend for power in the next round.

The continuing rise of right-wing populist and neo-fascist movements and their electoral victories in both the global North and the global South have added a new note that is reminiscent of the rise of fascism during the world revolution of 1917 (Chase-Dunn, Grimes et al. forthcoming). This raises the issue of the relationships between movements and counter-movements (Nagy 2018) and the possibility that the instrumentation and articulation of the global Left could be driven by the need to combat twenty-first century fascism. The glorification of strong leaders in the right-wing populist and neo-fascist movements was also seen in the twentieth century. But charismatic leaders have also been important in progressive movements in the past, and probably will be in the future, despite the 'leaderless' ideology of the horizontalists. The polarisation of politics provoked by the rise of neo-fascist politicians is increasingly providing a platform for more radical progressives in the mass media.

It is important to note that the rise of the right-wing populist movements has largely been a reaction against the neoliberal globalisation project. Dani Rodrik (2018) contends that the neoliberal globalisation project has had different political effects in Latin America from those in Europe and the US. In Latin America, the IMF's structural adjustment programmes requiring the cessation of social programmes led to the mobilisation and electoral successes of populist left politicians with the support of the urban informal sector – the Pink Tide. In Europe and the United States workers in older industries who had been decimated by capital flight to low-wage countries, were mobilised by right-wing politicians who blamed immigrants and liberals for what had happened during the neoliberal globalisation project. Contrary though these developments were, both were reactions against the neoliberal globalisation project.

Within the global Left there has always been a tension regarding anti-globalisation versus the idea of an alternative progressive form of globalisation. Samir Amin (1990) and Waldo Bello (2002) are important progressive advocates of deglobalisation and delinking the global South from the global North. Amin supported the idea of progressive national projects that would empower workers and farmers to carry out collective development projects that would serve the people. The alter-globalisation project has been articulated by Geoffrey Pleyers (2011). This globalist approach focuses on global justice and global inequalities and supports transnational social movements and engagement with international organisations.

While the United States has exercised a de facto global military empire since the demise of the Soviet Union, US economic hegemony[8] has been in decline since the 1970s. The proportion of the global domestic product that is accounted for by the US economy has declined since its peak in 1945 (Chase-Dunn et al. 2011). In the 1970s German and Japanese manufacturing caught up with US manufacturing, leading to global overcapacity and the expansion of finance capital. The rise of economic competitors from the semi periphery (China and India) has produced a multipolar global economy that will eventually be followed by a multipolar distribution of military power, because the current concentration of military capability under the control of the United States is very expensive, and has mainly been made possible by the survival of advantages accrued during the long period of US economic hegemony (Chase-Dunn and Inoue 2017). The coming of multipolarity may be an opportunity for countries in the global South but it could also be a very dangerous situation if rivalry for global domination among powerful states leads to interstate warfare.

What is needed is a capable instrument that can confront and contend with the global power structures of world capitalism and the popular reactionary movements that are emerging. This will involve overcoming the fragmentation of the progressive movements and some of the aspects of identity politics that have been consequences of the rise of possessive individualism, the internet, social media and precarious labour. The new organisational instrument should be designed to support contentious politics and institution-building at the local, national and global levels. I propose organising a vessel for the global Left based on struggles for human rights, climate justice, feminism, sharing networks, peace alliances, taking back the city, progressive nationalism and confronting and defeating neo-fascism.

THE VESSEL: FORGING AN ORGANISATIONAL INSTRUMENT FOR THE GLOBAL LEFT

A new discourse has emerged regarding possibilities for greater articulation among the movements of the global Left. This discourse often recounts and tries to derive lessons from the successes and failures of twentieth century united and popular fronts because of somewhat similar circumstances that the global Left found itself in in the first half of the twentieth century (Chase-Dunn et al. 2014).

The increasing tendency of progressive social movements to form around single issues and identity politics is seen as a problem that stands in the way of mobilising more effectively to become a significant player in world politics. This has been recognised and addressed in different ways by both activists and political theorists for the last twenty years (Sanbonmatsu 2004: 14). Leninists and neo-Leninists (Amin 2008, 2018; Dean 2012, 2016) have proposed a new communist international that would allow more than one legitimate group per country and would be more democratic than the Third International became under Stalin. The Amin and Dean versions differ in some respects regarding their notions of agency – Amin has long been a Third Worldist who sees the workers and farmers of the global South as the agents of a more decentralised and just world society, whereas Dean is more of a core-centric workerist. John Sanbonmatsu (2004) proposes a new political theory of agency that is similar in form to that advanced by Paul Mason (2015) and Heikki Patomäki (2019). Enlightened and creative individuals are claimed to be the agents who will carry forth the contemporary world revolution and build a post-capitalist world society.[9]

The World Social Forum held in Salvador, Brazil, in 2018 focused on how the social forum process could be reinvented to more effectively confront the rise of right-wing forces (Mestrum 2017, 2018). The demise of the US and European social forums may mean that the social forum process is running down. If that is the case, the question is then what could replace and improve upon the social forum process.

I contend that the anti-organisational beliefs that have been a salient part of the culture of progressive movements since 1968 have been a major fetter on the capability of progressive movements to effectively realise their own goals. But these sentiments and ideas run deep and so any effort to construct organisational forms that can facilitate progressive collective action must be cognisant of this embedded culture. The internet and social media, facilitating cheap and effective mass communications, have been blamed for producing specialised, single-issue movements. But communication technologies can also be harnessed to produce more sustained and integrated organisations that can be used to contend for power in the institutional halls of the world-system, as well as to develop prefigurative communities. The old reformist/revolutionary debate about whether to engage in electoral politics is another fetter on the ability of the global Left to effectively contend. States are not, and have never been, whole systems. They are organisations, like the Boy Scouts of America, except that they claim and exercise jurisdiction and try to monopolise legitimate violence. And their organisational resources can be used to facilitate the building of a post-capitalist global society. Progressive transnational social movements should be prepared to work with progressive regimes in order to try to change the rules of the global economic order (Evans 2009, 2010).

Rightly or wrongly, the culture of the global New Left strongly rejects vanguardism and the idea that political organisations should impose ideological uniformity on their members. The 'march-in-line' approach of the many competing vanguard parties is strongly rejected. In order to mobilise the global New Left an organisational instrument would have to be flexible, democratic, tolerant of dissent and encouraging of experimental projects.

Progressive transnational social movements should also be willing to work at the local level, with city governments, to implement progressive goals such as a universal basic income, as these cities would then serve as an emulative example (Lowrey 2018; Van Parijs and Vanderborght 2017; Wright 2010). This includes learning from cities in the global South and applying lessons learned in the global North. For instance, in the twenty-first century a universal basic income was piloted first in Kenya and Brazil, and now is being introduced in Stockton and Chicago. I agree with Paul Mason (2015) that the anti-utopianism of the Old Left and some in the New Left was a mistake. Prefiguration is a good idea. Sharing networks, co-ops, community banks, zero emissions homes, farms and industries are worthwhile endeavours for activists of the global Left.[10]

POLITICAL THEORY AND ORGANISATIONAL STRUCTURES

Horizontalism valorises leaderlessness and zero formal organisation, often paired with consensus decision making. Horizontalist organisation, also called 'self-organisation' (Prehofer and Bettstetter 2005) has several advantages: resilience (you can kill or repress some of the activists, but there is a lot of redundancy), flexibility and adaptability. Individual entities interact directly with one another, and there is no larger hierarchy that can be disrupted. These desirable characteristics are those that are stressed by advocates of horizontalist networks. But critics of horizontality point out that (as I have said above) structurelessness does not prevent the emergence of informal structures among groups of friends, and groups that embrace structurelessness have no mechanisms for regulating the power of these informal networks (Freeman 1972/73).

The idea of leaderless movements and organisations is an anarchist trope that has been critiqued by both Marxists (Epstein 2001) and feminists (Freeman 1972/73). Political organisations need to have institutionalised procedures for making decisions and for ways to hold leadership accountable so that mistakes can be rectified and so that those participants who are not inside the informal friendship network can have some say over decision making. These requisites are not so important when the world-system is humming along with business as usual but, when both conjunctural and systemic crises erupt, and powerful popular right-wing social movements and regimes emerge, *leaderlessness becomes an unacceptable luxury*. An alternative to 'march-in-line' must be found. While the culture of the contemporary global Left usually equates the idea of a political party with vanguard parties or electoral machines, there is a recent literature that argues that new forms of party organisation are possible in the age of internet communication (Carroll 2015; Dean 2012, 2016). Wiki farms facilitate the formation of virtual organisations that combine the virtues of open networks with leadership structures (data stewards) that allow groups to collectively author documents and to make group decisions (Wiki Organization n.d.).

Diagonalism argues for something that combines horizontalism with a centralised formal organisation that is itself democratic and flexible. A diagonal organisation is a complex of horizontally connected individuals, small groups and larger regional organisations with a decision-making structure by which groups can discuss and adopt policies and implement them. The hierarchy is as flat as is possible consistent with organisational capacity. Leadership is rotational and maximises opportunities for participatory democracy. Organisational bureaucracy is kept to a minimum, but legitimate representatives or delegates from horizontal groups make collective decisions and help to formulate policies and plan actions for the whole organisation.[11] This is The Vessel.[12]

The Vessel will be a *diagonal*[13] *network formed of project affinity groups that share the results of their experiments and constructions and coordinate with one another for political actions, including mass demonstrations and electoral campaigns*. Diagonalism links horizontal networks of individuals and groups with a legitimate leadership structure composed of designated delegates who are empowered to carry out the decisions of the organisation. Delegates make group decisions by a mixture of consensus and voting. The Council of The Vessel should combine horizontalism with a decision-making structure in which delegates are selected by local groups to represent the ideas and needs of the local groups in larger bodies that are tasked with decision making and carrying out policies.

The Vessel should not be a political party in the old sense, but it should be allowed, unlike the WSF, to adopt resolutions and to support campaigns. It should have a designated structure composed of a chosen facilitating delegate council to coordinate collective decision making and to deal with problems of security and communications. Digital organisations and the discourse on net governance make new forms of network organisation possible. The Vessel would declare itself in favour of horizontal authority structures and would allow local collectives to pick the particular structures and processes that they think will work best for them. Organisations also need to specify their boundaries and protect themselves against those who would like to disrupt them, or worse. These jobs are best done by all active members, but it may be found necessary to delegate security responsibilities to individuals or groups. Smart practices can be developed and shared as the struggle continues.

The Democracy in Europe Movement (DiEM25)[14] is a globalist organisation intending to democratise the European Union and structured along lines that are appealing to both intentional local communities and political activists who want to contend in world politics. It is a good organisational model that could be expanded, with some adjustments, to focus on global issues and to facilitate cooperation between progressive activists from the global South and those from the global North. The DiEM25 exemplifies what I mean by a diagonal organisation that combines self-organisation with vertical integration and that facilitates cooperation, coordination and global-level political action.[15]

ISSUE FOCI

The Vessel should focus on the articulation of several central issues and would discuss visions, strategies and tactics for the global Left and for collaboration among transnational, national and local projects.

The main issues that should constitute the focus of The Vessel are

- humans rights/anti-racism,
- climate justice,
- workers' rights,
- feminism,
- sharing networks,

- peace/anti-war alliances,
- taking back the city and
- anti-corporate transnationalism and democratic global governance.

The Vessel should also coordinate efforts to combat twenty-first century fascism and right-wing populism and should make alliances (united fronts; popular fronts) with NGOs and political parties that are willing to collaborate with these efforts.[16]

Human rights and anti-racism have been central in the network of movements participating in the social forum process. And global indigenism (Hall and Fenelon 2009) has been an important issue for the global Left (Chase-Dunn, Fenelon et al. forthcoming). The rights of colonised peoples, racial and ethnic minorities, indigenous peoples and people with minority gender and sexual orientations are central to the inclusive concerns of the global Left. The climate justice movement is already a collaborative project combining environmentalists with those who focus on the most vulnerable communities (Bond 2012; Foran 2018; Foran et al. 2017). Feminism has been one of the central movements in the social forum network of movements (Moghadam 2018). Sharing networks are a potentially potent tool for organising post-capitalist institutions that can transform the logic of global capitalism (Danaher and Gravitz 2017; Mason 2015). The peace/anti-war movements need local and national mobilisation against militarism (Benjamin 2013) as well as engagement with international governmental organisations in order to prevent the emergence of wars among core states in the coming multipolar world. The existing international political organisations are under attack from right-wing forces. The Vessel needs to advocate the strengthening and democratisation of global governance institutions that can help keep the peace as humanity passes through the coming multipolar phase of inter-imperial rivalry and to move in the direction of an eventual democratic and collectively rational form of global governance. The Take Back the City movement is an important venue for activists fighting for social justice in both the global North (Fasenfest 2018; Harvey 2012) and the global South (Davis 2006; Evans 2002). Progressive nationalism is an important fight-back against the appropriation of nationalism by right-wing populists and neo-fascists. For example, how could the national economy of the United States be reorganised to produce things needed abroad without destroying the environment and using the skills of those who have been left out of the economy by neoliberal globalisation? Nationalism is being reinvented as a response to the crises produced by the neoliberal globalisation process. The global Left has been resolutely cosmopolitan and internationalist, but how could it engage the rising wave of nationalism to propose more cooperative relations with peoples abroad and with the global South?

The Vessel also needs to provide analyses and strategies for local and national movements who are fighting against the rise of right-wing authoritarianism and the suppression of progressive popular movements.

CONCLUSION

Rather than wallowing in cynicism and resignation, the global Left needs to face up to the setbacks that have occurred in recent decades and to adopt a new strategy for moving humanity in a better direction. The next few decades will be chaotic, but the movements and institutions we build can make things better. Whether the big calamities all come at once or sequentially, we need to pursue a strategy of 'disaster post-capitalism' that plants the seeds of the future in the midst of the chaos. It is not the end, just one more age of chaos, and an opportunity for a transition to a much better world-system. The Vessel can take us there. Forging the Vessel could start with a foundational conference held under the auspices of the next World Social Forum.

NOTES

1   World revolutions are periods in world history during which rebellions and revolutions break out in many locations within the same decades. Symbolic years designate the signatures of each world revolution (1789, 1848, 1917, 1968, 1989, and 20xx). 20xx refers to the period of the rise of the global justice movement since the 1990s (Chase-Dunn and Niemeyer 2009). World revolutions have been named after a year that symbolizes the issues, events and the collective protagonists that signify the nature and culture of the revolts that clustered together over a period of time.

2   Thomas Jefferson claimed that a revolution was needed every 20 years to deal with the sclerosis issue. When new organisations can be easily organised, old sclerotic and conservative ones can be abandoned, and new radical ones formed.

3   Paul Mason is a British journalist who is well known to scholars of transnational social movements for his perceptive ethnographic coverage of the global justice movement (Mason 2013) and his proposal for a transition to a post-capitalist society based on free information (Mason 2015).

4   However, the fragility of these networked protests has been pointed out by other scholars studying them (Tufecki 2017) and by neo-Leninists arguing in favour of the re-establishment of more formal organisational instruments (Dean 2016).

5   The surveys were conducted at social forum meetings in Porto Alegre, Brazil, in 2005, Nairobi, Kenya, and Atlanta, Georgia, in 2007 and Detroit, Michigan, in 2010.

6   Our categorisation of reformist and antisystemic regimes in Latin America from 1959 to 2012 is contained in the Appendix to Chase-Dunn et al. (2015). See http://www.irows.ucr.edu/cd/appendices/pinktide/pinktideapp.htm (accessed 24 August 2019).

7   Valentine Moghadam (2017) shows how gender relations and women's mobilisations prior to the outbreak of the protests, along with differences in political institutions, civil society and international influences, explain most of the variance in the different outcomes of the Arab Spring.

8   The term hegemony is used here in the world-system sense of a predominant concentration of global economic power in a single core state. Ideological hegemony, as theorised by Antonio Gramsci, refers to the ideological class struggle and the power of the ruling class to impose its worldview on society. The Gramscian perspective has been extended to the global level by Robert Cox, Stephen Gill, William Carroll and other international relations scholars.

9   Sanbonmatsu's naming of a global political party – the Postmodern Prince – reflects his debt to Antonio Gramsci, but not to his devastating critique of postmodern philosophy, which he sees as a serious obstacle to moving forward toward an integrated egalitarian global society.

10 I doubt that Mason's (2015) version of post-capitalism, a global society in which wage labour has been replaced by the provision of free goods produced by networked machines, is a possibility for the next few decades, but I agree that this is a desirable goal for humanity.

11 Forms of representation that strike a balance between anarchist horizontality and the typical forms usually found in states are advocated by Teivo Teivainen (2016).

12 The new organisation should be named by those who want to create it. The Vessel is just one suggestion. Perhaps a better name would be the World Party/World Network, to designate its diagonal structure.

13 Keith Hayson (2014: 48–52) outlines an agenda for building an organisational diagonalism which is intended to produce a useful compromise between anarchistic horizontalism and organisational hierarchy that makes leadership and accountability possible.

14 See https://diem25.org/ (accessed 24 August 2019).

15 For more about the structure of the Movement, see https://diem25.org/organising-principles/ (accessed 7 February 2019).

16 This list is just a proposal for discussion. The development of a list of central issues should avoid the tendency to try to include everything. Simplicity is a virtue.

REFERENCES

Aldecoa, J., Chase-Dunn, C., Breckenridge-Jackson, I. and Herrera, J. 2019. 'Anarchism in the web of transnational social movements'. *Journal of World Systems Research* 25 (2). Accessed 7 February 2019, http://irows.ucr.edu/papers/irows107/irows107.htm.

Amin, S. 1990. *Delinking: Towards a Polycentric World*. London: Zed Press.

Amin, S. 2008. 'Towards the fifth international?' In K.S. Patomaki and M. Ulvila (eds), *Global Political Parties*. London: Zed Press, pp. 123–143.

Amin, S. 2018. 'Letter of intent for an inaugural meeting of the International of Workers and Peoples'. IDEAs network, 3 July. Accessed 7 February 2019, http://www.networkideas.org/featured-articles/2018/07/it-is-imperative-to-reconstruct-the-internationale-of-workers-and-peoples/.

Arrighi, G., Hopkins, T.K. and Wallerstein, I. 1989. *Antisystemic Movements*. London: Verso.

Bello, W. 2002. *Deglobalization*. London: Zed Books.

Benjamin, M. 2013. *Drone Warfare*. London: Verso.

Bond, P. 2012. *The Politics of Climate Justice: Paralysis Above, Movement Below.* Pietermaritzburg: University of KwaZulu-Natal Press.

Carroll, W.K. 2015. 'What radical means in the 21st century: Robust radicalism', *Review of Radical Political Economics* 47 (4): 1–6.

Carroll, W.K. 2016. *Expose, Oppose, Propose: Alternative Policy Groups and the Struggle for Global Justice.* New York: Zed Books.

Chase-Dunn, C., Reese, E., Herkenrath, M., Giem, R., Guttierrez, E., Kim, L. and Petit, C. 2008. 'North–South contradictions and bridges at the World Social Forum'. In R. Reuveny and W.R. Thompson (eds), *North and South in the World Political Economy.* Malden, MA: Blackwell, pp. 341–366.

Chase-Dunn, C. and Kaneshiro, M. 2009. 'Stability and change in the contours of alliances among movements in the social forum process'. In D. Fasenfest (ed.), *Engaging Social Justice.* Leiden: Brill, pp. 119–133.

Chase-Dunn, C. and Niemeyer, R.E. 2009. 'The world revolution of 20xx'. In M. Albert, G. Bluhm, H. Helmig, A. Leutzsch and J. Walter (eds), *Transnational Political Spaces.* Frankfurt/New York: Campus Verlag, pp. 35–57.

Chase-Dunn, C., Kwon, R., Lawrence, K. and Inoue, H. 2011. 'Last of the hegemons: U.S. decline and global governance', *International Review of Modern Sociology* 37 (1): 1–29.

Chase-Dunn, C., Stäbler, A-S., Breckenridge-Jackson, I. and Herrera, J. 2014. *Articulating the web of transnational social movements.* Working Paper No. 84. Institute for Research on World-Systems, University of California-Riverside. Accessed 7 February 2019, http://irows.ucr.edu/papers/irows84/irows84.htm.

Chase-Dunn, C., Morosin, A. and Álvarez, A. 2015. 'Social movements and progressive regimes in Latin America: World revolutions and semiperipheral development'. In P. Almeida and A. Cordero Ulate (eds), *Handbook of Social Movements across Latin America.* Dordrecht, NL: Springer, pp. 13–23.

Chase-Dunn, C. and Inoue, H. 2017. *Problems of peaceful change: Interregnum, deglobalization and the evolution of global governance.* Working Paper No. 69. Institute for Research on World-Systems, University of California-Riverside. Accessed 7 February 2019, http//:irows.ucr.edu/papers/irows117/irows117.htm.

Chase-Dunn, C., Fenelon, J., Hall, T.D., Breckenridge-Jackson, I. and Herrera, J. Forthcoming. 'Global indigenism and the web of transnational social movements'. In I. Rossi (ed.), *New Frontiers of Globalization.* Accessed 7 February 2019, http://irows.ucr.edu/papers/irows87/irows87.htm.

Chase-Dunn, C., Grimes, P. and Anderson, E.N. Forthcoming. 'Cyclical evolution of the global right'. *Canadian Review of Sociology.*

Danaher, K. and Gravitz, A. (eds). 2017. *The Green Festival Reader.* London: Routledge.

Davis, M. 2006. *Planet of Slums.* London: Verso.

Dean, J. 2012. *The Communist Horizon.* London: Verso.

Dean, J. 2016. *Crowds and Party.* London: Verso.

Epstein, B. 2001. 'Anarchism and the anti-globalization movement', *Monthly Review* 53 (4): 1–14.

Evans, P.B. 2002. *Livable Cities? Urban Struggles for Livelihood and Sustainability.* Berkeley: University of California Press.

Evans, P.B. 2009. 'From situations of dependency to globalized social democracy', *Studies in Comparative International Development* 44: 318–336.

Evans, P.B. 2010. 'Is it labor's turn to globalize? Twenty-first century opportunities and strategic responses', *Global Labour Journal* (1) 3: 352–379.

Fasenfest, D. 2018. *Detroit and New Urban Repertoires: Imagining the Co-operative City*. Bristol, UK: Policy Press.

Foran, J. 2018. *Taking or (Re)Making Power? The New Movements for Radical Social Change and Global Justice*. London: Zed Books.

Foran, J., Gray, S. and Grosse, K. 2017. '"Not yet the end of the world": Political cultures of opposition and creation in the global youth climate justice movement', *Interface: A Journal For and About Social Movements* 9 (2): 353–379.

Freeden, M. 2003. *Ideology: A Very Short Introduction*. Oxford: Oxford University Press.

Freeman, J. 1972/73. 'The tyranny of structurelessness', *Berkeley Journal of Sociology*, 17: 151–165.

Hall, T.D. and Fenelon, J.V. 2009. *Indigenous Peoples and Globalization: Resistance and Revitalization*. Boulder, CO: Paradigm Press.

Harvey, D. 2012. *Rebel Cities: From the Right to the City to the Urban Revolution*. London: Verso.

Hayson, K. 2014. *A Brief for Diagonalism: A Dialectical Take on David Graeber's* The Democracy Project. Accessed 7 February 2018, https://www.academia.edu/7289524/A_Brief_for_Diagonalism_-_A_Dialectical_Take_on_David_Graebers_The_Democracy_Project.

Hobsbawm, E.J. 1994. *The Age of Extremes: A History of the World, 1914–1991*. New York: Pantheon.

Korotayev, A.V. and Zinkina J.V. 2011. 'Egyptian revolution: A demographic structural analysis', *Entelequia, Revista Interdisciplinar* 13: 139–170.

Lowrey, A. 2018. *Give People Money: How a Universal Basic Income Would End Poverty, Revolutionize Work, and Remake the World*. New York, NY: Crown.

Mason, P. 2013. *Why It's Still Kicking off Everywhere: The New Global Revolution*. London: Verso.

Mason, P. 2015. *Postcapitalism*. New York: Farrer, Straus and Giroux.

McCarthy, J.D. and Zald, M.N. 1977. 'Resource mobilization and social movements: A partial theory', *American Journal of Sociology* 82 (6): 1212–1241.

Mestrum, F. 2017. 'Reinventing the World Social Forum: How powerful an idea can be'. Accessed 7 February 2019, https://opendemocracy.net/francine-mestrum/reinventing-world-social-forum-how-powerful-idea-can-be.

Mestrum, F. 2018. 'The World Social Forum is dead! Long live the World Social Forum?' Accessed 7 February 2019, http://www.alterinter.org/spip.php?article4654.

Meyer, J.W. 2009. *World Society: The Writings of John W. Meyer*. New York: Oxford University Press.

Michels, R. (1915) 1968. *Political Parties: A Sociological Study of the Oligarchical Tendencies of Modern Democracy*. New York: The Free Press.

Milkman, R., Luce, S. and Lewis, P. 2013. 'Changing the subject: A bottom-up account of Occupy Wall Street in New York City'. Accessed 7 February 2019, https://media.sps.cuny.edu/filestore/1/5/7/1_a05051d2117901d/1571_92f562221b8041e.pdf.

Moghadam, V.M. 2005. *Globalizing Women: Transnational Feminist Networks*. Baltimore: Johns Hopkins University Press.

Moghadam, V.M. 2017. 'Explaining divergent outcomes of the Arab Spring: The significance of gender and women's mobilizations', *Politics, Groups, and Identities* 6 (4): 666–681. Accessed 7 February 2019, http://dx.doi.org/10.1080/21565503.2016.1256824.

Moghadam, V.M . 2018. 'Feminism and the future of revolutions', *Socialism and Democracy* 32 (1): 31–53.

Nagy, S. 2018. 'Global swings of the political spectrum: Cyclically delayed mirror waves of revolutions and counter-revolutions'. Accessed 7 February 2019, https://irows.ucr.edu/papers/irows124/irows124.htm.

Patomäki, H. 2019. 'A world political party: The time has come'. Accessed 7 February 2019, https://greattransition.org/publication/world-political-party.

Pleyers, G. 2011. *Alter-Globalization: Becoming Actors in a Global Age*. Malden, MA: Polity Press.

Prehofer, C. and Bettstetter, C. 2005. 'Self-organization in communication networks: Principles and design paradigms', *IEEE Communications Magazine* 43 (7): 78–85.

Reitan, R. 2007. *Global Activism*. London: Routledge.

Rodrik, D. 2018. 'Populism and the economics of globalization', *Journal of International Business Policy* 1 (1/2): 1–22.

Sanbonmatsu, J. 2004. *The Postmodern Prince*. New York: Monthly Review Press.

SDS (Students for a Democratic Society). 1962. 'The Port Huron statement'. Accessed 7 February 2019, http://www2.iath.virginia.edu/sixties/HTML_docs/Resources/Primary/Manifestos/SDS_Port_Huron.html.

Sen, J. and Kumar, M. with Bond, P. and Waterman, P. 2007. *A Political Programme for the World Social Forum? Democracy, Substance and Debate in the Bamako Appeal and the Global Justice Movements*. New Delhi, India and Pietermaritzburg, South Africa: Indian Institute for Critical Action: Centre in Movement (CACIM) and the University of KwaZulu-Natal Centre for Civil Society (CCS). Accessed 7 February 2019, http://www.cacim.net/book/home.html.

Standing, G. 2014. *A Precariat Charter: From Denizens to Citizens*. London: Bloomsbury.

Steger, M., Goodman, J. and Wilson, E.K. 2013. *Justice Globalism: Ideology, Crises, Policy*. Thousand Oaks, CA: Sage.

Teivainen, T. 2016. 'Occupy representation and democratise prefiguration: Speaking for others in global justice movements', *Capital and Class* 40 (1): 19–36.

Tufecki, Z. 2017. *Twitter and Tear Gas: The Power and Fragility of Networked Protest*. New Haven, CT: Yale University Press.

Van Parijs, P. and Vanderborght, V. 2017. *Basic Income: A Radical Proposal for a Free Society and a Sane Economy*. Cambridge, MA: Harvard University Press.

Wallerstein, I. 2007. 'The World Social Forum: From defense to offense'. Accessed 7 February 2019, http://www.sociologistswithoutborders.org/documents/WallersteinCommentary.pdf.

Waterman, P. 2006. 'Toward a global labour charter for the 21st century'. Accessed 7 February 2019, http://www.choike.org/nuevo_eng/informes/4278.html.

Wiki Organization. n.d. 'Wikipedia: Formal organisation'. Accessed 7 February 2019, https://en.wikipedia.org/wiki/Wikipedia:Formal_organization.

WSF (World Social Forum). 2001. 'World Social Forum charter of principles'. Accessed 7 February 2019, http://www.universidadepopular.org/site/media/documentos/WSF_-_charter_of_Principles.pdf.

Wright, E.O. 2010. *Envisioning Real Utopias*. London: Verso.

Youngs, R. 2017. 'What are the meanings behind the worldwide rise in protest?' Accessed 7 February 2019, https://www.opendemocracy.net/protest/multiple-meanings-global-protest.

7

TOWARDS THE FIFTH INTERNATIONAL?

Samir Amin

C apitalism as an essential mode of production that defines modern time is based on the axial class conflict between labour and capital. The centrality of this concept is at the origin of the proletarian character proclaimed by the international organisations of the popular classes engaged in anti-capitalist social struggles, and in the socialist (or communist) horizons in which the proletariat in question has defined its liberation. Therefore I find that it is altogether natural that the proletarian International originated in the advanced centres of the system of global capitalism, in western Europe, in the nineteenth century.

Yet because of the imperialist character of the global expansion of capitalism, the affirmation of this dominating reality has also contributed to hiding other characteristics of social struggles in the peripheries of the system.

The diversity of social conditions and policies of the states and nations that constitute the global system is a consequence of the nature of the developments that characterise the global capitalist expansion, and more specifically (i) the inherent contrast between centres and peripheries in this development (in other words, the essentially imperialist nature of this expansion in all phases of its history), and (ii) the multiplicity of centres constituted as historic nation-states, which engage in a permanent competition positioning one against the other. Despite being subordinated to the demands of the accumulation in the centres of this system, the social formations of the peripheries have never been marked by the central position of the workers' proletariat in the whole organisation of production. Here the peasant societies and – to varying degrees – many other classes and social groups are also major victims of the system.

During the entire course of their formation, nations were always marked by their own particularities, regardless of their being dominating or dominated. The hegemonic blocs of classes and interests that helped capital establish its dominance, as well as the blocs that the victims of the system have built or tried to build to meet the challenge, have therefore always been different from one country to another, and one era to another. This has created political cultures that articulate value systems and 'traditions' of expression, organisation and struggle in their own ways. These, as well as the culture in which they are expressed, are all objective diversities. Finally, the development of the forces of production through scientific and technological revolutions has led to changes in the organisation of work and the various forms of subordination to capitalist exploitation.

Taken together, these diverse realities make it impossible to reduce political actors to bourgeoisie and proletariat. That simplification might work in polemical rhetoric, but it is useless for the elaboration of an effective policy. Because of its objectivity, the diversity results in a segmentation of the working classes and the dominated and exploited peoples, generating the weakening of their resistance and even of their offensive struggles whenever they succeed in changing the relations of force to their own advantage.

The diversity does not help to bring about a natural convergence of struggles against what only afterwards will be seen as the principal adversary. On the contrary, it causes potentially negative conflicts of interest between, for instance, urban and rural workers (over the prices of food products), or between nations (or dominating national blocs).

Strategies of reproduction of the dominant powers often successfully exploit the negative effects of the segmentation of interests and struggles. The flexibility of capitalism, which is often analysed as being an expression of its exceptional power (in comparison with the rigidity – effective or mythical – of other systems), is only the practical consequence of its reproduction as the dominant pole under the conditions of diversity and permanent evolution.

Nationalism frequently strengthens the successes of the strategies of capital and the hegemonic bloc of which it is the leader. In the centres of the imperialist system, this happens by way of rallying the political forces that benefit from the support of the working classes towards the global strategies of the dominant classes. The colonisation and the imperialist domination were legitimised in this way, yesterday by the discourse about the 'civilising mission', today by many of those who pretend to export democracy and defend human rights everywhere. The socialist parties and the social democrats have often practised this alignment and deserved the qualification of social-colonialists (or social-imperialists). This applies to the case of the social-liberal Atlanticists of contemporary Europe. Nationalism has sometimes also been aggravated by inter-imperialist conflicts. As we know, the working classes (at least the parties that represent them) have rallied behind their respective bourgeoisies in major conflicts, as happened during World War 1.

By contrast, the situation in the dominated peripheries typically generates reactions calling for national liberation. These are perfectly legitimate and positive when seen in a long-term perspective to abolish exploitation and oppression, but they also entail dangers and illusions. The position of representatives of the exploiting class may become too strong within the liberation front, either sooner or later.

This is a major and permanent problem in the globalised system of capitalism. The system, which is imperialist by nature, produces and reproduces the contrast between imperialist centres and dominated peripheries, and therefore imposes the national struggle as a necessary step towards further social progress.

THE HISTORIC LESSONS OF THE SOCIALIST AND COMMUNIST INTERNATIONALS

The diversity of the conditions of reproduction of the different partners of global capitalism has always constituted a major challenge to the success of struggles conducted by the victims of the system. The Internationals of the workers' movement were conceived precisely to surmount this major obstacle.

After a century and a half of the history of the Internationals it would be useful to draw some lessons that may clarify the present challenges and options for strategic action.

The first International, which was called the International Working Men's Association, was created precisely to surmount the negative effects shown by the national dispersion caused by the European revolutions of 1848. The new social subject, the primary victim of the expansion of capitalism in western and central Europe, which had expressed its socialist or communist dreams in the year 1848, ended up being broken by the counter-revolution. It called itself 'the proletariat', which at that time was composed of a minority assembled in the large factories and mines of the era, and a large circle of handicraft workers. The new proletarian class was exclusively localised in the north-west region of Europe, but spreading to the United States, meaning that the possibility of an intervention of the International made itself felt only within the borders of this region.

Despite its limitations, the first International was able to manage the diversity of social and political struggles in a democratic spirit, which placed it at the forefront of its generation. The association brought together organisations of varying nature and status, (embryonic) political parties, unions and cooperatives, civic associations and personalities (like Karl Marx, Pierre-Joseph Proudhon and Mikhail Bakunin). Their range of intervention, analysis of challenges, strategies, visions and mobilising ideologies were diverse – extremely so. The limitations of the ideas of this generation are easily enumerated: the patriarchal notion of the relations between men and women, the ignorance about the rest of the world, and so on. We could also thrash out one more time the nature of the conflicting ideologies (infant Marxism, anarchism, workers' spontaneity, etc.), their relevance and efficacy and so on, but this is certainly not the objective of this chapter. We should keep in mind the only lesson given by the first experience: the democratic respect for the principle of diversity.

This is an important lesson for us today.

The Second International was conceived on wholly different principles. The accelerated proletarianisation of the epoch had given birth to new forms of workers' parties with relatively important numbers of followers and influences on the working classes. The parties differed in many ways, ranging from English labour to the Marxist social democrats of Germany to French revolutionary trade unionism. Nevertheless, these parties rallied – at least at the beginning – to the objective of replacing the capitalist order with socialism. Of greater importance, however, was the principle of 'one' single party for each country, 'the' party that was supposed to be the exclusive representative of 'the' class that in itself was seen as the unique historical subject of social transformation, 'the' party that was potentially the bearer of 'the correct line', regardless of whether the party opted for – as history was later to show – moderate reform or revolution. Friedrich Engels and the first Marxist leaders (Karl Kautsky, Antonio Labriola and others) certainly considered these options as proof of progress in relation to the First International – as they probably were, at least in part. The new generation of leaders of the International did not always ignore the dangers of the main options of the time, as some were too hastily to observe (but that is not a matter of discussion in this chapter). Still, the limits to democratic practices in the political and social movements that were inspired by the parties of the Second International stemmed from these original fundamental options.

On the whole, these parties drifted towards imperialism and nationalism. The Second International very rarely addressed the colonial question and imperialist expansion. It often legitimised imperialism by claiming that its consequences were 'objectively' positive (that it forced retarded people to enter into capitalist modernity). This historical perspective, however, was refuted by the imperialist nature inherent in the global expansion of capitalism. 'Social imperialist' is an apt description of this alignment of social democratic parties with the linear bourgeois economism (which I claim Marxism has nothing in common with), and continued to be one of their features up until the period after World War 2 with their rallying Atlanticism and subsequently social liberalism.

The drift towards imperialism reinforced the chances of a parallel alignment with the nationalistic visions of the leaders of capitalism, at least in terms of international relations. As is well known, the parties of the Second International foundered in the chauvinism produced by World War 1.

The Third International was created to correct this drift, and it did, at least partially. It did in fact make its presence felt globally, supporting the creation of communist parties in all the peripheries of the world system and proclaiming the strategic character of the alliance of the 'Workers of the West' with the 'Peasants of the East'. Maoism expressed this development when it enlarged the call for internationalism to include the 'oppressed peoples' at the side of the 'workers of the world'. Later the alliance between the Third International (which had become Cominform), the Non-Aligned Movement following Bandung (1955) and the Tricontinental (1966) reinforced the idea and the practices of the globalisation of anti-capitalist struggles on a truly global scale.

Even so, the Third International not only conserved the organisational options of the Second, but also reinforced its traits: one 'single' party per country, and that party being the bearer of the one and only 'correct' line and the catalyst of all the demands the trade unions and mass organisations considered 'transmission belts'.

In addition, the Third International found itself in a situation that was unknown to the First or the Second: it had to protect the first socialist state, and later the camp of the socialist states. How this necessity evolved and what (negative) effects it had, in relation to the evolution of the Soviet system itself, are not the objects of this chapter.

The Fourth International, which reacted against this evolution, did not bring innovations with respect to the forms of organisation initiated by the Third. It wanted only to return to the origins of its forerunner.

BANDUNG AND THE FIRST GLOBALISATION OF STRUGGLES (1955–1980)

In Bandung, in 1955, the governments and the people of Asia and Africa proclaimed their desire to reconstruct the global system on the basis of recognition of the rights of nations that until then had been dominated. The 'right to development' set the foundation for a pattern of globalisation that was to be realised through multipolar negotiations, therefore compelling imperialism to adjust itself to the new demands. The success of Bandung – and not its failure, as is often thoughtlessly proclaimed – is at the origin of the enormous leaps forward by the people of the South in the domains of education and health, the construction of the modern state and the reduction of social inequalities, and the move into the era of industrialisation. Of course, the limitations of these gains, especially the democratic deficit of the national populist regimes that 'gave to the peoples' but never allowed them to organise themselves, must be considered seriously in the balance sheet of the epoch.

The Bandung system related itself to two other characteristic systems of the period following World War 2: the Soviet (and Maoist) system and the welfare state of the Western social democrats. These systems were certainly in competition and even in conflict (although the conflicts were not allowed to escalate beyond certain local limits), but they were certainly also complementary. In this situation it makes sense to talk about global struggles, since, for the first time in the history of capitalism, struggles took place in all the regions of the planet and inside all the nations, and interacted.

The proof of interdependence of the struggles and the historic compromises assuring stability in the management of concerned societies came with developments that followed the erosion of the potential in the three systems. The collapse of the Soviet system sparked the real social advances in the social democratic model that were the only possible way of facing the 'communist challenge'. The echo of the Chinese Cultural Revolution in Europe in 1968 should also be remembered.

The progress of industrialisation beginning in the era of Bandung was not a result of the unfolding of imperialism but was imposed by the victories of the peoples of the South. Without doubt this progress fed the illusion of a 'catching up', but imperialism, which had to adjust itself to the development of the peripheries, in reality rebuilt itself around new forms of domination. The old dichotomy between imperialist/dominated countries, which was a synonym for the dichotomy of industrialised/non-industrialised countries, was slowly replaced by a new dichotomy founded on 'the five new monopolies' of the imperialist centres: the control of new technology, natural resources, financial flows, information and weapons of mass destruction.

The accomplishments of the period as well as its limits take us back to the central question of the future of the bourgeoisie and capitalism in the peripheries of the system. This is an enduring question inasmuch as the global unfolding of capitalism, by virtue of the polarising effects due to its imperialist nature, leads to a basic inequality between the centre and the periphery with respect to a potential bourgeois and capitalist development. In other words, is the bourgeoisie of the peripheries constrained to subject itself to the requirements of this unequal development? Is it necessarily a comprador bourgeoisie? Is the capitalist road, in these conditions, necessarily a dead end? Or does the margin of autonomy that the bourgeoisie in certain circumstances has at its disposal (a margin that needs to be specified) allow a national capitalist development that is autonomous and able to advance in the direction of the 'catching up'? Where are the limits of these possibilities? At what point do these limits force us to qualify the capitalist option as an illusion?

Several doctrinaire and one-sided responses to these questions have been offered, first in one and then in the opposite direction, but in the end they were always adjusting to evolutions that neither the dominating forces nor the popular classes had foreseen correctly. In the aftermath of World War 2 the communism of the Third International qualified all the bourgeoisies of the South as comprador, and Maoism proclaimed that the road to liberation could be opened only by a socialist revolution which advanced in stages that were directed by the proletariat and its allies (the rural working classes in particular), and especially by their avant-garde, the Communist Party. Bandung set out to prove that this judgement was hasty and that under the direction of the bourgeoisie a hegemonic national populist bloc was capable of bringing about some of the desired development. Once the neoliberal offensive of the oligopolies of the imperialist centre (the triad: the United States, Europe, Japan) had put an end to the Bandung era in the 1980s, however, the bourgeoisies of the South appeared again to be ready to adopt a subordinate comprador role and to accept unilateral adjustment (this adjustment of the peripheries to the centre is in a way the inverse of the adjustment of the centres to the peripheries during the era of Bandung). But this reversal of tendency had barely occurred before a new window of opportunity for the national capitalist option again seemed to open in the so-called 'emerging countries', especially in China, but also in other countries such as India and Brazil. Without a deepened analysis of these potential advances and their contradictions and limits it will not be possible to build effective strategies of convergence of the local and global struggles.

NEW ERA, NEW CHALLENGES?

The era of the Internationals and of Bandung has come to an end. The three dominating systems of the period following World War 2 no longer exist. This has paved the way for a triumphant capitalist offensive. Capitalism and imperialism have entered into a new phase with qualitatively new features. The task of identifying these transformations and their real significance should be at the centre of our debate. Important works on these questions already exist but discussing them and their conclusions is not the object of this chapter.

Let me recall some central theses that I have advanced concerning these transformations:

- The transformations of the organisation of work and of the stratification of classes and social groups in relation to the technological revolution in progress (information, genetic, space, nuclear) and to the accelerated industrialisation in the emerging peripheries have resulted in a set of multiple social and political actors that are articulated in a new manner in their possible conflicts and alliances. The precise identification of these new subjects of the social transformation, of their interests and their aspirations, of their visions of the challenges and of the responses that they have brought, of the conflicts that separate them and make obstacles for their convergence in their diversity, is the first condition for a fruitful debate on local and global strategy.

- The centre/periphery opposition is no longer a synonym of the dichotomy industrialised countries/non-industrialised countries. The polarisation of centres/peripheries that gave the expansion of global capitalism its imperialistic character continues and even deepens because of the above-mentioned 'five new monopolies' enjoyed by the imperialist centres. Under these conditions the projects for accelerated development, which have been undertaken with immediate and indisputable success in the emerging peripheries (in China in the first place, but also in other countries of the South), cannot abolish the imperialist domination. These projects contribute to the establishment of a new centre/periphery dichotomy, but it does not surpass its predecessor.

- The noun imperialism is no longer to be declined in the plural as it used to be in previous historical periods. From now on it is a 'collective imperialism' of the triad (United States, Europe, Japan). This means that the common interests of the oligopolies based in the triad are stronger than their eventual conflicting ('commercial') interests. This collective nature of imperialism expresses itself through the use of the common instruments of the triad in the management of the global system: at the economic level, the World Trade Organization (WTO) (Colonial Ministry of the triad), the International Monetary Fund (collective Colonial Monetary Agency), the World Bank (Propaganda Ministry), the Organisation for Economic Co-operation and Development and the European Union (conceived to prevent Europe abandoning liberalism), and at the political level, the G7/G8, the US Army and the North Atlantice Treaty Organization (NATO), its instrument (the marginalisation/domestication of the UN completes the picture).

- The hegemonic project of the United States, which operates through a programme of military control over the planet (which among other things implies the abrogation of international law and the self-proclaimed right of Washington to wage preventive wars whenever it wants to), articulates itself in the collective imperialism and gives the US leadership the means to over-compensate for its economic weaknesses.

I would also like to briefly mention the main conclusions of some further reflections on these ongoing transformations of capitalism:

- It is said that the scientific revolution will lead to the replacement of types of work that are done under vertical hierarchies of command with 'network organisations' of free individuals. In this new science-dominated mode of production the individual is thought to become the real subject of history, taking over the tasks of the previous historic subjects, such as the classes and nations.
- Furthermore, it is being maintained that the era of imperialism has come to an end and that, in the present post-imperialist globalisation system, the 'centre is everywhere and nowhere'. In accordance with this idea, confrontations between multiple economic and social powers have replaced those of the states, which in earlier times made up the framework for relatively stable blocs of hegemonic power.
- Emphasis is being put on the 'financialisation' of management of the new 'patrimonial' capitalism, which is not analysed in terms of specific conjunctural phenomena belonging to the present moment of 'transition' (a transition that leads to a new system whose nature is therefore in itself an object of discussion), but as stable features of the new system being built.

I am not hiding the fact that I, for my part, have strong reservations with regard to these theses. What I propose in the following is not a thorough discussion of these questions – indisputably necessary – but only to make some observations concerning the political method that is needed to make these debates serve the positive construction of an alternative based on the principle of convergence in the diversity.

HOW TO 'DO POLITICS'?

Following the end of the twentieth century the new generation of militants and the movements definitely rejected the way of doing politics that had characterised the earlier critical movements on the Left (in particular the Second, Third and Fourth Internationals). The traditional way is justly reproached for the not-so-democratic practices on which it was built: the refusal of diversity, the pretence of one or another to hold the secret of a 'correct line' that has been deduced by way of 'scientific' (and thus impeccable) analysis, the excessive centralisation of organisation and the power of decision (in parties, unions and associated movements) and the ensuing fatal bureaucratic and doctrinaire deviations. The concept of the 'avant-garde' is considered to be dangerous and is, in consequence, rejected.

This criticism should be taken seriously and accepted in its essential parts. In this sense the principle of opening to the diversity, and to the democratic way of handling the diversity that is at the origin of the convergence of 'social movements' in the global, regional and national 'social forums', should be strictly respected.

The diversity in question is multidimensional, and concerns both theory and the practice.

The diversity of explicit or implicit analysis is present not only in the wide range of the contemporary movements but also very often within the particular movements. In order to gain an idea of this diversity one may take a look at the extreme positions held by the one or another concerning the relation between theory and practice.

At one extreme we find those who put forward a (probably simplified) Leninist thesis, affirming that the 'theory' (which has to be as 'scientific', that is to say true, as possible) must be conveyed to the movement from 'the outside'. Others associate it with the dream world of a creative utopia. At the other extreme are those who state that the future can only be the natural and almost spontaneous result of a movement that is free from concerns about systematic formulations in advance.

Accepting this diversity certainly means tolerating a whole range of opinions which, in turn, means adopting the perspective that the future is produced both by means of pre-formulated concepts and by the movement. For my part, I define the objective – which I will continue to call socialism/communism – as the simultaneous product of the theory and the practice, the product of their gradual convergence. This proposal does not imply a theory that has been ordained 'correct' a priori, or with any predefined vision of the final goal.

I will go even further and propose that we admit that the diversity concerns both the visions of the future themselves and their ethical and cultural foundations.

'Marxism' (in the singular or plural), 'radical reformism', 'liberation theology', 'anarchism', 'radical ecologism', 'radical feminism' all have their place in the necessary effort to build a convergence in the diversity.

This being so, organising the convergence while respecting the diversity does not exclude debate between opposing points of view, but implies it, on the condition that the aim of the confrontation is not to cast the miscreants out.

Having reached this point, I should like to formulate my own propositions. In itself and in its spontaneity, the movement cannot produce any desirable future; it does not provide an exit from chaos – all the more so if the movement declares itself to be apolitical. We know that, for perfectly respectable ethical reasons and because history provides real examples of how 'power corrupts', part of the movement rejects the idea that it should 'come to power'. The enthusiasm for the Neo-Zapatism of Subcomandante Marcos stemmed, for a good part, from this position, which, undoubtedly, is sometimes justifiable. It cannot, however, form the basis of a general rule that may be applied in the future (or even in the present situation). More generally, the apolitical option that Hardt and Negri have formulated (together with – not by chance – their 'post-imperialist' thesis) is naive at best; at worst it signals that they are accepting the notion of an apolitical civil society belonging to reactionary US political culture.

The way of doing politics that I believe is needed to challenge the present capitalistic/imperialistic system and to produce a positive alternative consists of treating the diversity as the First International did, and not as it was treated in the Second, Third and Fourth Internationals. Incidentally, I find that the debates within the First International show a striking analogy with those within the World Social Forum (WSF).

OBJECTIVES AND MEANS OF A STRATEGY
FOR CONVERGENCE IN DIVERSITY

My starting point is that the system in place (capitalism in the era of the collective imperialism of the triad under the command of the US leader, supported by subordinate bourgeoisies of the South) is not sustainable.

Capitalism has reached a stage in its development where its victim (its adversary) is no longer exclusively the class of proletarians whose work it exploits; rather, it is all of humanity whose survival is threatened. At this stage the system deserves to be called senile and therefore its only future is to cede its place to 'another world' that may be better or worse.

From now on, the further accumulation of capital actually requires the destruction of peasant societies (in which half of humanity lives) through a policy of 'enclosures' that is to be implemented on a planetary scale. Yet the system does not have the capacity to absorb the peasants whom it has chased from the fields into industrial activities. It also leads to the rapid exhaustion of non-renewable resources, to the accelerated destruction of biodiversity and to exacerbating the threat to the present ecological balance essential for the reproduction of life on the planet. A consequence of the devaluation of the labour force is that a greater contribution is demanded from the women who do the care work. We could continue the list of areas where the destructive consequences of capitalist expansion vastly predominate over its creative effects. The pursuit of capital accumulation has become an obstacle to the production of wealth made possible by the development of science and technology.

This evolution signifies that the historic subject that is the bearer of the desired transformation must henceforth be conceived in the plural. The movements of resistance and protest are intervening in a growing number of areas. But this plurality of anti-capitalistic subjects, which is the expression of a potentially invincible power of social movements, is, at the same time, the manifestation of the immediate weakness of that same movement. The sum of the demands – however legitimate they may be, and they are legitimate – and of the struggles conceived in their name do not constitute the efficient alternative that is needed to unleash a series of successive advances.

Thus the challenge is serious and will be met only on the condition that a victorious coalition, an alternative hegemonic bloc, is formed.

The challenge is such that those who want to act efficiently can hardly satisfy it with immediate and partial responses (in order to achieve 'capitalism with a human face'), without a perspective that goes 'beyond' capitalism. Without doubt every strategy of the real struggles must include objectives for the short term and others for the long term, in order to be able to identify the steps in the progression of the movement. The mere affirmation of a far-off objective (such as, for example, 'socialism') is not only insufficient, but may also be discouraging. Immediate goals must be set and action organised to guarantee that the militant mobilisations achieve victories. But this is not sufficient. It is ever more necessary to re-establish the legitimacy and the credibility of a long perspective, that of socialism/communism.

In the aftermath of the collapse of the Soviet system, China abandoned Maoism to embark on the path we know, and when the populist regimes of the Bandung era went off course, even the term socialism lost all its sense of credibility and legitimacy. The regimes which had emerged from revolutions made in the name of socialism, and the state powers that had been established by the victorious national liberation movements, had gradually engaged in disgraceful and sometimes also criminal activities. They lived in the midst of lies and a crooked, repetitive rhetoric. Therefore, these regimes and states are responsible for the collapse of hope, from which capitalism immediately profited. No wonder the re-emerging 'movement' of the 1990s accepted capitalism as the impassable horizon of the foreseeable future (if not the end of history) and chose to ignore imperialism's violations of the rights of nations.

But it is time to understand that this moment should be transcended. It is time to be radical. It is time to comprehend that the savage neoliberal offensive only reveals the true face of capitalism and of imperialism.

In this frame the issue of the European institutions poses a central challenge to Europe. These institutions were conceived to set Europe on the road of economic liberalism and political Atlanticism for ever, and the Commission is, in this sense, the perfect guarantor of the durability of the power of the European reaction. The call for 'another Europe' or 'a social Europe' is a pure incantation as long as this institutional construct is not thoroughly questioned.

The European institution annihilated state sovereignty, without which democracy turns into a surreal farce. State sovereignty has not been replaced by a federal power or confederation; the necessary conditions for that are lacking anyway. It obviously reduced the real Europe to a European dimension of the American political project (Atlanticism and the decisive role of NATO, led by Washington, in the foreign policy of Europe). And as long as the action of the collective imperialism of the triad continues the present liberal globalisation, the European institution will serve as one of its instruments.

The 'plural Left', as it is called in Europe, is certainly not the means whereby the peoples of this continent can reach the end of the tunnel. It is built on the principle of 'alternation' with the Right, within limits imposed by the liberal and Atlanticist European institutions (and therefore it is not an alternative). The reconstruction of 'another Left' is a condition without which it is difficult to imagine that Europe could be ruled by the European peoples. Will contradictions between 'Europe' and the United States manifest themselves with growing force? Some find economic conflicts of interest between the dominant firms in the two countries/regions to be highly probable. I am not persuaded by this argument. I believe that the contradiction lies elsewhere, in the contrast between the political culture of Europe and that of the United States, which will lead to a political conflict of which the first manifestations are already visible. In my opinion, the new upsurge of the European political cultures, which are threatened by 'Americanisation', can result in the rebirth of a Left that is up to the challenge, that is to say, an anti-liberal and anti-Atlanticist Left.

On the other hand the peoples of the three continents (Asia, Africa, Latin America) are today confronted with a system analogous in many respects to that in place at the end of World War 2: a colonial system that does not recognise their sovereign rights, and imposes an economic system that suits the expansion of the oligopolies of the imperialist centres, and corresponding political systems. The expansion of the so-called neoliberal global imperialist system is nothing less than the construction of 'apartheid on a global scale'.

At Bandung in 1955, the nations and states of Asia and Africa responded to this same challenge. Those states came into existence after the victory of revolutions made under the banner of socialism or powerful liberation movements, and which therefore benefited from an established legitimacy. The coalitions that constituted the revolutionary blocs, and the national liberation movements, always included important bourgeois segments aspiring to become the rulers of new society, even if they could not rule alone. This bourgeois dimension of Bandung, which manifested itself in the vision of economic development typical of the time, rehabilitated the 'national bourgeoisie' whose historic role appeared to have come to its end in the early post-war period. The decades of the Bandung era were deeply marked by the tension between the ambitions of these bourgeois elements and the aspirations of the popular classes.

The new imperialist order will be challenged. By whom? What will be the result? These are the questions that the states and the peoples of the periphery will have to answer.

The ruling classes of the South have largely accepted the role of subordinate comprador. They are not capable of questioning the dominating reality. The peoples, who are engaged in the daily struggle for survival, also seem ready to accept their lot – or, worse, swallow new illusions that the same ruling classes are feeding them (political Islam is the most dramatic example). But, on the other hand, the mobilisation of movements of resistance and the struggles against capitalism and imperialism across the three continents, the successes and electoral victories of the New Lefts in Latin America (whatever limits those victories may have), the progressive radicalisation of many of these movements, the critical positions that the governments of the South are beginning to take in the WTO – all prove that 'another world', better than the present one, is becoming possible.

An offensive strategy is needed for the reconstruction of the front of the peoples of the South. This requires a radicalisation of the social resistance to imperialist capital.

It requires the politicisation of the resistance, the capacity to make the struggles of peasants, women, workers, the unemployed, the 'informals' and democratic intellectuals converge and assign to the entire popular movement objectives for democratisation and social progress (these are indissolubly associated) that are possible in the present term and in the long term. It requires that the values that give this movement legitimacy are applicable universally (in a socialist perspective), therefore surpassing cleavages that see peoples of the South in opposition to one another (Muslims and Hindus, for example). Para-religious or para-ethnic 'culturalisms' (for instance, political Islam, political Hinduism) cannot be allies in the fight for an alternative to imperialism. On the contrary, they are the principal reactionary allies of the dominating imperialist forces.

There is a possibility that the mobilisation and the advances of the popular struggles will inflect the policies of the powers in place in the countries of the South, and even change these powers for the better. Such inflections are beginning to show in, for instance, the formation of the Group of 20 and the Group of 99 within the WTO, even if this crystallisation of diverse (converging or diverging) interests may entail ambiguities.

The ruling classes of certain countries of the South have visibly opted for another strategy. Their strategy is neither one of passive submission to the dominant forces in the global system, nor one of declared opposition. It is a strategy of active interventions followed by a hope for accelerated development of their countries.

China was better equipped than others to make this choice and achieve incontestably brilliant results. China benefited from the solidity of its nation as a result of the revolution and Maoism, from the decision to keep control over its currency and its capital flows, and from its refusal to abandon the state ownership of land (the main achievement of the peasant revolution). Can this experience be continued? And what are its limits? The analysis of the contradictions of this option brings me to the conclusion that the project of a national capitalism capable of imposing itself as an equal with the major powers of the global system is largely built on illusions. The objective conditions inherent in its history do not permit such a historic social compromise between capital, workers and peasants that would guarantee the stability of the system. The system will necessarily slide towards the Right (and will therefore confront a growing social movement of the popular classes), or evolve towards the Left, building a 'market socialism' as one step in the long transition towards socialism.

The apparently analogous choices of the ruling classes in other 'emergent' countries are even more fragile. Neither Brazil nor India is capable of resisting with enough force the combination of imperialism and local reactionary classes, because they have not made a radical revolution, as has China. That the WTO made these two governments take sides with the liberal globalisation (in Hong Kong in

December 2005) incontestably helped imperialism to avoid the disaster that was waiting for it, and dealt a hard blow to the emerging front of the countries of the South. This supreme error – if it is not something worse – serves only the interests of the most reactionary local classes (the Brazilian and Indian big landowners!) who are imperialism's natural allies and sworn enemies of the popular classes of these countries. The hopes that a part of the historic Left of Latin America has invested in the social democratic model are founded on a major error of assessment: European social democracy was able to achieve what it did because it could turn social-imperialist. That is not a viable option under the conditions obtaining in Brazil and the other countries of the South.

TOWARDS A FIFTH INTERNATIONAL?

The globalisation of capitalism's strategies creates the need for a counter-strategy from its victims. Should we conclude that a new International is needed to assure the convergence of the struggles of the people against capital?

I do not hesitate to give a positive answer to this question, on the condition that the envisioned new International is conceived in the same way as the First, but not as the Second, the Third or the Fourth Internationals. It should be a socialist/ communist International open to all who want to act together to create convergence in diversity. Socialism (or communism) would thus be seen as the product of the movement, and not as something that is deduced from a previous definition. This proposition does not exclude the formulation of theoretical concepts for the society to come. Instead, it evokes precise formulations of such concepts, and it excludes the monopoly of one concept over the right way and phases of transition.

It is certainly difficult to achieve these fundamental democratic principles. The exercise of democracy is always difficult. We should draw 'limits', accept that defining the strategic objectives implies making choices and that there is no predetermined way of handling the relation of a majority to one or more minorities.

In order not to go against the principles that I have just formulated, I shall not try to answer these questions. I shall only propose some major strategic goals for the battle ahead, arranging them in three sections:

1. Roll back liberalism at all levels, nationally and globally. To this end, a number of immediate goals can be formulated – for instance, the exclusion of agriculture from the agenda of the WTO, the abrogation of decisions by the imperialist powers on intellectual and technological property rights, the abrogation of

decisions that hamper the development of a non-commercial management of natural resources and public services, the abrogation of the bans on regulation of capital flows, the proclamation of the right of states to cancel debts that, after audit, are proved to be immoral or despicable, and so on.

2. Dismantle the programme of control of the planet by the military forces of the United States and/or of NATO. The repudiation of international law by the United States, and the 'authorisation' that it gives itself to conduct preventive wars, must be condemned without reservations. The functions of the UN must be restored. There must be an unconditional and immediate withdrawal of the occupying army stationed in Iraq, and of the Israeli administration of the occupied Palestine. All military bases of the United States that are dispersed across the continents must be dismantled. As long as this project to control the planet is not morally, diplomatically, politically and militarily defeated, any democratic and social advances will remain vulnerable, the people under threat of being bombed by the US Air Force.

3. Repeal the liberal and Atlanticist concept upon which the institutions of the European Union are based. This implies reconsidering the whole European institutional framework and the dissolution of NATO.

Initiatives aiming at formulating a strategy of convergence corresponding to the general vision proposed here have already been taken.

In Bamako, on 18 January 2006, on the eve of the polycentric World Social Forum (Bamako and Caracas), the day was devoted to debates on the strategy and construction of convergence in diversity. The fact that this meeting could be held and that it produced interesting results shows that the global social movement is already moving in this direction.

The sketched Fifth International or, more modestly, the strategic actions proposed in the Bamako Appeal which I am here referring to, should contribute to the construction of the internationalism of the peoples. It should embrace all peoples from North to South, not only the proletariat, but all social classes and popular strata that are victims of the system whose survival is threatened, and thus humankind as a whole. The proposed internationalism should strengthen and complete 'another internationalism', namely the solidarity between the peoples on the three continents (Asia, Africa, Latin America) against the aggressive imperialism of the triad. The solidarity of the people in the North and in the South cannot be based on charity. It should be based on common action against imperialism.

The reinforcement of the internationalism of the peoples will facilitate advancements in three directions that, taken together, form the alternative: social progress, democratisation and strengthening of national autonomy through a negotiated globalisation.

Who will subscribe to this perspective? At this point we must return to the question of 'limits'. The Fifth International should not be an assembly for political parties only; it should welcome all organisations and resistance movements of the people and guarantee both their voluntary participation in the construction of common strategies and their independence of decision making. Thus political parties (or their factions) should certainly not be excluded. Whether we like it or not, the parties remain important gathering points for civic action.

The fundamental principle may be formulated in the following two complementary phrases: (i) no socialism without democracy (and therefore no progress towards socialism without democratic practices); (ii) no democratic progress without social progress.

Thus it becomes understandable that it will not be just a few, small groups of political extremists and some goodwilled NGOs who will join this perspective. Many big movements (trade unions, peasant associations, women's organisations, citizens' movements) know from experience that 'there is strength in numbers'. The parties of the Third and Fourth Internationals will also find themselves a place, if they stop being self-proclaimed avant-gardes! Many democratic, social and anti-imperialist parties of the peripheries will certainly understand the advantages of coordinated anti-imperialist struggles. Unfortunately, the parties of the Second International that take sides with liberalism and Atlanticism have excluded themselves from this prospect.

This is not the place to go further into the issue of the 'conditions' for membership (in analogy with the famous 21 conditions to be fulfilled by the members of the Third International). Serious debates on these principles and the statutes of the International are indispensable. We only ask for reflection on these issues.

The WSF will certainly count as one of the friends of this International, if it comes into existence. The fundamental democratic principle of the WSF – that everybody who accepts its charter is welcomed without reservation – makes it possible for the members of the new International to coexist with organisations that contribute to the convergence in diversity, even if they do not adhere to a socialist perspective, as well as with organisations that decide not to participate in the formulation of common strategies. This diversity gives strength to the movement and should be preserved.

Nevertheless, the idea of a Fifth International has its adversaries, and their number will increase if it becomes a reality. There are already those who wish to maintain the WSF in a state of maximum impotence. The ideologies by which they want to legitimise the inactivity are well known. One of their propositions is the claimed equivalence of the diversity of the Forum and that of the self-proclaimed 'plural Left' (in Europe, principally). Another is the thesis of the apolitical civil society (or even anti-political civil society). This thesis, which has always been typical of the political culture of the United States, has attracted a number of NGOs over the past decades.

Their goal is to turn the WSF into a complement to the Davos forum. In other words, instead of questioning the principles of liberalism, capitalism and imperialist globalisation, they are giving these principles new legitimacy through a minimum of 'social demands' (such as the 'struggle against poverty'). Associations (as apolitical as possible) of the so-called 'civil society' are considered instrumental in the formulation of such demands.

There are already a number of such adverse initiatives, supported by the Davos establishment, the G7, the big foundations in the United States and the institutions of the European Union. The Mediterranean Forum (the so-called Barcelona initiative promoted by the European Union) and the Arab Democracy Forum (later called the Future Forum) promoted by US agencies, and the coalitions of hand-picked NGOs formed on the initiative of international institutions (principally the UN and the World Bank) in order to follow the big conferences organised by the institutions of the system (the WTO and others), are probably meant to divide the social forums, or maybe to make them break down, or at least stop their potential development, growth and radicalisation.

ACKNOWLEDGEMENT

This chapter was first published in English as Samir Amin, 'Towards the Fifth International', Chapter 7, in *Global Political Parties*, edited by Katarina Sehm-Patomäki and Marko Ulvila, 2007, published by Zed Books. Reproduced with permission of the Licensor through PLSclear.

8

THE CAMPAIGN TO DISMANTLE CORPORATE POWER

Keamogetswe Seipato

The growing power of transnational corporations and their extension of power through privatization, deregulation and the rolling back of the State also mean that it is now time to develop binding legal norms that hold corporations to human rights standards and circumscribe potential abuses of their position of power.

Jean Ziegler (2003)

The terms 'transnational corporation' (TNC) and 'multinational corporation' (MNC) are often used interchangeably, but there are key differences between them. Transnational corporations are corporations that have headquarters in one country, mostly in the global North, and operate in the global North and the global South. The corporation based in the global South is not necessarily a subsidiary of the mother company. It can be autonomous from a branding perspective and/or a production perspective. A good example is Coca Cola, which is based in several countries around the world, where some of the beverages sold by the corporation are either country or region specific. A multinational corporation, on the other hand, is based (has its headquarters) in one country and operates or has subsidiaries in other countries. Often, headquarters are in the global North and the subsidiaries are in the global South. An example of this is Apple Inc., which has iPhones designed in California, assembled in China, and sold globally. However, the differences between TNCs and MNCs have disappeared with the introduction and intensification of globalisation and the mobility of capital.

The earliest historical origins of TNCs can be traced back to the sixteenth century with colonial and imperial expeditions to countries outside of Europe, for example the British East India Company. TNCs have provided one key avenue through which capitalism has spread, in the process causing massive destruction, all in the name of profit. When states from the global North could no longer play a direct role in the extraction of resources and the exploitation of people through slavery and colonisation, TNCs and the Bretton Woods Institutions became the new instruments to accumulate wealth within the context of globalisation.

This chapter looks at how the power of TNCs has been left unchecked and shows how the masses seek to roll back corporate power and replace it with people's power. There is a plethora of examples of corporate abuse around the world, but the gross human rights violations and economic repercussions of corporate abuse are particularly jarring in southern Africa and in the African continent as a whole. After giving an historical account of the rise of TNCs, the chapter brings to the fore the invisible structure that exists solely to facilitate corporate impunity. In order to highlight the immense material implications of corporate abuse, the chapter also examines cases such as the Marikana Massacre that took place in 2012 in South Africa. People's power and resistance globally and in the southern African region is foregrounded as part of the conclusion.

THE BRETTON WOODS BROTHERS AND GLOBALISATION: FERTILE SOIL FOR MULTINATIONAL CORPORATIONS

After World War 2, Europe had to rebuild itself and countries like Britain were no longer at the top of the global economic food chain. While the whole of Europe was at war with itself, the United States was growing, building its industries and becoming an economic superpower, which made it a natural strategic ally in the eyes of the British. Both the US and Britain agreed that the world economy had to be a stable one, unlike its unstable condition during the pre-World War 2 era (Buckman 2004: 23).

As a means to rebuild the economy, an Anglo-American agreement was established between Britain and the United States. The agreement led to the Bretton Woods Conference of 1944, attended by 730 representatives from 44 countries around the world, which gave rise to institutions such as the International Monetary

Fund (IMF) and the World Bank. During the Bretton Woods Conference, it was determined that these institutions would be the pillars of the new world economy and would work towards a prosperous global economy.[1]

To ensure that money flowed beyond just loans to countries, trade became key. A body to ensure cross-border trade also became pertinent, thus the General Agreement on Trade and Tarriffs (GATT) was established. It was created to regulate world trade in an effort to aid economic growth.[2] Due to the limitations of GATT and the initial idea of forming a third institution to complement the IMF and World Bank, the GATT was replaced by the World Trade Organization (WTO) in 1995.

All three of these bodies – the IMF, the World Bank and the WTO – can be seen as the engines of globalisation. They laid a concrete foundation for corporations based in the North to advance into other markets beyond their home country borders. The cross-border flow of goods, services and money facilitated by all three of these bodies gave rise to modern economic globalisation. The fertile trade and investment soil created by economic globalisation nurtured the growth of TNCs and corporate power.

THE FIRST BATTLE AGAINST MULTINATIONAL POWER: THE NEW INTERNATIONAL ECONOMIC ORDER

Dependency theorists like Raúl Prebisch and Hans W. Singer in the 1950s postulated that development taking place in the First World was happening at the expense of countries in the Third World, and in addition, the economic growth in the First World depended on the grotesque extraction of natural resources in the Third World, with no benefit to these Third World states. Theories about the world system, such as dependency theory, and the dysfunctional economic growth of former colonies in comparison to that of imperial powers provided the political and economic impetus to create the demand for a New International Economic Order (NIEO) in the early 1970s. The NIEO came into existence as a result of a sequence of events between the 1950s and the early 1960s that organised the power of the global South within the decolonising world order. This included the launch of the Non-Aligned Movement (NAM) in 1961. The NAM was a multilateral rejection of the Cold War bilateral alliances that continued to enforce the unequal development paradigm of that time. Moreover, the establishment of the United Nations Commission on Trade and Development (UNCTAD) was crucial. It was created to deal with matters related to international trade and industrialisation to ensure inclusion of the Third World in the international trade system – not only as the cogs but also as beneficiaries of the system.

NAM, UNCTAD and the NIEO can be viewed as the global South's first step in challenging corporate power – the corporations that were central to the global North's success in the economic growth race. These platforms, particularly UNCTAD and the NAM, were spaces where the growing power of corporates was exposed and challenged. UNCTAD released a series of World Investment Reports assessing international development and policy and tracking key trends in relation to TNCs and their power. Through its reports and under its auspices it created the framework that highlighted the growing disparities in development and growth between the First World and the Third World. The eminence of corporate power led the G77 and Third World countries to call for a special session of the UN General Assembly. Resolution 3201 – a declaration on the establishment of an NIEO – was tabled at this special session.

In 1974 the General Assembly adopted the declaration. It was an extremely progressive declaration in relation to matters of corporate power. It wanted TNCs to be regulated and supervised. To achieve this principle, it was resolved that an international code of conduct for TNCs should be formulated and adopted. This led to the 'Draft United Nations Code of Conduct on Transnational Corporations' in 1983.[3] The draft code of conduct established the means by which TNCs could be regulated by stipulating the responsibilities of TNCs around matters such as environmental protection and respect for the domestic laws of the host country in which the TNC operates. What is particularly interesting is that it also addressed matters of taxation and transfer pricing, which tackles issues related to illicit financial flows.

Much can be said about the success of the NIEO, the demands it put forth and how they were implemented. Many speak of how most of the demands of the NIEO were a push to radicalise the world system. However, those in power would not allow that disruption and/or there was lack of political will to implement the demands. The leaders in the North treated the NIEO as a general crisis of the economic system of the time, and individual leaders in the North viewed the NIEO in the same way as they had viewed domestic unrest (as a revolt in a colony) and tackled the demands as such (Gilman 2015). The fire started by the NIEO was extinguished by the economic crisis that followed in the mid- and late 1970s. Many of the Third World elite that had propagated Third Worldism were silenced. The deepening crisis pushed the global South into the hands of the same institutions that they were fighting; the global North and its Bretton Woods Institutions were able to push many countries into debt traps with structural adjustment programmes.

THE UNITED NATIONS AND ITS SHIFTS:
THE RISE OF CORPORATE POWER

Before the 1970s, the world's general view of TNCs had been a fairly positive one: TNCs were seen as a means to accelerate development (Emmerij and Jolly 2007). This changed in the early 1970s when the involvement of the International Telephone and Telegraph Corporation (ITT) in presidential politics in Chile and the matters of bribery by TNCs around the world were exposed. These scandals provided the first glimpse of the extent to which corporations wielded power. It revealed that TNCs can meddle in politics to ensure that their interests are protected.

In 1972, against the backdrop of these scandals, Philippe de Seynes, the Under Secretary General of the UN's Economic and Social Council, worked on tabling a resolution that called together a Group of Eminent Persons who were tasked with looking at the impact of TNCs on development and international relations. Their work was housed at the UN's Economic and Social Council (Moran 2009).

The group's goal was to develop a new international economic world order and its work led to the establishment of the United Nations Commission on Transnational Corporations (UNCTC) in 1974. The focus of UNCTC was on forming a code of conduct to regulate transnational corporations (UNCTC 1983). The body of the UNCTC's work took place at the time when there was a growing Third World movement that found expression through the development of the NIEO. This fuelled the UNCTC's work, which reached its apex with the drafting of the 'Draft United Nations Code of Conduct on Transnational Corporations' in 1983. Instead of intensifying the powers of the UNCTC and setting it up as a regulatory body that could hold TNCs accountable in the wake of the above scandals, the UNCTC was abolished and its functions dissolved into UNCTAD in 1993 (Emmerij and Jolly 2007).

The change in economic landscape in the late 1980s saw the proactive stance that the UN had taken towards TNCs and their impacts on the world dissipate. The change may be attributed to the move toward neoliberal economic policies in countries that are key players in the UN. Therefore, actively working to curtail the power of TNCs was not in the interests of the UN. A key example, indicative of this shift, is demonstrated by the standing ovation that the General Assembly gave to Salvador Allende's speech in the 1970s asserting that 'the world community, organised under the principles of the UN, does not accept an interpretation of international law subordinated to the interests of capitalism', while in the early 2000s it was content to hear Ban Ki-moon say, 'Now, a new set of crises requires a renewed sense of mission . . .' and thereafter called his audience to sign up to inclusive capitalism: 'a new constellation of international cooperation – governments, civil society and the private sector, working together for a collective global good' (Zubizarreta and Ramiro 2016: 9).

The power of TNCs accelerated in the 1980s – they became stronger global actors without the limitations of international law that block nation-states from directly being key players in the global economic playing field. The rise in the power of TNCs is mapped out in the World Investment Reports of UNCTAD. The 1991 report, which used a substantial amount of data produced in the 1980s, reveals that TNCs dominated the foreign direct investment flows amounting to US$196 billion in 1989 (UNCTAD 1991). The report also mentions that TNCs played a major role in the international trade of high technology products, which, since technology is a key determinant of economic growth, means that TNCs played a significant role in shaping and controlling the economic landscape of the 1980s.

One might argue that a key reason for the clear shift in the UN's approach to TNCs is based on the fact that they were major global actors within the process of privatisation. Countries in Africa were facing major economic challenges and in order to qualify for bailouts they had to implement structural adjustment programmes. One of the many policies the Bretton Woods Institutions implemented through these programmes is the privatisation of public services/goods. This, in turn, made it possible for TNCs to virtually run the economies of these countries because they were the largest suppliers of the foreign direct investment that created an inflow of money for any crisis-ridden country. The excitement around the economic prosperity guaranteed by TNCs is seen in the language used in the World Investment Reports of UNCTAD. The 1992 report illustrates this through a diagram that positions TNCs at the centre of economic growth of any 'host economy' in which they operate (UNCTAD 1992: 13).

THE ARCHITECTURE OF IMPUNITY

'The evolution of global capitalism from the mid-nineteenth century to the present has served to consolidate and strengthen the pivotal role of TNCs in the global economy, as well as their increasing dominance over multiple areas of life' (Zubizarreta 2015: 7). To believe the notion that corporate abuses and crimes are just a phenomenon and that only a few outlier corporations are implicated is naïve, when there is a structure of corporate law and trade treaties designed to protect the interests of corporations, above even human rights.

The amount of power that corporations wield has led to an asymmetrical legal system known as the *lex mercatoria*. The *lex mercatoria* is characterised by several trade treaties – multilateral and bilateral trade agreements, investment protection agreements, policies imposed by the IMF, conditional loans by the World Bank, investor–state dispute settlement systems and trade measures enforced by the WTO (Zubizarreta and Ramiro 2016).

Looking into the history of the WTO reveals that each ministerial meeting enforced trade rules in areas that contributed to the growing power of TNCs. These rules were designed to ensure that the goods and services of TNCs were not undercut by the availability of cheaper goods and services in poor countries (Buckman 2004: 48) The investor–state dispute settlement mechanism is a cog in the huge machinery of the *lex mercatoria* which allows TNCs to sue a government for passing laws that can affect their future or present profits. The grounds on which a TNC can sue are very fluid. For example, in cases where corporations have taken governments to court for passing laws or measures that could harm their present or future profits, the cases are heard, regardless of how ludicrous their grounds are (George 2016).

The Transatlantic Trade and Investment Partnership (TTIP), which has been negotiated behind closed doors, is one of the crudest examples of these trade agreements that form the basis of corporate impunity. Once the TTIP is signed, it is set to lead to the abolishment of 'barriers' to corporate profits and to allow US-based companies to sue the UK government or any other government in the EU through arbitration courts. The trade agreement is forecast to lead to a race to the bottom in food, environmental and labour standards in the EU (War on Want n.d). In essence the TTIP looks as promising as the North American Free Trade Agreement (NAFTA) looked – on paper. NAFTA promised prosperity and economic growth for Mexico, Canada and the US, but in Canada, for example, the agreement brought nothing but a US$250 million lawsuit after the people of Quebec voted against fracking and a company sued the Canadian government for loss of profits (War on Want n.d).

Rules such as the most-favoured-nation principle of the WTO ensure that 'everyone is treated equally', which means that no country can legislate any law to guarantee that national corporations will receive subsidies from their governments, and also prevents any preferential treatment of national corporations within a specific market in which a TNC is also operating in that territory. In addition, the existence of international arbitration tribunals and the effectiveness of their rulings strengthens corporate law (Zubizarreta and Ramiro 2016: 17). This strength, juxtaposed with corporate social responsibility, codes of ethics and international human rights law, relegates the protection of nature and society as a whole to the status of soft law. It is particularly interesting to observe that most disputes are raised by TNCs in the extractive industries which of course are not interested in the development of countries in the global South.

There are three key tools that help build and strengthen the *lex mercatoria*, namely lobbying – when experts and lawyers work on moulding national and international policies in favour of the revolving-doors interests of TNCs, thus enabling high-level people to move between the public and private sectors without problems related to a conflict of interest; corporate diplomacy and bribery. Often a corporation seeking to operate in new territories offers the officials in the potential host countries 'financial incentives' or bribes to facilitate its operations. Several high-level cases of bribery or corporate corruption have been reported over the years. For instance, in 2008 Siemens was ordered to pay the US government US$1.6 billion for violating the country's anti-corruption laws. The assistant attorney general at that time was quoted in a newspaper as saying 'Bribery was nothing less than standard operating procedure at Siemens' (O'Reilly and Matussek 2008).

The balance of power within a neoliberal framework guarantees that the interests of TNCs are central and assures legal certainty for their business, at the cost of protecting the fundamental rights of the majority. Examples of how Chevron has taken Ecuador to several international arbitration tribunals because Chevron was required to pay compensation to those impacted by its pollution in the Amazon is a clear depiction of this (Zubizarreta and Ramiro 2016: 7). The strength of the *lex mercatoria* is reinforced through the Chevron case, which started in 1993 and has led to back-and-forth court battles with Chevron losing each time. However, the mere fact that Chevron has been to several international arbitration tribunals to fight this over the past 25 years, highlights how the corporation trusts the process and believes that it will win. In 2018, there were several judgments that found Chevron guilty, but they have been overruled by the Permanent Court of Arbitration in the Hague. The judgment stated that the Ecuadorian government was liable for 'denying' Chevron justice and violating the company's fundamental procedural rights (Business and Human Rights Resource Centre 2018).

CORPORATE IMPUNITY: THE CASE STUDY

On 16 August 2012, South Africa witnessed the Marikana Massacre, in which 34 striking mine workers were gunned down by police. The mine workers at Lonmin Platinum were on strike for a wage increase, demanding a living wage. After the massacre then President Zuma called for a commission of inquiry, which revealed what had taken place on 16 August and the days leading up to the massacre. It became clear that the police had been working with Lonmin Platinum and that high-level officials at the time gave police orders to squash the strike. Recordings and emails presented as evidence during the Farlam Commission of Inquiry implicated several government officials, including then deputy president, Cyril Ramaphosa.

Lonmin Platinum is a TNC that operates in South Africa, with its main headquarters in London and its operational headquarters in Johannesburg. Founded in 1909 as part of the London and Rhodesian Mining and Land Company Limited, Lonmin PLC was the mining division of the company. In 2012, the deputy president had acquired a large shareholding in the company through a loan from the mother company in London. When the miners started striking for a living wage and the company started losing revenue the investors became uneasy and, in the true fashion of corporate impunity and revolving doors, the deputy president had to intervene and send direct orders to the minister of police to do something about the strike. State resources like helicopters were used to fly over the area and the company's security worked together with the police.

The epitome of soft-law practices is the establishment of truth commissions or commissions of inquiry that lead to no prosecutions and end with recommendations – the Farlam Commission of Inquiry falls perfectly into this category. Under the guise of corporate social responsibility, Lonmin promised to start an education fund for the children of those who were deceased. The company promised to give jobs to those who had lost their loved ones and to build new houses (houses that were already meant to have been built back in 2006). On the seventh anniversary of the massacre the CEO of Lonmin spoke in a radio interview on a local radio station. He mentioned the progress that Lonmin had made since 2012 (Magara 2018). However, the widows and mine workers who were injured during the strike have not yet received any reparations.

The fact that Lonmin was given access to state resources like the police services and that Cyril Ramaphosa felt that it was necessary to send out a direct order to the police minister to do something about the strike speaks directly to how corporate power works and how those that benefit from it will protect the interests of big business, by any means necessary. The fact that the company was not held accountable for the mine workers' deaths also highlights how the architecture of impunity is designed.

IN THE ABSENCE OF A REGULATORY BODY: PEOPLE'S POWER

In 2000, after the abolishment of the UNCTC in 1993 and in the absence of any regulatory body to monitor the activities of TNCs, the then Secretary General of the UN, Kofi Annan, launched the Global Compact. The Global Compact is a voluntary partnership between the UN, corporations and NGOs that embraces the ten principles (Emmerij and Jolly 2007). The ten principles fall within four categories derived from the UN bodies' principles and declarations, such as the United Nations Convention Against Corruption.

In the millennium the matter of TNCs and their power came into question once more, so in 2005 John Ruggie was mandated by the UN Secretary General to look at matters of business and human rights because TNCs were not satisfied with the draft 'Norms and Responsibilities of Transnational Corporations and other Business Enterprises'. TNCs stated that the norms placed the responsibilities of states on corporations and that the norms undermined the interests and rights of private enterprises. Ruggie concluded his findings in 2011, publishing a report calling for the implementation of the 'Protect, Respect and Remedy Framework' through the UN's *Guiding Principles on Business and Human Rights*[4] (Zubizarreta 2015).

The Global Compact and the UN *Guiding Principles* are instruments that could have regulated or even held TNCs accountable, but because they operate within soft law they have no weight in really effecting change or pushing for any form of accountability. The demise of the UNCTC had left a vacuum, and the disappointing guidelines that came out of the Ruggie process – social movements and progressive NGOs had hoped the process would be a concrete step towards halting corporate impunity – pushed NGOs and social movements that had been challenging corporate power and globalisation to work collectively on ways to dismantle and stop corporate impunity.

The Global Campaign to Reclaim Peoples Sovereignty, Dismantle Corporate Power and Stop Impunity (hereafter the Global Campaign) was formed in 2012. The international call to action on the website of the global campaign states: 'The time has come to unite the hundreds of struggles, campaigns, networks, movements and organisations that are combating the different ways TNCs are appropriating our destinies, natural heritage and rights, dismantling public services, destroying the commons and endangering food sovereignty in every corner of the planet.'[5] The Global Campaign is a network of over 200 social movements, networks, organisations and affected communities resisting land grabs, extractive mining, exploitative wages and environmental destruction caused by TNCs. The campaign's work focuses on developing a virtual observatory on TNCs. Through working with other groups like the Treaty Alliance it participates in campaigns for a binding UN treaty to regulate TNCs and stop human rights abuses. The campaign is also proposing an 'International Peoples Treaty', which will epitomise people's power because usually treaties are signed by states. The treaty aims to create a political framework to support social and civic movements and communities in their acts of resistance and to support practices alternative to corporate power.

THE CHALLENGES IN DISMANTLING CORPORATE POWER

Mobilising globally has its inherent challenges no matter what the issue might be, but for a campaign that seeks to disrupt the economic foundations that the current system is built on, the challenges are great indeed. Bringing together the voices of diverse people from different corners of the world and making sure that each voice is clearly articulated – even amplified – is a major challenge. However, this is also the challenge of any global campaign.

One of the major stumbling blocks of the global campaign is mapping out what will take place if the process of the open-ended intergovernmental working group (OEIWG) on TNCs and human rights is derailed and the process stops with a draft treaty. In 2017, the positive gains then made seemed a bit murky because of the change in government in Ecuador, which was leading the work of the OEIWG in Geneva, Switzerland. The change in government forecasted that Ecuador would no longer take the progressive stance it had in the previous sessions. This then meant that energy had to be spent on working with another progressive actor within the process, which in this case is South Africa, the second country leading the process of the binding treaty.

This challenge highlights the volatility of working as a campaign at a UN level. It shows that the gains made after years of planning and activity can be lost in an instant if there is no political will. This also then speaks to another challenge that the campaign might face in the long run, if the treaty process becomes a lengthy one. Academics and other groups speculate that we have five to ten years before the treaty is ratified. This can lead to campaign fatigue and a loss of momentum. Thus far, the Global Campaign has been attending each session and organising a 'peoples' process outside the Palace of Nations in Geneva, but if this continues for five more years without any major successes, mobilising people to take part in the 'Week of Peoples Mobilisation' in Geneva might prove to be extremely difficult because of general campaign fatigue and the high costs of travelling to Switzerland. The Global Campaign and its partners would need to strengthen its interventions to dismantle corporate power from other pressure points, beyond UN lobbying. This could include starting global working groups that would tackle the corporate plunder of key corporations that operate in the same way as Lonmin and that would push for domestic and international means to hold such corporations accountable for their crimes.

PEOPLE'S POWER IN THE REGION

It became apparent that the fight against corporate power could not just take place at a global level with key regional blocks pushing for corporate accountability from their corners of the world. The Southern African Campaign to Dismantle Corporate Power (hereafter Southern African Campaign) was established in 2016 as the regional leg of the Global Campaign. The launch of the Southern African Campaign took place when the campaign hosted the very first Permanent People's Tribunal (PPT) on TNCs in southern Africa, in Manzini, Swaziland (the second session of the PPT was held in Johannesburg, South Africa in August 2017). The PPT is a public opinion tribunal that is independent from state authorities. Its work is based on the principles of the Universal Declaration of the Rights of Peoples proclaimed in Algiers in 1976. The tribunal applies international human rights law to the cases presented before it. The tribunals serve as platforms for communities and movements to present their grievances and create awareness of their struggles among a larger southern African and global audience.

Cases presented at the 2016 and 2017 sessions brought to the fore how corporate plunder manifests itself in the region and how it disrupts communities' way of life. Often the introduction of a development project led by a TNC results in land grabs and the mass displacement of people. From Penhalonga, Zimbabwe, community members gave chilling accounts of how the bones of their loved ones were exhumed, without their knowledge, through the mining process of a Chinese mining company operating on the river bank close to a site that the community used for burials. Community members from Tete, Mozambique, recounted how the government worked with Jindal (an Indian steel corporation) and Vale (a Brazilian mining corporation) to repress the community when it resisted the commencement of their operation in their area.

From Malawi, the Rural Women's Assembly spoke about how Monsanto (an American mega agrochemical corporation) has captured the Farmer Input Subsidy Programme, making sure that the Malawian government spends the bulk of the funds in the programme on importing and offering only Monsanto's hybrid seeds to smallholder farmers. One of the major challenges with these hybrid seeds is that they destroy indigenous seed systems. Most of the cases also highlighted how women bear the brunt of corporate impunity. Women from different walks of life spoke in front of each jury panel about how they have to walk for hours to fetch drinking water because a mining company has cut off their access to the nearest water source; how they have to take care of family members who are now ill from working underground and have lost their jobs at the mines due to their sickness.

After each session a juror statement is produced. The statement is a consolidation of the jurors' deliberations which then gives recommendations on what can be done to hold these corporations to account through international law. The first statement, after the 2016 session, highlighted issues related to women and extractivism and the second statement, after the 2017 session, highlighted issues around development and the environment.[6]

In addition to the tribunal process, the Southern African Campaign also aims to strengthen the joint struggles fought by communities against TNCs and bring partner organisations, affected communities and movements together to confront and break down the corporate systems which destroy their livelihoods, homes and health and violate their basic rights, as well as the state policies which enable this. Several communities affected by mining are uniting in action against extractivism. During the testimonies made during the sittings of the tribunal it became clear that the Right to Say No campaign, based on the UN-recognised right of indigenous people to Free Prior and Informed Consent (FPIC), has potential to unite a wider range of communities and popular organisations. FPIC places the development decision in the hands of the community.

To realise this right, the community's decision should be made free from any obligation, duty, force or coercion and must include access to information that is understandable to such a community. Ideally, various development options should be presented to the affected community to ensure that their decision is based on a real choice. An affected community should make development choices without being influenced by decisions already made by government, financial institutions or investors. In other words, the community's right to FPIC is not realised if they are presented with a project as a fait accompli. Again, access to sufficient information to understand the nature and scope of the project, including its projected environmental, social, cultural and economic impacts is critical. Such information should be objective and based on the principle of full disclosure.

The Right to Say No Campaign resonates with the struggle for alternatives to the current extractive development paradigm. Communities and social movements around the world, and particularly in the southern African region, seek to preserve their sovereignty and protect the environment. Based on this collective energy, the tribunal process of the Southern African Campaign has given way to the development of the Right to Say No Campaign. The voices of community members, movements, peasants and small-scale farmers have been ignored for decades to protect corporate power and to uphold the destructive capitalist status quo, but the dream of a different world fuels those that have been on the oppressed side of capitalism.

The dream of self-determination beyond the nation-state, of a sustainable way of life, a living wage and basic services has fuelled social movements today. The dream of reclaiming people's power and notions of power from below have gathered enough momentum to build campaigns. Initiatives such as the Global Campaign to Reclaim Peoples Sovereignty, Dismantle Corporate Power and Stop Impunity, and its regional leg – the Southern African Campaign to Dismantle Corporate Power – create platforms where those who have been under the thumb of corporate power and its impunity can unite to challenge these corporations and claim back their sovereignty.

NOTES

1 See https://www.imf.org/en/About/Factsheets/Sheets/2016/07/27/15/31/IMF-World-Bank (accessed 4 October 2018).
2 See https://www.investopedia.com/terms/g/gatt.asp (accessed 4 October 2018).
3 Available at https://digitallibrary.un.org/record/75478#record-files-collapse-header (accessed 9 September 2019).
4 See https://www.ohchr.org/documents/publications/GuidingprinciplesBusinesshr_eN.pdf (accessed 26 August 2019).
5 See https://www.stopcorporateimpunity.org/call-to-international-action/ (accessed 4 October 2018).
6 Both statements are available online. For the 2016 statement, see http://aidc.org.za/download/campaign_to_dismantle_corporate_power/PPT-TNC-Swaziland-.pdf (accessed 26 August 2019). For the 2017 statement, see : http://aidc.org.za/download/campaign_to_dismantle_corporate_power/PPT_JHB_August-2017-Final-Version-.pdf (accessed 26 August 2019).

REFERENCES

Buckman, G. 2004. *Globalization: Tame it or Scrap it: Mapping the Alternatives of the Anti-globalization Movement*. London: Zed Books.
Business and Human Rights Resource Centre. 2018. 'Texaco/Chevron lawsuits (re Ecuador)'. Accessed 4 December 2018, https://www.businesshumanrights.org/en/texacochevron-lawsuits-re-ecuador.
Emmerij, L. and Jolly, R. 2007. *The UN and Transnational Corporations*. UN Intellectual History Project. Briefing Note No. 17. Accessed 3 October 2010, http://www.unhistory.org/briefing/17TNCs.pdf.
George, S. 2016. Interview about HHRR and TNCs treaty process (online video). Accessed 13 September 2019, https://www.youtube.com/watch?v=nmkvY7xtf1Y.
Gilman, N. 2015. 'The new international economic order: A reintroduction', *Humanity: An International Journal of Human Rights, Humanitarianism and Development* 6 (1): 1–16. Accessed 30 November 2018, http://humanityjournal.org/issue6-1/the-new-international-economic-order-a-reintroduction/.

Magara, B. 2018. 'We have made progress in delivering on our promises to Marikana – Lonmin CEO'. Interviewed by Bruce Whitfield, *The Money Show, 702*, 16 August. Accessed 27 September 2018, http://www.702.co.za/articles/315724/we-have-made-progress-in-delivering-on-our-promises-to-marikana-lonmin-ceo-ben-magara.

Moran, T.H. 2009. 'The United Nations and transnational corporations: A review and a perspective', *Transnational Corporations* 18 (2): 91–112. Accessed 2 December 2018, https://unctad.org/en/docs/diaeiia200910_a4en.pdf.

O'Reilly, C. and Matussek, K. 2008. 'Siemens to pay $1.6 billion to settle bribery cases', *Washington Post*, 15 December. Accessed 1 December 2018, http://www.washington-post.com/wpdyn/content/article/2008/12/15/AR2008121502926.html?noredirect=on.

War on Want. n.d. 'What is TTIP?' Accessed 1 December 2018, https://waronwant.org/what-ttip.

UNCTAD (United Nations Conference on Trade and Development). 1991. *World Investment Report: The Triad in Foreign Direct Investment*. New York: UN. Accessed 27 November 2018, https://unctad.org/en/Docs/wir1.

UNCTAD. 1992. *World Investment Report: Transnational Corporations as Engines*. New York: UN. Accessed 9 September 2019, https://unctad.org/en/Docs/wir1992overview_en.pdf.

UNCTC (United Nations Commission on Transnational Corporations). 1983. 'Information paper on the negotiations to complete the code of conduct on transnational corporations', *International Legal Materials* 22 (1): 177–191.

Ziegler, J. 2003. 'The Right to Food'. Report of the Special Rapporteur of the Commission on Human Rights (A/58/330). United Nations. Accessed 18 January 2019, https://undocs.org/A/58/330.

Zubizarreta, J.H. 2015. 'The new global corporate law'. In N. Buxton and M Bélanger Dumontier (eds), *State of Power 2015: An Annual Anthology on Global Power and Resistance*. Amsterdam: Transnational Institute, pp. 6–16.

Zubizarreta, J.H. and Ramiro, P. 2016. *Against the 'Lex Mercatoria': Proposals and Alternatives for Controlling Transnational Corporations*. Barcelona: Icaria Editorial. Accessed 20 September 2018, http://omal.info/IMG/pdf/against_lex_mercatoria.pdf.

9

MASS STRIKES IN A GLOBAL CONJUNCTURE OF CRISIS: A LUXEMBURGIAN ANALYSIS

Alexander Gallas

On 8 and 9 January 2019, an event occurred in India that was not covered much by the media outside the country. What took place was probably one of the largest strikes in global history. According to estimates, 150–200 million workers took part. Ten main union federations – different party affiliations notwithstanding – supported the two-day general strike. The main demands were that the Modi government revoke plans to liberalise labour law and abandon the idea to further flexibilise labour markets in a country with a vast informal sector, roll out a national minimum wage of ₹18 000 and stop privatisation measures. In 2015 and 2016, Indian workers had already staged general strikes of a similar magnitude (Chattopadhyay and Marik 2016; Hensman 2017: 173; Miyamura 2016: 1922; Shyam Sundar 2019; Woodcock 2019).

The Indian general strikes follow a pattern that is currently visible in many parts of the world: there are large-scale stoppages framed as political confrontations between working people and governments (see Gallas and Nowak 2016; Nowak and Gallas 2014). For instance, there was a general strike on 14 November 2012 throughout Portugal and Spain, which was directed against the politics of austerity imposed on the two countries in order to address the sovereign debt crisis in the Eurozone. Again, this was historic because it was based on a truly transnational mobilisation. Similarly, there was a strike wave in the South African platinum belt in recent years. It started with the events leading up to the Marikana massacre in 2012 and included a five-month stoppage in 2014–2015. This was not only the longest and most costly labour dispute in South African history, it also represented an (at times very violent) confrontation between the repressive state apparatus and tens of thousands of workers.

What comes to mind, in this context, is Rosa Luxemburg's famous pamphlet *The Mass Strike* (1906). In it, she provides a conjunctural analysis of workers' struggles in the run-up to the first Russian Revolution in 1905 and discusses the strategic implications of the events for the labour movement in Germany and beyond. Obviously, it would be a mistake to draw simplistic analogies between struggles that took place in just one country in the early 1900s and those that occur all around the world over 100 years later, at the time of a global crisis of capitalism – all the more since Russia was about to experience a revolution, whereas at present, labour movements seem to be on the defensive in most parts of the world. But there are also a number of similarities: the struggles are based on mass mobilisations; they have a wide geographical spread; they impact directly on the political scene and they articulate different forms of protest. The similarities suggest that there are general conditions and patterns of the mass strike in capitalist surroundings, which may be relevant for understanding why it emerges in the current political conjuncture, and what its effects are. Correspondingly, my wager in this chapter is that some of Luxemburg's insights help us explain the present-day strategic significance of mass strikes for labour.

THE MASS STRIKE FROM A LUXEMBURGIAN PERSPECTIVE

According to Luxemburg, there are two features that set the mass strike apart from other modes of labour struggle, most importantly the sectoral economic strike for higher wages. First – and this is obvious – the mass strike is characterised by mass participation. Second, we are not looking at a singular, clearly defined instance of protest action, but at waves of stoppages and other forms of protest that are connected because they all contribute to creating a thrust towards revolution. This becomes clear when we look at Luxemburg's observations on the Russian Revolution:

> Political and economic strikes, mass strikes and partial strikes, demonstrative strikes and fighting strikes, general strikes of individual branches of industry and general strikes in individual towns, peaceful wage struggles and street massacres, barricade fighting – all these run through one another, run side by side, cross one another, flow in and over one another – it is a

ceaselessly moving, changing sea of phenomena. And the law of motion of these phenomena is clear: it does not lie in the mass strike itself nor in its technical details, but in the political and social proportions of the forces of the revolution. (Luxemburg 1906: 140–141)

It follows that the 'mass strike' in a Luxemburgian understanding is an umbrella term for a range of practices of protest connected through a general political thrust, and the fact that they are carried out by workers and are somehow associated with their capacity to exercise power through the refusal to work.

Jörg Nowak (2019: 49–50) argues that Luxemburg's description allows us to identify five features that characterise the mass strike as a mode of struggle. This concerns, first of all, its aims, which are neither strictly economic nor strictly political but shift back and forth over time. It follows that the mass strike is a form of conducting working-class politics that is an alternative to operating within the official channels of political decision making often used by workers' parties (Cortés-Chirino 2016: 379). Consequently, it questions the separation between the economic and political domination that is constitutive of the capitalist mode of production (see Poulantzas 1978: 54).

This also suggests, second, that the mass strike disrupts the political scene. It directly impacts on political discourses and decision making, and politicians, in one or way or another, will react to it.

Third, it has a mobilising effect on workers as a class, not just on specific sectors – and it results in a class confrontation that is discernible as such for the workers involved. Put differently, the mass strike is a collective practice of workers that acts as a catalyst of working-class formation: through engaging in struggles, they develop what Luxemburg calls 'class feeling' (1906: 129). They experience that they are connected to fellow workers, and that their collective interest is opposed to the interests of capital.

Fourth, it expands beyond localised focal points and proliferates.

Significantly, features one to four all have potentially destabilising effects on the capitalist mode of production. So fifth, and most importantly, the mass strike takes place in the context of a revolutionary conjuncture and is a mode of struggle reflecting the revolutionary aspirations of the working class.

All of this suggests that the mass strike is a highly specific mode of struggle, and that not every strike with mass participation qualifies as mass strike, according to Luxemburg. In order to avoid misunderstandings, it makes sense to speak of a revolutionary mass strike, which is offensive and driven by class feeling and working-class politics.

The implication is that the mass strike as a mode of struggle was the adequate response of workers to the tendencies at work at the level of the conjuncture in Luxemburg's day – adequate in the sense that their strategic choices were likely to bring results in line with their collective interests. This also suggests that it cannot be transferred easily to other times and places, which is in line with Luxemburg's critique of anarchist, voluntarist positions that simply want to 'switch on' the revolution by promoting the idea of a mass strike (1906: 115–116). In Luxemburg's words, 'the mass strike does not produce the revolution, but the revolution produces the mass strike' (1906: 147). Luxemburg suggests here that conjunctural circumstances invite specific modes of struggle, not the other way round – and that any strategic reflection must start from assessing those circumstances and finding out how to best intervene in them. In other words, the mass strike as defined by Luxemburg may function as a driver of working-class formation in revolutionary conjunctures. It would be a grave mistake, however, to believe that it would emerge under other conjunctural circumstances if one simply called for it.

THE GLOBAL CONJUNCTURE: AN ONGOING CRISIS

Luxemburg's line of argument suggests that the Russian mass strike was successful insofar as it contributed to a revolution under the leadership of the working class. In fact, her optimism about the prospects of labour-led insurrections seemed vindicated when the October Revolution shook up Russia and the world in 1917. And yet, the failure of revolutionary movements across Europe in subsequent years – including the smashing of the Spartacus Revolt in Germany in January 1919 that culminated in the murder of Luxemburg and Karl Liebknecht – and the rise of the far right in Italy and Germany signalled the end of the revolutionary conjuncture in early twentieth century Europe. The working class was now on the defensive, and what represented adequate modes of struggle had shifted.

In his book *Fascism and Dictatorship* (1970: 156–165), Nicos Poulantzas shows that the failure of leading representatives of party communism to understand this conjunctural shift and to embrace an adequate, defensive mode of struggle in the new conjuncture – the united front – paved the way for the victory of fascism. This suggests that asking what the lessons of Luxemburg's analysis are for the struggles of today requires us, firstly, to gain an understanding of the current political conjuncture and secondly, to evaluate whether the collective activities of workers are adequate to it.

When I speak of the current political conjuncture, this gives rise to the question of scale. Conjunctural analyses are often conducted at the national level (see,

185

for example, Ege and Gallas 2019) – in particular since many institutions heavily affecting class relations are still national institutions. If we consider the spread of the crisis of capitalism in the last ten years, however, it makes sense to speak of a global political conjuncture.

Obviously, it is beyond the scope of a book chapter to provide a detailed conjunctural analysis of the state of labour in global capitalism. Nevertheless, my wager is that it is possible to circumnavigate the insurmountable challenge of producing a complete picture. I propose identifying key elements of the global conjuncture of labour through taking a two-staged approach: as a first approximation, I provide a rough sketch of important labour struggles in the age of crisis from around the world; and in a second step, I compare labour struggles in the US and India – two countries that represent the global North and South respectively and play a key role in global geopolitics. If it is possible to discern common trends in these vastly different countries that also resonate with the global picture, it can be argued that they have a general relevance.

But before launching into a detailed discussion of labour struggles, I would like to make three general, admittedly impressionistic, remarks about the current global conjuncture. First of all, it is still marked by a protracted crisis of financial capitalism, compounded by a deep ecological crisis. The magnitude of the latter is only starting to come into view, and the international community and national governments have failed, so far, to curb carbon emissions (Satgar 2018). The former first emerged in 2007, in the form of a global banking crisis. Global GDP growth may have picked up since then, but the institutions of global capitalism have not been restructured much. Scholars point out that attempts to re-regulate the financial sector have been limited (Christophers 2016; Rixen 2013); that the 'too big to fail' problem has not been addressed properly; that profitability in the banking sector remains weak (Bell and Hindmoor 2018) and that attempts to act against financial crime have been lacklustre (Ryder 2016). Put differently, the crisis is ongoing, and financial capitalists have so far been able to defend the deep integration of finance across national boundaries and its leading position. Correspondingly, finance-oriented accumulation strategies still dominate at the level of economic, fiscal and monetary policy (see Palley 2016: 124–127; Scherrer 2011). As a consequence, the room for manoeuvre of organised labour is seriously constrained. In recent decades, a scalar incongruence has emerged between the often global networks of capital and the mainly local and national associations of workers. Under conditions of a deep crisis and the resultant insecurity for capital, the negative effects of this incongruence for workers are magnified. They are exposed to even fiercer international competition, and productivist arrangements with capital, which are characterised by relative surplus value production and the translation of productivity gains into increasing living standards, are difficult to achieve.

Second, there is a realignment at the level of geopolitics – with a move from a unipolar world characterised by US supremacy to a multipolar world under US dominance. There are new contender states such as China and Germany playing a key geopolitical role in their region and beyond – and an old adversary of the US, Russia, that has gained weight again in recent years. The global predominance of the US is not seriously threatened due to US military might, the US economy still being the largest in the world and the US dollar serving as world money (see Panitch and Gindin 2012). But there are various frontiers where it is tested and contested – not just in geopolitical conflict zones like Syria and the Ukraine, but also inside international organisations marked by US predominance. This concerns, most importantly, the North Atlantic Treaty Organization (NATO), the UN and the World Trade Organization (WTO). The stance of the Trump administration on countries like Iran and Syria, international trade and the Paris Agreement has been met with open opposition from countries usually seen as reliable allies of the US. In the context of heightening geopolitical tensions, there is extra room for nationalist interpellations, which work directly against working-class formation – across but also within national boundaries.

Third, concerning class politics, power blocs across the world are launching fierce attacks on labour – be it in the form of attacks on the right to strike, austerity agendas hitting public spending or direct attacks on organised labour involving repressive state apparatuses. Left organisations and parties have, on the whole, been unsuccessful in terms of thwarting these offensives, and there is a rightwards trend in politics in countries across the globe. Accordingly, authoritarian populist political leaders such as Jair Bolsonaro, Rodrigo Duterte, Sebastian Kurz, Viktor Orbán, Narendra Modi and Donald Trump can build on broad popular support, including the support of certain groups of workers.

THE POLITICS OF THE MASS STRIKE

In the wake of the crisis, governments across the globe have been working to restore the profitability of investments for capital. Attacks on organised labour have been an integral part of this mode of crisis management. There have been direct attacks, such as the imposition of restrictions on the right to strike, but also indirect attacks such as decreases in the social wage resulting from cuts to state expenditure.

In this situation, a pattern of resistance from labour has emerged that resembles the revolutionary mass strike in Luxemburg's sense, but is fundamentally different in its purpose. This is the defensive mass strike. I use the term to refer to a politicised strike wave, with a mobilising effect on the entire working class, that is aimed at thwarting government interventions made on behalf of capital. It is a collective act of resistance that builds on mass participation and disrupts official politics. In other words, it contributes to working-class formation – just like its revolutionary counterpart.

Importantly, strikes with mass participation become politicised in the current conjuncture almost by default – either from the outside, that is, through other political actors, or by the workers themselves (see Gallas 2018: 239–240). On the one hand, the repression against organised labour is an important driver of politicisation. As Luxemburg (1906: 150) observed with reference to Russia, 'In a state in which every form and expression of the labor movement is forbidden, in which the simplest strike is a political crime, it must logically follow that every economic struggle will become a political one.' More generally speaking, one can say that any strike wave of a certain size becomes a pertinent political issue because it disrupts everyday life to such a degree that political actors will feel compelled to comment on it, be it approvingly or disapprovingly. On the other hand, strikes also become politicised through the strikers themselves. The neoliberal age is marked by a supremacy of capital that is reflected at the political level in the neoliberal turns of social democratic parties; the erection of legal and institutional safeguards that shield the field of monetary and fiscal policy from political interventions not in line with neoliberal orthodoxy, for example through the existence of independent central banks and debt brakes that are enshrined in constitutions; and, most importantly, through people's difficulty in envisaging an alternative political project. Under these circumstances, it is hard for workers to air political grievances through official political channels, which creates a strong incentive to use the strike weapon for political ends.

Against this backdrop, it becomes clear that the defensive mass strike has great significance for organised labour in the conjuncture of crisis. In a nutshell, a defensive but political mode of struggle with mass participation is the adequate reaction of labour to the dominant pattern of political crisis management.

MASS STRIKES AROUND THE GLOBE

Despite the fact that strike incidence has been falling in the US and Europe for a long time, there have been politically charged strike waves with mass participation in the global North in recent years. Among them are general strikes against austerity in western Europe, which took place in Belgium, Britain, Greece, Iceland, Italy, Portugal and Spain (see Gallas and Nowak 2016; Nowak and Gallas 2014); a strike wave in Germany in 2015 that mostly affected the railways, the postal service and childcare (Birke 2018) and triggered broad political debates on the right to strike and on care work; and the 2018 stoppage in France, which was directed against Emmanuel Macron's decision to restructure labour relations in the railway sector and open it up to foreign companies competing with the state-owned railway service SNCF.

Likewise, there have been huge strikes in the global South, and like the strikes in the North, they are often politically charged – either because they take place in countries controlled by authoritarian regimes or because they are similar to the strikes in the North in the sense that they are directed against neoliberalisation and neoliberal crisis management.

When it comes to mass strikes under conditions of authoritarianism, the Egyptian case stands out: strikes with mass participation played a crucial role in the emergence of a revolutionary movement in 2011 (Adbelrahman 2012; Alexander 2011; McNally 2011; Schwartz 2011; Zemni et al. 2013). Large strike waves are also visible in East and Southeast Asian countries with authoritarian governments that have been integrated into global production networks in recent decades. In Vietnam, there have been 6 000 illegal strikes since the country enacted a Labour Code in 1995 (Thi Thu 2017). For example, 90 000 workers in Ho Chi Minh City downed tools in order to protest changes to social insurance in 2015 (Anner 2018: 63; Bell 2017). Likewise, there have been several waves of strikes in Cambodia, with mass participation of garment workers, against poor wages and working conditions and authoritarian politics, and for the right to unionise. In late 2013 and early 2014, 350 000 workers went on strike for two weeks, protesting against what they saw as a rigged general election a few months earlier, and for a significant increase in the minimum wage, in the course of which several workers were killed by armed forces (Pratap and Bose 2015: 3; Reuters 2014; Thul 2014). In China, there have been significant strikes as well. A well-known strike took place in 2010 at a Honda factory in Guangdong, which kick-started a strike wave throughout the province, resulting in significant wage increases for workers of up to 40 per cent. In 2014 in Dongguan, a city in the Pearl River Delta, 40 000 workers in seven shoe factories run by a company called Yue Yen, which supplied Nike and Adidas, went on a successful strike over pay and social security contributions (Pringle 2016: 139; Yunxue 2018: 45).

But the dynamics of labour struggles do not neatly map on the divide between authoritarian and formally democratic regimes. Arguably, there is an authoritarian convergence: formally democratic regimes are curbing civil and labour rights in the name of security and economic prosperity, and despotic regimes are accommodating for the fact that working-class agency cannot be suppressed fully. Correspondingly, labour struggles in formally democratic countries in the global North and South are often about asserting the right of workers to organise and collectively fight for their interests.

In Indonesia – a country generally seen as a democracy, but one with a long history of repression against labour movements – there were general strikes in 2012 and 2013 with two and three million participants respectively demanding not just a hefty increase in the minimum wage and an end to outsourcing, but also legal changes in favour of labour (Panimbang and Mufakhir 2018: 26–28; Pratap and Bose 2015: 4–10). Between 2011 and 2014, there was a strike wave in the Brazilian construction sector over wages and working conditions, which was the largest since the downfall of the military dictatorship in 1985 and involved hundreds of thousands of workers. It had a political dimension not just because of police repression against the strikers, but because many of the stoppages took place at building sites for large-scale, state-funded infrastructure projects (Nowak 2018: 115–116, 127). Last but not least, in Argentina in April and December 2017, general strikes directed against the restructuring of labour relations under the Macri government took place.

Admittedly, this description is impressionistic, but it is also backed up by data. Obviously, strike incidence at the global level is hard to measure. Based on a systematic examination of coverage in five key newspapers from the Anglophone world, Şahan Savaş Karataşlı et al. (2015) argue that there was a global explosion of social protest from 1991 to 2011, and that labour struggles played a key role in driving up numbers. Similarly, Fernando Cortés-Chirino (2016) asserts that political mass strikes increased significantly between 1919 and 2014 across the world, and that they spread from Europe to the global semi-periphery and periphery.

From a qualitative perspective, one may argue that there have been waves of defensive mass strikes against neoliberalism and neoliberal crisis management across the globe. In the conjuncture of crisis, in particular, a politicisation of industrial action has occurred from the inside. Workers are using the strike weapon as a means of political protest, and their interventions are often loosely linked with other protest movements that have sprung up in the course of the crisis. From a Luxemburgian perspective, the questions that emerge against this backdrop are: what patterns of labour struggle are visible in the conjuncture of crisis, and are they adequate to it?

THE US: REARGUARD ACTION AND NEW FRONTS

In the US case, the claim that the working class has been on the defensive for a long time is hard to refute. Important indicators point to this direction: union density fell from 20.1 per cent in 1983 to 10.7 per cent in 2017 (BLS 2018a). Strike incidence has also decreased significantly, which, under conditions of shrinking labour organisations and weak wage development for workers in the US in the last 40 years (Palley 2016: 120), can be seen as a sign of working-class agency being curbed. In 1983, there were 83 strikes involving more than 1 000 workers and lasting for more than one shift; in 2017, the figure was seven, the second lowest number since records began in 1947 (BLS 2018b). For 20 odd years, labour scholars have been discussing strategies aimed at revitalising US labour (see, for example, Clawson and Clawson 1999; Milkman 2006; Milkman and Voss 2004; Voss and Sherman 2000), with a heavy emphasis on the importance of organising strategies for unions.

From a Luxemburgian perspective, these debates should surely be welcomed. But following Luxemburg, tactics and strategies of labour cannot be chosen at will and always have to be discussed in the context of a conjunctural analysis. Ideally, such an analysis should operate across scales. In light of this, it may be worth shifting the focus of the debates somewhat: one could focus on identifying patterns of labour struggle that are garnering mass support, examine their situatedness in a distinct national-cum-global conjuncture and assess their class effects – no matter whether they are taking place inside unions, on their periphery or outside of fixed organisations.

In my view, at the moment there are at least three patterns of labour struggle in the US worth mentioning. First of all, there have been several waves of struggle in the public sector in recent years. These struggles are hugely important for the overall strength of organised labour in the US today because union density in the public sector is far higher than in the private sector – 34.4 per cent as opposed to 6.5 per cent in 2017 (BLS 2018a). In 1954, union density in the private sector was still 39 per cent (Clawson and Clawson 1999: 97), and its decline can be attributed to the fact that the US power bloc orchestrated an offensive against labour from the 1970s onwards (see Clawson and Clawson 1999: 102–103; Cohen 2006: 62–65). This was accompanied by financial market liberalisation, labour market flexibilisation, de-industrialisation and the proliferation of precarious work, which all contributed to union decline, in particular in the private sector. Importantly, in the global conjuncture of crisis, these trends have not subsided, quite the contrary.

Generally, the struggles in the US public sector are about defending the institutional supports of public-sector trade unionism and improving working conditions in areas of service provision that have been starved of funds thanks to the predominance of free-market ideas, enmity to public expenditure and neoliberal practices of crisis management.

In 2011 in Wisconsin, there was a wave of protests against a 'right to work' bill joined by tens of thousands of public-sector workers and their supporters. The bill was aimed at banning public-sector unions from collecting fees from non-members benefiting from collective bargaining agreements. It also contained provisions that seriously restrained their collective bargaining rights. The protests included not so much traditional strikes, but 'sick-ins' where public-sector workers took to declaring themselves not well and staying away from work in order to join demonstrations . The demonstrations attracted people not just from the public sector, but from a range of constituencies. In the course of the protest, the state Capitol was occupied (Collins 2012: 6, 10, 11; Moody 2012). The protests were unsuccessful in terms of thwarting the legislative drive against public-sector unions. As a consequence of the new law coming into force in 2015, union density at the state level had dropped, by the end of 2016, by 3.5 percentage points (Manzo and Bruno 2017: 3). But the protesting workers still managed to influence public opinion significantly and, in so doing, contributed to national debates on workers' rights and the role of organised labour in US society.

In 2012, teachers in Chicago walked out; again this was not an economic strike in a narrow sense because they did not only protest against poor pay and working conditions, but also against the corporate influence over education and for better learning conditions (Cantor and Gutierrez 2012; Kamper 2018: 157–158). Similarly, there were teacher strikes in Arizona, Kentucky, Oklahoma and West Virginia in 2018 that also connected the economic issue of low pay with the political issue of poor learning conditions in public institutions. Remarkably, there was a dispute in Los Angeles in January 2019 where teachers clearly prioritised their political over their economic demands: they went on strike for better learning conditions for students and won significant improvements (Wong 2019).

Against this backdrop, a significant legal challenge to US public-sector unions has emerged – the ruling in a Supreme Court case called *Janus vs. American Federation of State, County, and Municipal Employees* (AFSCME). The case was decided in June 2018 and ruled on an issue already at stake in the Wisconsin protests: it prohibits public-sector unions from collecting fees from people who are not members but still benefit from collective bargaining agreements (Richman 2018; Scheiber and Vogel 2018). The implications of the ruling are ambiguous: the abolition of 'agency fees' could heavily dent union funding, but there is also a possibility that unions will start to reject no-strike deals (which are common today) and embrace more militant strategies (Richman 2018). After all, some of the recent actions by teachers were wildcat strikes, and they had a political dimension insofar as they highlighted the importance of public education, the threat of privatisation and lack of sufficient funding for schools. These recent public-sector struggles can be said to contribute to restoring and consolidating working-class agency.

Second, there have been serious attempts to extend union coverage in the private sector by achieving recognition at non-unionised production sites in the US South. German telecommunications company T-Mobile, an enterprise known for using union-busting techniques in the US, has faced a campaign for union recognition carried by the Communication Workers of America (CWA), which was supported by German public- and service-sector union ver.di (Compa 2015: 19–22; Daley 2014; Scheytt 2012). Likewise, in recent years the United Automobile Workers union (UAW) has campaigned for recognition at a Volkswagen plant in Tennessee and a Nissan plant in Mississippi (Brooks 2017, 2018; Fichter 2018; Scheiber 2017). On paper, these drives have not achieved their aims so far, and questions can be asked about whether a legalistic orientation towards recognition is the way forward (Kamper 2018: 161; Richard 2017). But they have contributed to politicising the issues of poor working conditions and collective rights of workers (see Sanders 2017), potentially preparing the ground for future attempts to expand working-class agency.

Third, struggles of precarious workers have sprung up in recent years, and they take a distinct form. A campaign that has made headlines is Fight for $15. The two main demands of the campaign are a living wage for workers of US$15 an hour and the right to unionise. It was launched in 2012 by fast food workers in New York with the support of community organisers and the Service Employees International Union (SEIU) and quickly spread to other sectors, in particular retail. The campaign involves demonstrations, strikes and other types of protest. From a union perspective, it amounts to a shift in strategy. The primary target of interventions is not employers, but legislators, and activists aim to build broad coalitions that also involve organisations and platforms usually not seen as being linked to labour. In 2017, on the forty-ninth anniversary of Martin Luther King's assassination, Fight for $15 and Black Lives Matter activists joined forces for demonstrations and teach-ins under the slogan 'Fight Racism, Raise Pay'. Importantly, the campaign has produced tangible results: by the end of 2017, the states of California and New York and several big cities (which can set minimum wage rates in some states) had passed legislation aimed at increasing minimum wages to US$15 an hour (Chen 2015: 43; Hannah 2016; Luce 2015: 72–75; NELP 2017). However, it remains a critical issue that the campaign has not contributed to unionisation or to stable forms of organisation in the sectors affected (Kamper 2018: 158).

In sum, we are mostly seeing rearguard action and attempts to resist attacks by capital in the US. In class theoretical terms, the conjuncture of crisis in the country is characterised by the prevalence of defensive mass strikes for the protection and restoration of working-class agency. They are not revolutionary mass strikes in Luxemburg's sense, but aim at defending and rebuilding organised labour as a collective actor. In so doing, they are politically charged and signal fundamental dissent to the neoliberal status quo, according to which rights at work are individual, not collective rights. In a nutshell, the dominant mode of struggle appears, on the whole, adequate to the conjuncture. But considering that the relations of forces are heavily favouring capital at the moment, the question remains how stronger links between different sites of struggle can be established so that it becomes possible to stop the barrage of onslaughts on labour orchestrated by the US power bloc. In all likelihood, attacks by capital will intensify in the next years because it is emboldened by the Trump administration. And yet, the Trump era has already given rise to some of the biggest social mobilisations in US history. If organised workers manage to build alliances with other actors, it may be possible to shift the relations of forces somewhat in favour of labour.

INDIA: MASS ACTION AND NEW LABOUR ORGANISATIONS

After India shook off the yoke of colonialism and became an independent country in 1947, the socialist and nationalist Indian Congress Party dominated the political scene. The country's economic policy was characterised by a mixed economy approach that aimed to establish a large state-owned sector and constrained markets with the help of state interventionism, quantitative restrictions and economic plans. In the mid-1980s, the Congress took first steps towards liberalisation when it reduced corporate and import taxes, removed price controls, eased access to loans for large corporations and opened up the public sector for private investment. Foreshadowing the neoliberal turns of centre-left parties in the global North in the 1990s and 2000s, prime minister PV Narasimha Rao, also representing Congress, triggered a full regime shift in 1991. He instigated the transition of India to a market economy. This created the political environment in which Hindu nationalism began to thrive. Between 1998 and 2004, during the first government led by the far-right Bharatiya Janata Party (BJP), threats were made to directly attack workers' rights, which did not really come to fruition. After another ten-year period of Congress rule, the BJP, now under the leadership of Modi, won an absolute majority in 2014. As in other countries across the globe, the conjuncture of crisis has resulted in rights of workers coming under attack. After taking power, the Modi government has made consistent attempts to undermine the consultation rights of trade unions and to flexibilise labour relations. For example, it liberalised child labour in 2016. At the level of states, new bans on cattle slaughter and the consumption of beef have come into force, which have thrown hundreds of thousands of Muslim and Dalit workers in the meat and leather industries out of work. Likewise, the decision of the government to abolish ₹500 and ₹1 000 notes, allegedly in order to combat corruption and forgery, had the effect of stripping the poorest segments of the population of jobs, wages and savings (Hensman 2010: 112–113; Hensman 2017: 173–174; Ms 2019; Remesh 2017: 106; Sarker 2014: 417–418). It follows that as is the case in the US, workers in India are on the defensive.

What has remained in place throughout this whole period, however, are two deep divides in the Indian workforce that have been enshrined in law since independence, as Satoshi Miyamura (2016) observes: first, the divide between formal and informal employment – with the latter, as of 2011, accounting for 92 per cent of the Indian workforce; and second, the divide between the 'organised' and the 'unorganised' sectors of the economy, that is, large and medium-sized as opposed to small business units. Notably, even in the organised sector, only 45 per cent of workers were formally employed in 2012, down from 62 per cent in 2000. Indeed, there appears to be a strategic pattern on the side of India-based capital of responding to the existence of organisations forcefully representing the interests of workers by replacing formal with informal employment. This is also motivated by the fact that under the dominant understanding of Indian labour law, collective rights, such as the right to be represented by a union that engages in collective bargaining, apply to only formal workers (Miyamura 2016: 1923–1925; Monaco 2017: 129). In other words, the fact that labour is on the defensive is also reflected in the ongoing process of informalisation that is taking place in an economy already characterised by a huge informal sector.

These divides characterising the Indian working class are also visible in a much discussed strike wave, which has been taking place in the country's automotive sector since the mid-2000s. The stoppages are of strategic relevance both for organised labour and for the power bloc because the sector is responsible for seven per cent of India's GDP, and the country is the seventh biggest manufacturer of automobiles in the world (Remesh 2017: 105). In recent years there have been strikes or slowdowns at the plants of well-known corporations, such as Ford, General Motors, Honda and Hyundai (Sinha 2017: 214). Probably the most fiercely fought conflict, however, erupted in 2011 at a Maruti Suzuki plant located in Manesar, which is close to New Delhi. Here, confrontations were triggered when management tried to block the establishment of an independent union at the plant, to which both formal and informal workers responded with strikes and protests. In 2012, these culminated in physical confrontations at the plant, during which an HR manager was killed. The circumstances of his death are not entirely clear, but the events had severe effects on the workers: more than 2 000 of them were sacked and 148 arrested. Whereas the big, party-affiliated trade unions were ambivalent about supporting the workers, smaller political groups, left-wing intellectuals and the grassroots-oriented New Trade Union Initiative (NTUI) did. The strike transformed itself into a political protest against the repression of organised labour by the authorities – and workers politicised themselves in the process, as Nowak's detailed account of a protest march in 2014 shows.

In 2017, 117 of the people arrested at the Manesar plant were acquitted – and 13 were sentenced to life for the murder of the HR manager, among them 12 representatives of the union. The sentences led to a one-hour strike in the region and protests in 35 cities across India (Hensman 2017: 172–173; Miyamura 2016: 1933–1934; Monaco 2017: 132–133; Nowak 2014, 2016, 2017a: 970–974, 2017b). In keeping with Luxemburg's argument, a strike triggered an openly political struggle due to the repressive environment in which it took place – and it involved both formal and informal workers from the plant, plus the mass support of other workers and activists. Furthermore, the types of intervention shifted over time and consisted of picketing, sit-in strikes, demonstrations and riots. The overall thrust of the action was to assert workers' rights in the context of the power bloc's sustained attack on labour.

Similar points can be made about the general strikes in recent years. In total, there have been 18 demonstrative general strikes in India in the last quarter of a century, culminating in the 2019 mass protest against the attempts of the Modi government to change labour law. What is remarkable about this most recent general strike is its breadth and size. Ten of the main union confederations supported it – as well as a number of smaller, rank-and-file initiatives (Woodcock 2019).

Notably, other social groups also carry out large-scale protests in India. Examples are a march of 100 000 farmers to Delhi in November 2018, demanding higher prices for their produce and debt relief, and a human chain, 620 km long, formed by millions of women in the southern state of Kerala in support of two female worshippers who entered a Hindu temple that had not been open to women before (*The Economic Times* 30 November 2018; Withnall 2019). This raises the question of how the struggles of agrarian and non-agrarian workers can become articulated, and what role women's rights play in the struggles of organised labour (see Shyam Sundar 2019: 24).

What becomes clear is that Indian workers are attempting to find new, politicised forms of action and organisation in response to the offensive of the power bloc. Similar to the US case, their activities can be seen as efforts to defend and restore working-class agency – and in this sense, they are adequate to the conjuncture. Importantly, however, labour in India remains fragmented – due to the divides inherent in the organisation of the economy; due to the fact that there are numerous union umbrellas with widely diverging political standpoints, among them a large Hindu nationalist organisation; and due to the fracturing of the left at the party political level. The general strikes have served to bring workers together, albeit for a very short period of time. The principal problem with this type of mobilisation is that even if turnout is high, it is fairly easy for a government to ride it out (see Shyam Sundar 2019: 24).

Consequently, the challenge for labour in India remains to translate the impulses to resist attacks from the power bloc into more permanent and wide-ranging alliances. The Modi government is pursuing a right-wing authoritarian project that is serious about constraining the rights not just of workers, but of various groups and individuals in Indian civil society who do not fit into the Hindu nationalist agenda. In light of this, organised labour will have to find ways of connecting with other social movements voicing fundamental dissent (see Hensman 2017).

CONCLUSION

Luxemburg's pamphlet on *The Mass Strike* is informed by an implicit theorisation of working-class formation and agency that is highly useful for analysing the state of labour in the global conjuncture of crisis. As is visible in a number of countries around the world, among them the hugely different cases of the US and India, governments are exploiting the global crisis to deepen neoliberalisation and attack workers' rights. Channels used by working classes to influence political decision making have been closed. In this situation, defensive political mass strikes emerge that manifest worker discontent with neoliberalism and the neoliberal and authoritarian political management of the ongoing crisis. In class-analytical terms, they contribute to working-class formation insofar as their general thrust is to exercise and strengthen forms of action that amount to the exercise of working-class agency.

But the question of the age remains how these mass strikes can be amplified and extended to such a degree that they pose a real challenge to the power blocs around the globe. In the conjuncture of crisis, workers, activists and other groups of people discontented with the status quo have not managed to seriously threaten the existing modes of crisis management or even the existing structures of social domination. As Luxemburg made clear, it would be a serious mistake to resort to voluntarism in this situation and simply call for all-out resistance or even a revolution. Quite to the contrary: the task is to analyse the global conjuncture together with national cases in order to identify cracks in the prevalent government strategies and to find narratives and forms of action, in an experimental fashion, that promise to expand working-class agency and the agency of any subaltern forces prepared to challenge the status quo. In this context, it would be important for workers to find effective ways of using the strike weapon politically.

REFERENCES

Abdelrahman, M. 2012. 'A hierarchy of struggles? The "economic" and the "political" in Egypt's revolution', *Review of African Political Economy* 39 (134): 614–628.

Alexander, A. 2011. 'The growing social soul of Egypt's democratic revolution', *International Socialism*, 28 June. Accessed 29 July 2018, http://isj.org.uk/the-growing-social-soul-of-egypts-democratic-revolution/.

Anner, M. 2018. 'Strikes in Vietnam'. In J. Nowak, M. Dutta and P. Birke (eds), *Workers' Movements and Strikes in the Twenty-First Century*. London: Rowman & Littlefield, pp. 63–80.

Bell, E. 2017. 'Đình công tự phát: Wildcat strikes in postsocialist Vietnam'. *Chuang* blog post, 31 May. Accessed 29 July 2018, http://chuangcn.org/2017/05/dinh-cong-tu-phat-wildcat-strikes-in-post-socialist-vietnam/.

Bell, S. and Hindmoor, A. 2018. 'Are the major global banks now safer? Structural continuities and change in banking and finance since the 2008 crisis', *Review of International Political Economy* 25 (1): 1–27.

Birke, P. 2018. 'The strike wave of 2015 in Germany'. In J. Nowak, M. Dutta and P. Birke (eds), *Workers' Movements and Strikes in the Twenty-First Century*. London: Rowman & Littlefield, pp. 221–236.

BLS. 2018a. 'Union members – 2017'. News release, Bureau of Labor Statistics, 19 January. Accessed 29 July 2018, https://www.bls.gov/news.release/pdf/union2.pdf.

BLS. 2018b. 'Major work stoppages in 2017'. News release, Bureau of Labor Statistics, 9 February. Accessed 29 July 2018, https://www.bls.gov/news.release/pdf/wkstp.pdf.

Brooks, C. 2017. 'After Nissan: Can we organize the South?', *Labor Notes*, 1 September. Accessed 29 July 2018, http://www.labornotes.org/2017/09/after-nissan-can-we-organize-south.

Brooks, C. 2018. 'Trump's labor board likely to strip auto workers of southern victory', *Labor Notes*, 10 January. Accessed 29 July 2018, http://labornotes.org/2018/01/trumps-labor-board-likely-strip-auto-workers-southern-victory.

Cantor, P. and Gutierrez, R.R. 2012. 'Striking teachers, parents join forces to oppose "Corporate Education Model" in Chicago', *Democracy Now!*, 10 September. Accessed 29 July 2018, https://www.democracynow.org/2012/9/10/striking_teachers_parents_join_forces_to.

Chattopadhyay, K. and Marik, S. 2016. 'India on strike', *Jacobin*, 10 April. Accessed 29 July 2018, https://www.jacobinmag.com/2016/10/indian-workers-general-strike.

Chen, M. 2015. 'Vote for $15', *Dissent*, 63 (3): 42–46.

Christophers, B. 2016. 'Geographies of finance III: Regulation and 'after-crisis' financial futures', *Progress in Human Geography* 40 (1): 138–148.

Clawson, D. and Clawson, M.A. 1999. 'What has happened to the US labor movement? Union decline and renewal', *Annual Review of Sociology* 25: 95–119.

Cohen, S. 2006. *Ramparts of Resistance: Why Workers Lost Their Power and How to Get It Back*. London: Pluto.

Collins, J. 2012. 'Theorizing Wisconsin's 2011 protests: Community-based unionism confronts accumulation by dispossession', *American Ethnologist* 29 (1): 6–20.

Compa, L. 2015. 'Corporate hypocrisy: Violations of trade union rights by European multinational companies in the United States', *Revista Derecho Social y Empresa* 4: 15–32.

Cortés-Chirino, F. 2016. 'Political mass strikes: Workers' countermobilization to capitalist enforcement', *Working USA* 19: 377–394.

Daley, T. 2014. 'The German war on American workers: Deutsche Telekom in the United States', *Socialism and Democracy* 28 (2): 166–182.

Ege, M. and Gallas, A. 2019. 'The exhaustion of Merkelism: A conjunctural analysis', *New Formations* 96/97: 89–131.

Fichter, M. 2018. 'Building union power across borders: The transnational partnership initiative of IG Metall and the UAW', *Global Labour Journal* 9 (2): 182–198.

Gallas, A. 2018. 'The politics of striking: On the shifting dynamics of workers' struggles in Britain'. In J. Nowak, M. Dutta and P. Birke (eds), *Workers' Movements and Strikes in the Twenty-First Century*. London: Rowman & Littlefield, pp. 237–254.

Gallas, A. and Nowak, J. 2016. 'Introduction: Mass strikes in the global crisis', *Workers of the World* 8: 6–15.

Hannah, M. 2016. 'The "Fight for 15": Can the organizing model that helped pass Seattle's $15 minimum wage legislation fill the gap left by the decline in unions?', *Journal of Law and Policy* 51: 257–277.

Hensman, R. 2010. 'Labour and globalization: Union responses in India', *Global Labour Journal* 1 (1): 112–131.

Hensman, R. 2017. 'The labour movement in an increasingly authoritarian Hindu Nationalist State', *Global Labour Journal* 8 (2): 171–179.

Kamper, D. 2018. 'The United States: Worker agency and innovation in the midst of crisis'. In J. Nowak, M. Dutta and P. Birke (eds), *Workers' Movements and Strikes in the Twenty-First Century*. London: Rowman & Littlefield, pp. 151–168.

Karataşlı, Ş.S., Kumral, S., Scully, B. and Upadhyay, S. 2015. 'Class, crisis and the 2011 protest wave: Cyclical and secular trends in global labor unrest'. In I. Wallerstein, C. Chase-Dunn and C. Suter (eds), *Overcoming Global Inequalities*. London: Paradigm Publishers, pp. 184–200.

Luce, S. 2015. '$15 per hour or bust: An appraisal of the higher wages movement', *New Labor Forum* 24 (2): 72–79.

Luxemburg, R. (1906) 2008. 'The mass strike'. *The Essential Rosa Luxemburg*, edited by H. Scott. Chicago: Haymarket.

Manzo, F. and Bruno, R. 2017. *The impact of "Right-to-Work" laws on labor market outcomes in three Midwest states: Evidence from Indiana, Michigan, and Wisconsin (2010–2016)*. Project for Middle Class Renewal, School of Labor and Employment Relations, University of Illinois.

McNally, D. 2011. 'Mubarak's folly: The rising of Egypt's workers', 11 February. Accessed 29 July 2018, http://davidmcnally.org/?p=354.

Milkman, R. 2006. *L.A. Story: Immigrant Workers and the Future of the U.S. Labor Movement.* New York: Russell Sage Foundation.

Milkman, R. and K. Voss. 2004. *Rebuilding Labor: Organizing and Organizers in the New Union Movement.* Ithaca: ILR Press.

Miyamura, S. 2016. 'Diverse trajectories of industrial restructuring and labour organising in India', *Third World Quarterly* 37 (10): 1921–1941.

Monaco, L. 2017. 'Where lean may shake: Challenges to casualisation in the Indian Auto Industry', *Global Labour Journal* 8 (2): 120–138.

Moody, K. 2012. 'General strikes, mass strikes', *Solidarity.* Accessed 29 July 2018, https://solidarity-us.org/atc/160/p3679/.

Ms, N. 2019. 'Trade unions protest against Modi's "pro-corporate" and "anti-people" labour reforms', *The Caravan*, 6 January. Accessed 1 February 2019, https://caravanmagazine.in/policy/trade-unions-against-modi-labour-policies.

NELP (National Employment Law Project). 2017. 'Raises from coast to coast in 2018: Workers in 18 states and 19 cities and counties seeing minimum wage increases on January 1, many of them to rates of $12 to $15 an hour'. Accessed 29 July 2018, https://www.nelp.org/publication/raises-from-coast-to-coast-in-2018-minimum-wage-increases/.

Nowak, J. 2014. 'March for justice: The protest of India's Maruti Suzuki auto workers against imprisonment and dismissals', *Working USA*, 17: 579–586.

Nowak, J. 2016. 'Class coalitions or struggles within the working class? Social unrest in India and Brazil during the global crisis', *Workers of the World* 8: 71–98.

Nowak, J. 2017a. 'Mass strikes in India and Brazil as the terrain for a new social movement unionism', *Development and Change* 48 (5): 965–986.

Nowak, J. 2017b. 'Dreizehn Mal lebenslänglich: Die Repression ist massiv', *Analyse & Kritik* 626: 22.

Nowak, J. 2018. 'Mass strikes in the Brazilian construction sector, 2011–2014'. In J. Nowak, M. Dutta and P. Birke (eds), *Workers' Movements and Strikes in the Twenty-First Century*. London: Rowman & Littlefield, pp. 115–132.

Nowak, J. 2019. *Mass Strikes and Social Movements in Brazil and India: Popular Mobilisation in the Long Depression.* Basingstoke: Palgrave.

Nowak, J. and Gallas, A. 2014. 'Mass strikes against austerity in Western Europe: A strategic assessment', *Global Labour Journal* 5 (3): 306–321.

Palley, T. 2016. 'The US economy: Explaining stagnation and why it will persist.' In A. Gallas, H. Herr, F. Hoffer and C. Scherrer (eds), *Combating Inequality: The Global North and South.* London: Routledge, pp. 113–131.

Panimbang, F. and Mufakhir, A. 2018. 'Labour strikes in post-authoritarian Indonesia, 1998–2013'. In J. Nowak, M. Dutta and P. Birke (eds), *Workers' Movements and Strikes in the Twenty-First Century.* London: Rowman & Littlefield, pp. 21–44.

Panitch, L. and Gindin, S. 2012. *The Making of Global Capitalism: The Political Economy of the American Empire.* London: Verso.

Poulantzas, N. 1970. *Fascism and Dictatorship.* London: NLB.

Poulantzas, N. 1978. *State, Power, Socialism.* London: NLB.

Pratap, S. and Bose, A.J.C. 2015. 'Issues of labour unrest in Asia: A comparative study of hotspots and flashpoints', *Journal of Indian Research* 3 (1): 1–23.

Pringle, T. 2016. 'Strikes and labour relations in China', *Workers of the World* 8: 122–142.

Remesh, B.P. 2017. 'An automotive revolution in neoliberal India: Evolution, industrial structure, trends and prospects'. In R. Traub-Merz (ed.), *The Automotive Sector in Emerging Economies: Industrial Policies, Market Dynamics and Trade Unions.* Berlin: Friedrich Ebert Stiftung, pp. 105–126.

Reuters 2014. 'Cambodia: Garment workers end strike', *New York Times*, 7 January. Accessed 29 July 2018, https://www.nytimes.com/2014/01/08/world/asia/cambodia-garment-workers-end-strike.html.

Richard, J. 2017. 'Not just signing cards', *Jacobin*, 18 August. Accessed 29 July 2018, https://www.jacobinmag.com/2017/08/nissan-uaw-union-canton-mississippi-labor-history.

Richman, S. 2018. 'If the Supreme Court rules against unions, conservatives won't like what happens next', *The Washington Post*, 1 March. Accessed 29 July 2018, https://www.washingtonpost.com/news/posteverything/wp/2018/03/01/if-the-supreme-court-rules-against-unions-conservatives-wont-like-what-happens-next/?noredirect=on&utmterm=.842d973a2c37.

Rixen, T. 2013. 'Why reregulation after the crisis is feeble: Shadow banking, offshore financial centers, and jurisdictional competition', *Regulation & Governance* 7: 435–459.

Ryder, N. 2016. '"Greed, for lack of a better word, is good. Greed is right. Greed works": A contemporary and comparative review of the relationship between the global financial crisis, financial crime and white collar criminals in the U.S. and the U.K.', *British Journal of White Collar Crime* 1 (1): 3–47.

Sanders, B. 2017. Nissan dispute could go down as most vicious anti-union crusade in decades, *The Guardian*, 3 August. Accessed 29 July 2018, https://www.theguardian.com/us-news/2017/aug/03/nissan-workers-union-bernie-sanders.

Sarker, K. 2014. 'Neoliberal state, austerity, and workers' resistance in India', *Interface* 6 (1): 416–440.

Satgar, V. 2018. 'The climate crisis and systemic alternatives'. In V. Satgar (ed.), *The Climate Crisis: South African and Global Democratic Eco-Socialist Alternatives*. Johannesburg: Wits University Press, pp. 1–27.

Scheiber, N. 2017. 'UAW accuses Nissan of "scare tactics" as workers reject union bid', *New York Times*, 5 August. Accessed 29 July 2018, https://www.nytimes.com/2017/08/05/business/nissan-united-auto-workers-union-mississippi.html.

Scheiber, N. and Vogel, K.P. 2018. 'Behind a key anti-labor case, a web of conservative donors', *New York Times*, 25 February. Accessed 29 July 2018, https://www.nytimes.com/2018/02/25/business/economy/labor-court-conservatives.html.

Scherrer, C. 2011. 'Reproducing hegemony: US finance capital and the 2008 crisis', *Critical Policy Studies* 5 (3): 219–246.

Scheytt, S. 2012. 'Staying non-unionised by all means possible', *Mitbestimmung*. Accessed 29 July 2018, https://www.boeckler.de/66359_40699.htm.

Schwartz, M. 2011. 'The Egyptian uprising: The mass strike in the time of neoliberal globalization', *New Labor Forum* 20 (3): 33–43.

Shyam Sundar, K.R. 2019. 'Dynamics of general strikes in India', *Economic & Political Weekly*, 54 (3): 22–24.

Sinha, P. 2017. 'Trade unions and industrial relations in the car industry in India'. In R. Traub-Merz (ed.), *The Automotive Sector in Emerging Economies: Industrial Policies, Market Dynamics and Trade Unions*. Berlin: Friedrich Ebert Stiftung, pp. 206–219.

The Economic Times 2018. 'Why the farmers have stormed Delhi, what they want', 30 November. Accessed 1 February 2019, https://economictimes.indiatimes.com/news/et-explains/why-the-farmers-have-stormed-delhi-what-they-want/articleshow/66881527.cms.

Thi Thu, P. 2017. 'Why always wildcat strikes in Vietnam?', *Global Labour Column* 290. Accessed 29 July 2018, http://column.global-labour-university.org/2017/10/why-always-wildcat-strikes-in-vietnam.html.

Thul, P.C. 2014. 'Cambodian forces open fire as factory strikes turn violent', Reuters, 3 January. Accessed 29 July 2018, https://www.reuters.com/article/us-cambodia-protest/cambodian-forces-open-fire-as-factory-strikes-turn-violent-idUSBREA0203H20140103.

Voss, K. and Sherman, R. 2000. 'Breaking the iron law of oligarchy: Union revitalization in the American labor movement', *American Journal of Sociology* 106 (2): 303–349.

Withnall, A. 2019 'Protesters form 620km "women's wall" in India as female devotees pray at Hindu temple for first time', *The Independent*, 2 January. Accessed 1 February 2019, https://www.independent.co.uk/news/world/asia/womens-wall-protest-india-kerala-temple-hindu-pray-supreme-court-sexism-a8708381.html.

Wong, A. 2019. 'L.A.'s teachers got what they wanted – for their students', *The Atlantic*, 25 January. Accessed 1 February 2019, https://www.theatlantic.com/education/archive/2019/01/the-la-teachers-strike-settlement-is-a-victory-for-students/581197/.

Woodcock, J. 2019. 'India general strike 2019: Report from Bangalore', *Notes from Below*, 10 January. Accessed 1 February 2019, https://notesfrombelow.org/article/india-general-strike-2019.

Yunxue, D. 2018. 'Space and strike diffusion in a decentralised authoritarian country: A study of the auto parts industry in South China'. In J. Nowak, M. Dutta and P. Birke (eds), *Workers' Movements and Strikes in the Twenty-First Century*. London: Rowman & Littlefield, pp. 45–62.

Zemni, S., De Smet, B. and Boegaerd, K. 2013. 'Luxemburg on Tahrir Square: Reading the Arab revolutions with Rosa Luxemburg's *The Mass Strike*', *Antipode* 45 (4): 888–907.

10

THE NOVEL IN A TIME OF NEOLIBERALISM

Nivedita Majumdar

Theories of cultural production engaging with the global South often suffer from a debilitating conceptual problem. They tend to conflate the phenomenon of neoliberal globalisation with neocolonialism. The two phenomena, I argue, even if they share some common ground, are politically distinct. I exemplify the problem of conflation with a discussion of two acclaimed literary texts, Kiran Desai's *The Inheritance of Loss* (2006) and, published two years later, Arvind Adiga's *The White Tiger* (2008). Both were awarded the prestigious Man Booker Prize.

The critical reception of these texts celebrates them as statements of resistance against the scourge of neocolonialism while glossing over the specificities of the phenomenon. This is not surprising, given that critics draw on the consensus in fields like Cultural and Post-colonial Studies, which are characterised by a lack of rigour in their analysis of both neocolonialism and neoliberalism. This chapter argues that dominant positions in cultural analyses are not necessarily borne out by historical facts, much like the trajectory of economic development in large parts of Asia. Further, through a reading of the texts, I show that what passes for resistance to neocolonialism, actually suppresses conflicts and resistance against the reign of neoliberal capital.

NOVELS: THE CRITICAL CONTEXT

The 150-year-old chequered history of Indian Anglophone literature is, in crucial ways, defined by a colonial history. The peculiar conditions of its production – the use of a language that's both colonial and elite, the often deracinated social position of the writers, the catering to an audience largely untutored in Indian realities, the lure of a lucrative Western market – produced a body of literature that tended to foreground ethnic identity in ways that cater to immigrant nostalgia and offer images of the nation that are packaged for easy consumption in the West. There is, however, definitely a different trend emerging in the genre, now characterised by a generation of writers with no personal experience of colonialism and coming of age in a different and arguably more complex global and national political terrain. I briefly discuss Desai's and Adiga's novels, both of which exemplify this trend, and allow for a larger reflection on questions of neocolonialism, neoliberal capitalism and cultural production.

Critics hailed both novels as products of writerly subjectivities framed by a fierce sense of justice and depicting the darker aspects of a post-colonial reality, the predicament of the wretched of the nation, the plight of the rejects of a globalised world order, and the lingering toxicity of a colonial past. There is certainly much substance to the similarities in the characterisation of the narratives as recognised both by critics and by illustrious award panels. I will, however, point to a central difference in the authorial perspectives that shaped the novels – a distinction that has gone unremarked by their critical reception.

While both novels, albeit in varying degrees, engage with the plight of the indigent and the powerless in the contemporary globalised world, there is a significant point of divergence in the authorial perspectives on what it is that *causes* the suffering of multitudes in this world. If for Desai, it is the continuing economic and cultural domination of the West in a neocolonial world order, for Adiga, it's the reign of neoliberal capital personified by the domestic bourgeoisie that is responsible for the suffering and injustice portrayed in the novels. This crucial distinction produces narratives sharply divergent not simply in their approach to social conflicts and personal relationships, but also in determining who is embraced in each of the novel's ambit of sympathy and who is excluded. The fact that the critical commentary on the novels glosses over the specificity of the phenomena of neocolonialism and neoliberalism speaks to a larger issue of insufficient political engagement with these issues in Cultural Studies in general, and in the post-colonial field in particular.

The absence of any discussion of the specificities of either neocolonialism or neoliberalism as they relate to the novels is very much in consonance with the contemporary critical climate.[1] The assessment of cultural products like novels is shaped by a critical consensus emerging from the broad field of Cultural Studies. The field, with its various branches, was ensconced in academia during the sixties and seventies in the context of progressive social movements leading to fundamental shifts in the content of education, away from canonical texts to a democratisation of curriculum. In crucial ways, Cultural Studies articulated the liberal-Left ethos of the time. The milieu, however, was shaped just as much by a tacit acceptance of the defeat of labour. If labour unions and socialist organisations of varied stripes had gained strength in a different political climate in the wake of the depression of the thirties, after the next economic downturn of the seventies, the arc moved in the opposite direction – towards economic and political conservatism. The neo-liberal doctrine, with its deregulation of markets, free trade and the decimation of labour unions, became the reigning doctrine in the seventies and eighties. The liberal-Left turn in universities in the same era offered no meaningful challenge to the neoliberal consensus. The disciplines of Cultural and Post-colonial Studies, products of this political trend, encapsulate the contradictory pulls of liberalism and conservatism.

Critiques of cultural products such as novels, influenced by the reigning assumptions of academic disciplines, are often shorn of a rigorous analytical frame that accounts for the larger economic and political dynamics shaping the products. In the following sections, I situate the concept of neocolonialism in the larger context of neoliberal capital, and offer readings of Desai's and Adiga's novels grounded in that discussion.

THE CLAIM OF NEOCOLONIALISM

The notion of neocolonialism is often loosely deployed by theorists of various persuasions to signify the continuity of colonial rule in the global South under a different guise. Cultural critics draw on world systems and dependency theories viewing the contemporary world order as divided between the West/North, the centre of capitalism, and the East/South, the periphery exploited and left under-developed by capitalism; the division thus recreates the older divide between the coloniser and the colonised. The position was articulated by Kwame Nkrumah in his *Neocolonialism: The Last Stage of Imperialism* (1965) written at a time of despair. Krumah was trying to theorise the failure of post-colonial Ghana to transition into a self-reliant, socialist economy. He lays the blame for the failed policies of his government on the continuing influence of erstwhile colonising powers. Under such a regime, Nkrumah asserts that the state 'in the grip of neo-colonialism is not master of its own destiny' (1965: xi). The West continues to harness the economies of the South, and this relationship, Nkrumah holds, is what is responsible for the post-war boom in the West.

The Post-colonial Studies field draws on thinkers like Nkrumah to explain the national bourgeoisie's failure to carry out progressive national projects in the erst-while colonies. Post-colonial theorists subscribe to the idea of continuing Western oppression as responsible for the failure. Gayatri Spivak, for instance, holds that the 'contemporary international division of labour is a displacement of the divided field of nineteenth-century territorial imperialism . . . [wherein] the third-world pro-vide the field for investment, both through the subordinate indigenous capitalists and through their ill-protected and shifting labor force' (2010: 41). In this reading, the operation of capital in the South is carried out by a comprador bourgeoisie functioning in the interests of the West. Similarly, Partha Chatterjee claims that colonialism was never fully eradicated but only took on a new avatar in the form of neoliberal capital:

> From the early nineteenth to the early twentieth centuries, anticolonial nationalism struggled to enshrine the nation-state, which came to a place of dominance only after the end of World War II, as the universally legitimate form of the state. Once this was recognised, you would think that empire should have vanished. *But it does not.* One of my arguments is that already in the nineteenth century, you have a range of imperial practices and exer-cises of power that do not require direct territorial colonisation. Imperial power can be and was established through a range of other means (emphasis added). (2013: 188–189)

Chatterjee's argument here is that since empire never necessarily required territo-rial colonisation, political independence does not result in freedom from empire. Thus, there is a continuing line of imperial dominance from the colonial to the post-colonial period.

Like post-colonialists, theorists such as Anibal Quijano (2000) and Walter Mignolo (2011) address the continuing influence of colonialism, but they do so under a somewhat different rubric. They view capitalism in the South as an expres-sion of 'economic coloniality'. Drawing a distinction between colonialism and coloniality, they argue that while colonialism as a political phenomenon may not exist anymore, the logic of domination that supposedly generates it – coloniality – remains a strong force shaping the contemporary world. While there are several axes along which the West continues to maintain its dominance in the global South, capitalism is the economic aspect of the logic of coloniality. Quijano describes the functioning of capital in the global South as the 'coloniality of labor control deter-mined by the geographic distribution of labor in global capitalism' (2000: 539).

There is a measure of difference in the analysis of capitalism in the global South by post-colonial theorists like Spivak and Chatterjee, on the one hand, and by theorists subscribing to the notion of coloniality. Post-colonialists hold that the mandate of capital in the South, even if it is carried out by a native ruling class, functions in the greater interests of the North. But theorists like Mignolo acknowledge that the non-Western bourgeoisie has carved out a path where it no longer performs merely as a subsidiary to the West. By functioning independently of Western capitalist interests, the non-European bourgeoisie of colour has enacted what Mignolo (2012) calls a 'racial revolution'. The independent functioning of a non-European capitalist class is part of the process of de-Westernisation and viewed as a necessary stage towards the ultimate goal of decoloniality – when capitalism will be replaced by another indigenously developed economic order.

The difference between post-colonial theorists and those subscribing to the idea of coloniality notwithstanding, both draw on the assumption that capitalism is fundamentally a Western rather than a global phenomenon. If for Spivak, the 'comprador bourgeoisie' is a puppet of Western capital, Mignolo asserts the independence of the native capitalist class from Western economic interests. However, economic independence, Mignolo insists, is gained only in the context of a larger capitulation to the Western logic of coloniality, as manifest in the capitalist system. Thus, for both schools of thought – post-colonial and decolonial – the operation of capital in the South is a function of neocolonialism.

I'd contend that the identification of capitalism as a Western phenomenon is in fact responsible for the elision of the difference between the specificities of neocolonialism and neoliberalism that I mentioned earlier. If neoliberalism – a manifestation of late capitalism – is understood only as an aspect of neocolonialism – the continuing domination of the West or of coloniality – then there remains no reason to focus on the distinctiveness of the two phenomena. In the following section, I argue that capitalism in the global South functions neither as a subsidiary of Western capital, nor is it an instance of what Mignolo applauds as a 'racial revolution'. The non-Western bourgeoisie is neither a comprador one serving its Western masters, nor is it a force that is on a 'decolonial' path to constructing an indigenous economic system.

THE MYTH OF NEOCOLONIALISM

Post-colonialists, despite their professed faith in heterogeneity and cultural difference, paint the entire global South as neocolonial. Gayatri Spivak, for instance, describes neocolonialism as a phenomenon that develops after colonialism and is 'more economic and less territorial' (1991: 221). And while noting the vast disparity in the economic situation in the industrialised Asian countries like South Korea, Taiwan and Japan on the one hand and countries like India and Algeria on the other, she maintains that both regions are operating under neocolonialism. Similarly, Deepika Bahri opines that the turn towards a neoliberal frame in countries like India testifies to the fact that 'decolonization generally has failed' (1995: 62). Robert Young contends that even though the 'new system that replaced [colonialism] . . . was more subtle' neocolonialism denotes a 'continuing economic hegemony [of] . . . the former masters' (2001: 44–45).

To the extent that neocolonialism refers to the undue hold of both economic and political Western interests, strong enough to shape economies of the global South, it is certainly a phenomenon that has made its mark. The US has a solid track record of such intervention in South American countries like Haiti, Guatemala and Argentina. Similarly, the devastation wrought by the history of structural adjustment programmes in West African countries corroborates continuing Western dominance, albeit along a different route from that of the old colonial order. However, in the countries which did undergo this form of external takeover of vital economic and political sectors, the role played by their native bourgeoisie, by indigenous institutions, and the contestations and resistances to the external takeover, make the phenomenon far more complex than can be explained by the broad brush stroke of neocolonialism. More significantly, for vast parts of the South, such prevalence of Western influence played little or no role in their recent history.

The much discussed instance of the Asian Tigers Hong Kong, Singapore, Taiwan, and South Korea – newly industrialised economies that developed at exceptionally high growth rates – belies the paradigm of neocolonialism. The countries successfully followed their own trajectories of political and economic policies to become advanced economies, comparable to the US and western Europe, by the early part of this century. Other Southeast Asian countries – Indonesia, Malaysia, the Philippines, Thailand and Vietnam – often referred to as the 'tiger cubs', have attempted to follow the same export-driven path of economic development as the Asian Tigers, with varying degrees of success. Another notable instance of an economic formation outside of the US and western Europe is the BRICS, comprising what have been called the 'emerging economies': Brazil, Russia, India, China and South Africa. Together, the countries are home to 40 per cent of the world's population and cover more than 25 per cent of the world's land, with a combined GDP of US$20 trillion. These countries have sought to chart out an ambitious economic agenda, and it's worth noting that 'between 1990 to 2014, they went from accounting for 11 percent of the world's GDP to almost 30 percent' (Bremmer 2017). These are just a few instances of economies which point to a complex and heterogeneous terrain where economies of the South, while very much part of the global circuit of capital, are by no means subject to what can be called a neocolonial logic.

Participation in the global capital market also subjects these economies to the risks and recessions intrinsic to the logic of capital. For instance, the Asian financial crisis of 1997, triggered by the collapse of the Thai baht resulting from the circuitry of international capital and an asset bubble, not only wreaked havoc in the regional economies but generated shock signals across the globe. And, as CP Chandrasekhar and Jayati Ghosh rightly observe, the eventual recovery of the region, with its V-shaped growth trajectory, is based on IMF-directed stabilisation strategies that lead precisely to the kind of financial fragility that produced the crisis in the first place (2013: 323). Similarly, the impressive growth of the BRICS economies notwithstanding, the massive state debts and the general reliance on global capital keeps them vulnerable to the logic of crises. But what is noteworthy is that the fragility and risks of these non-Western economies result mainly from the political choices of the ruling classes in these countries, rather than from an imposition by the West. And because they choose global capital, they remain vulnerable to the same logic of crises and recessions that is intrinsic to capital everywhere.

I'll now look at the post-colonial Indian case in a little more detail to explore the claims of coloniality. By any measure, 70 years after independence, India still remains a poor country, with one third of the world's population living below the poverty line. Per capita income remains below US$2 000 at actual exchange rates, with inadequate job creation and more than 95 per cent of workers in the informal sector, and more than half of all workers in low productivity agriculture (Ghosh 2014). The country's poverty explains widespread poor nutrition indicators, and the inadequate provision of housing, electricity and health services as well as low investment in and expansion of education.

The prevalence of large-scale poverty and inequality, however, must be situated in the context of a country that has maintained a respectable level of economic growth and development. Soon after independence in 1947, the country undertook an ambitious and expansive plan of industrial development based on economic planning. While the history of state planning and the performance of the national bourgeoisie has yielded mixed results,[2] the country did develop a large and deep industrial base and has vastly expanded its technological and service sectors in the past three decades. In addition, it has sustained a rapid increase in GDP for most of the last two decades. It is true that India embraced a neoliberal economic model in the early nineties, with the reliance on global capital that this entails. It needs to be remembered, however, that the drive for liberalisation of the economy came from within the country, and not outside. A growing capitalist base demanded the freedom from institutional strictures that came with the post-colonial state's commitment to discipline capital. The economic development project, to the extent that it has been a successful one, has relied on the nation's robust political and legal institutions. India exhibits a combination of economic backwardness along with a record in democratic governance and an independent judiciary comparable to that of any advanced nation.

The central issue with theories premised on the failure of post-colonial states and the claim of continuing (neo)colonial subjugation is that it is not borne out by facts. The history of post-colonial India was very much shaped within a political and ideological framework free of Western intervention. Owing to a mass-based independence movement, a genuinely anti-colonial leadership and the country's geopolitical location, the responsibility for India's post-colonial successes and failures reside within the nation. This history of post-colonial India, along with that of other Asian countries, shows that the path of economic development followed by these countries for over 70 years was characterised both by successfully carving out a trajectory that was independent of Western interests and, in great measure, by strong state disciplining of domestic capital. This history belies generalised claims about the failure of post-colonial states, as well as the idea that they remain trapped in the colonial paradigm.

Unlike post-colonial theorists, the votaries of coloniality do acknowledge the independent trajectory of capitalist development in the South. They in fact applaud the phenomenon as evidence of a 'racial revolution', and hold that it is a desirable step towards the ultimate objective of an indigenous economic system and a decolonial order. The notion of indigenous capitalism as 'racial revolution' is premised on a fundamental confusion regarding the very nature of capitalism. Capitalism, unlike a *racial* order like white supremacy, *primarily* functions in the interest of a *class, not of a race*. This is not to deny the intersection of race and class, especially in countries with a deep racialised history such as South Africa, or of caste and class in India. But because within capitalism, the *fundamental* conflict is between capital and labour, even if the dominant racial character of the ruling class is transformed – whether with black or Dalit capitalists – it does not alter that fundamental conflict. In the South, as in the North, capitalism operates by exploiting workers in the interests of the ruling class; thus, workers in the South have not benefited from this alleged revolution. Similarly, the idea that 'de-Westernised' capital will pave the way to some desirable indigenous system is equally fallacious. Capitalists in the South, much like their counterparts in the West, function only to further consolidate their power and interests and not to move towards some other system. The experience of neoliberal capital in India bears out these facts.

If we were to abide by the theorists of coloniality, the trajectory of de-Westernised capital in India should have paved the way in its 70-year history for a fair and desirable indigenous system. Not surprisingly, the actual movement has been in the opposite direction. Studies show that during '1980–2012, the share of total emoluments to workers declined from 51.1 per cent to 27.9 per cent and the share of wages declined from 33 per cent to 13 per cent. Correspondingly, there has been a steady increase of profit share' (Abraham and Sasikumar 2017: 41; Goldar 2013). Not coincidentally, since the 1990s there has also been a decline in the power of trade unions as the political establishment increasingly shifts its support away from the working class in favour of employers (Sen Gupta 2003). This quick snapshot is enough to dismantle the notion that indigenous capitalism in the South functions in the interests of a race or the nation as a whole.

Ideas of neocolonialism and coloniality serve to erase the inherent oppression of non-Western capitalism, as well as the resistance to it. The only political opposition that such a perspective can envision is one between the imperial West, with its institutions of dominance, and the global South. Neocolonialism and related constructs are characterised by the dual move of generalising and centralising a colonial-era conflict between the coloniser and the colonised, and suppressing actual conflicts, oppressions and resistance in the global South.

THE NOVELS

Let us now return to the two earlier-mentioned novels to discuss how intellectual trends centralising the idea of coloniality can shape cultural production, and conversely, explore a work that instead foregrounds post-colonial realities beyond the colonial shadow.

The Inheritance of Loss subscribes to the idea that colonialism shaped the world in such a way that continuing human suffering would be the destiny of those who were on the wrong side of the colonial divide. The novel explores the lives of a few individuals in disparate settings – from the hills of India to the streets of colonial England and the shadow world of poor immigrants in New York. Sai, the central character, a young woman and an orphan, lives with her grandfather in Darjeeling. She falls in love with her tutor, Gyan, who belongs to the local Gorkha community. Gyan's identity becomes the trope for exploring the political conflict ravaging the region. Sai's grandfather, a Cambridge-educated retired judge, is an Anglophile much like some of his equally affluent neighbours who've made the hills an oasis for themselves. Meanwhile, Biju, the son of the grandfather's cook, struggles to make a basic living in the kitchens of New York restaurants along with other poor, illegal immigrants. Through these characters, Desai weaves a tale of individual suffering and of a globalised world gone terribly awry.

The narrative is invested in challenging the subject formation of the post-colonial elite, its deracinated lifestyle and its assumed innocence of historical injustices. The grandfather, for instance, epitomising the anglicised, affluent class, is a target of narrative judgement both for the centrality of class status in his public life and even more for his failings in his private life, like abandoning his wife whom he could no longer connect with after his cultural transformation in England. That his transformation in England is much like that of a servant adopting the ways of his master, not out of coercion but out of a desire for acceptance, does not mitigate the narrative judgement. The judge's Anglophilia, similar to that of his neighbours Lola and Noni, is subjected to harsh ridicule. These affluent characters, having created little cocoons of colonial comforts and manners for themselves, live not so much in oblivion of their surrounding destitute and wretched communities, as with a sense of their disconnected superiority.

In the novel, set in Darjeeling of the mid 1980s, the Gorkha insurgency becomes the narrative device for forcing the elite to face the consequences of their material status and clueless subjectivities. The Gorkhas, the original inhabitants of the land, have had a chequered history of economic and social marginalisation, starting during the colonial era and continuing into the post-colonial period. Based on a sense of alienation from the nation, the demand for a separate state of Gorkhaland is one of several movements for regional autonomy that the Indian state has had to negotiate. It is of course ironic for a post-colonial state to be accused of generating the sense of alienation reminiscent of the colonial period. The added irony in the instance of the Gorkha movement was that it developed in West Bengal, a state ruled by communists, with their doctrine of economic development and cultural inclusion.

Led by the Gorkha National Liberation Front (GNLF), the movement emerging in the 1980s with its demand for a separate state of Gorkhaland, was built to address the region's lack of economic development; its serious infrastructural problems (such as the inadequate supply of drinking water, creating virtual droughts and impacting on tourism – a mainstay of the local economy); its poorly built roads leading to routine landslides during the monsoons; its chronic power shortage; the lack of investment in higher education for the local population and discrimination against Gorkhas in public employment. Further, the lack of economic planning led to the problem of deforestation on a massive scale, aggravating the issues of landslides and drinking-water shortages, and also harming local agriculture. The GNLF successfully mobilised the deep-seated grievances of the people, rooted in neglect and deprivation, and built a militant movement around identity and autonomy.

The Gorkhas, in Desai's novel, are both peripheral and defining for the central actions. Even though the agitation is depicted only as backdrop, it serves to highlight the crucial tensions in the lives of the central characters. The novel opens with the scene of a group of Gorkha agitators forcibly intruding into Sai's grandfather's house to acquire guns and other more quotidian essentials like cold cream. The patrician grandfather is insulted and humiliated by the activists; he's forced to utter slogans in support of the movement and even more ignominiously, made to prepare tea for the intruders. Other affluent characters in the novel like Lola, Noni and Bose suffer from a state of heightened anxiety, with the Gorkha movement gaining in strength. These characters are fully cognisant of the poverty and sense of disenfranchisement that fuels the movement, as well as how they and their lavish lifestyles are implicated.

The encounter between the grandfather and the Gorkha activists in the introductory chapter offers a crystallised instance of the larger narrative stance on underlying issues. There is both a narrative judgement of the grandfather for his elitist lifestyle and sympathy for the injustices fuelling the Gorkha rebellion; however, both these positions are qualified in ways that result in their morphing into something else altogether. Because of the humiliation meted out to the grandfather, however deserved, he becomes an object of sympathy. Similarly, the Gorkha raid on his house, whatever its historic justification, becomes an act evoking censure. This dual move – an acknowledgement of class and class-related conflicts on the one hand, and a narrative embrace of the privileged on the other – is carried out through many instances in the narrative. Thus Noni, a character ridiculed for her almost comical love of everything British, is also redeemed because of her realisation that the age-old class divide is unjust, and that she and her dear ones will have to pay the price for it.

Conversely, while the Gorkhas are certainly depicted as being on the wrong end of history both in relation to their colonial and their post-colonial rulers, their movement is harshly critiqued for being motivated by the desire for power and for its violent means. Thus, even though Gyan, the only Gorkha to have some interiority in the novel, comes from an indigent background and remains unemployed in spite of an education, his embrace of the movement becomes a deeper occasion for critiquing its orientation. Interestingly, when critiqued, the movement loses its historicity and is cast in universal terms: 'they [Gyan and his fellow activists] found the hate pure, purer than it could ever have been before, because the grief of the past was gone. Just the fury remained, distilled, liberating. It was theirs by birthright, it could take them so high, it was a drug' (Desai 2006: 161). The privileged characters remain very much within the sympathetic ambit of the novel. Grandfather, Lola, and Noni may be ridiculed for their ways, but the narrative remains sympathetically invested in their subjective lives. In contrast, although there may be an abstract recognition of the historic injustice meted out to the Gorkhas, they remain outside the narrative orbit of empathy.

In fact, the only subaltern character receiving unqualified narrative sympathy is Biju, the cook's son, who navigates the back streets of New York as an illegal immigrant. Biju represents the underbelly of globalisation since he works for exploitative employers in filthy restaurants, desperately trying to eke out a living. 'It was horrible what happened to Indians abroad,' the narrative voice reminds us, 'and nobody knew but other Indians abroad. It was a dirty little rodent secret' (Desai 2006: 138). While the observation refers immediately to Biju, it also includes the judge's experience in England. Both the judge and Biju leave their country for the West and its promise of advancement as young men, and return with a legacy of pain and loss. The judge, too, had experienced the pain of racial otherness in the England of 1940s. There, he had seen old ladies on buses shun him because 'whatever they had, they were secure in their conviction that it wasn't even remotely as bad as what he had' (Desai 2006: 45). Having once been subjected to such experiences of isolation and non-belonging, it becomes part of the judge's destiny.

The easy parallel that the narrative draws between an affluent retired judge and an illegal immigrant foregrounds its underlying politics. People in and from the global South continue to suffer because of 'certain moves made long ago' (Desai 2006: 217). It is resonant with the idea of coloniality in subscribing to the notion that post-colonial nations continue to suffer because of the inheritance of a colonial way of being. The problem with casting colonialism as the sole culprit is that then there is no further blame to be assigned in any meaningful way to local actors. The judge, after all, carries the scars of a colonial past as much as a Biju or a Gyan. So in spite of all his issues that we might legitimately ridicule and judge, he's absolved of any defining blame. He and people of his class are depicted as victims of the same history that has supposedly relegated the Gorkhas to their lot of destitution. Once the central battleground of history has been painted with the West forever on the one side and with the (post)colonised on the other, it follows that other battles are of little consequence. Thus, to the extent that the Gorkha movement is targeted not at the West but at the post-colonial state and its agents like the retired judge, it is acknowledged, only to be discredited in the narrative.

The question that arises then is whose interests are served by claiming coloniality to be the central culprit and by the related suppression of conflicts within the nation. Such a reading of history offers no consolation to the subalterns in Desai's narrative, which refuses to address the legitimate economic and political grievances highlighted by the GNLF against the Indian state. Nor does it help Biju to know that his exploitative Indian employers in New York are as much victims of coloniality as he is. On the other hand, the idea of coloniality does serve the interests of the retired judge, of Lola and Noni and others of their class and persuasion by ultimately absolving them of blame and responsibility.

In contrast to *The Inheritance of Loss*, *The White Tiger* steers clear of the idea of coloniality and centralises class conflict in a neoliberal India. The narrative is offered from the perspective of its narrator, an uneducated young man from a poverty-stricken village who ends up as a successful businessman in Bangalore, the hub of neoliberal India. While Balram's story seemingly testifies to the promises of riches embedded in the new economic order, it does hide a dirty secret. Balram has murdered his employer and stolen his money to get started on his own path of success. The narrative uncovering the motivation behind Balram's criminal act is also the story of the dirty underbelly of neoliberal India.

Balram begins his journey in what is called 'the darkness' (Adiga 2008: 12), that is, rural India. The forgotten India is vividly portrayed in all its deprivation – its crumbling schools, its non-existent hospitals, a grinding poverty that has seeped into and stunted human relationships. At the outskirts of the village live the ruling elite, enjoying lavish lifestyles while engaging in every possible form of corruption and exploitation of the villagers. The dark portrayal of the realm of darkness notwithstanding, Adiga reserves his wrath for the nerve centres of the new India, its cities like Delhi and Bangalore. Balram, hired as a driver, is brought to Delhi by his employers. Much of the narrative takes place in post-liberalised Delhi, with its snazzy shopping malls, spectacular night life, expensive hotels and gated communities providing an oasis of material comfort and a wretched underclass that makes it all possible.

The narrative highlights the dehumanised status of an underclass that is included in the affluence of centres of wealth and power, but only as perpetual servants. The vicious hierarchy of a feudal culture that the country is deeply familiar with, has been transposed onto urban centres undergoing a neoliberal transformation. In the rush to a particular form of modernity, the disenfranchisement of the underclass is normalised in routine practices like the denial of access into shopping malls for anyone demonstrating visible signs of poverty. Illegal discrimination and the privatisation of public space have been normalised by both classes.

Balram describes the 'great Indian rooster coop' (Adiga 2008: 149) where the underclass is trapped in their lives of perpetual servitude. Once inside the coop, the idea of emancipation becomes suspect. The ideology of servitude, working with a combination of ideas, force and fear, prevents the typical member of the underclass from breaking free. Like all ideology, it is practised by all members of the dominant class, even the most well-intentioned. Balram's immediate employer, Ashok, for instance, is educated in the West and has liberal ideas. He treats Balram well, speaks to him kindly, gives him routine raises and often defends him against others in his family. Yet all this, we're given to understand, is strictly within the parameters of the master–servant relationship.

Consistent with his class loyalty, Ashok participates with the rest of his family in framing Balram for a murder, actually committed by one of their own family members. It is in fact not uncommon, we're given to understand, for a servant to be framed for the crimes of their employer; this too is normalised. In the end, Balram does commit a murder and justifies it as his only chance of getting out of the rooster coop. Even as Balram is depicted as an amoral narrator, the narrative sympathies are squarely invested in him and the entire narrative resonates with moral outrage at a system and a culture thriving on the dehumanisation of the larger part of the population.

CONCLUSION

The shift of focus from coloniality in *The Inheritance of Loss* to class in *The White Tiger* is not merely a theoretical exercise of foregrounding one or another idea of a social order. While both narratives portray the travails of the post-colonial nation, the difference in the underlying framework informs each author's writing, determines who the narrative is sympathetically invested in and who is castigated. If for Desai, both the haves and have-nots of the post-colonial nation equally suffer from the continuing ravages of a colonial past, and violent upsurges by the disenfranchised are ultimately purposeless, Adiga offers a different vision. For him, the central conflict is of a deeply unjust economic system with a corresponding feudal culture of inegalitarianism, both located firmly within the nation. The structures of dominance are not Western impositions, as Quijano (2000) would have it. The domestic ruling class cannot be absolved of the crimes of either the economic order of capitalism or the deep-rooted inegalitarianism of a feudal culture. If the Gorkha rebellion is perfunctorily acknowledged by Desai as a product of material and social disenfranchisement but ultimately denigrated for its violence and a base drive for power, for Adiga, the violence of the underclass cannot be judged, only contextualised as the understandable outgrowth of a deeply inhumane system. In this narrative, the wretched and the disenfranchised are not victims of a past order, but are being actively exploited by the ruling class of the post-colonial nation. And unlike in Desai's novel, there is no empathy for the exploitative elite.

My intention has not been to offer a comprehensive comparative critique of the two novels because a discussion of how the novels fare on multiple literary registers is beyond the scope of this paper. Instead, I have tried to foreground a failure in the critical commentary on the texts: glossing over the novelists' diverging treatment of neocolonialism and neoliberalism – an issue that shapes both texts. I have argued that this particular failure needs to be located within a broader intellectual milieu where the flourishing myth of neocolonialism disallows a rigorous critique of neoliberalism. Fundamentally, the myth refuses to acknowledge the independent and universal logic of neoliberal capital, and consequently, it is also unable to do justice to the different forms of resistance against the corrosive logic of neoliberalism in the global South. Historically rooted analyses of both neocolonialism and neoliberal globalisation are urgently necessary for the radical transformation that Left cultural theories claim as their agenda.

NOTES

1   For an exception to this general trend, see Nagesh Rao (2000).
2   See Vivek Chibber (2006).

REFERENCES

Abraham, V. and Sasikumar, S.K. 2017. *Declining wage share in India's organized manufacturing sector: Trends, patterns and determinants*. ILO Asia-Pacific Working Paper Series. Accessed 25 July 2018, http://www.ilo.org/wcmsp5/groups/public/---asia/---ro-bangkok/---sro-new_delhi/documents/publication/wcms_614777.pdf.

Adiga, A. 2008. *The White Tiger*. New York: Free Press.

Bahri, D. 1995. 'Once more with feeling: What is postcolonialism?' *ARIEL: A Review of International English Literature* 26 (1): 51–82.

Bremmer, I. 2017. 'The mixed fortunes of the BRICS countries, in 5 Facts', *Time*, 1 September.

Chandrasekhar, C.P. and Ghosh, J. 2013. 'The Asian financial crisis, financial restructuring and the problem of contagion'. In M.H. Wolfson and G.A. Epstein (eds), *The Handbook of the Political Economy of Financial Crises*. New York: Oxford University Press, pp. 311–325.

Chatterjee, P. 2013. 'Partha Chatterjee interviewed by Manu Goswami', *Public Culture* 25 (1): 177–189.

Chibber, V. 2006. *Locked in Place: State-Building and Late Industrialization in India*. Princeton: Princeton University Press.

Desai, K. 2006. *The Inheritance of Loss*. New York: Grove Press.

Ghosh, J. 2014. 'Is India still a developing country?' *The Guardian*, 6 April.

Goldar, B. 2013. 'Wages and wage share in India during the post-reform period', *Indian Journal of Labour Economics* 56: 75–94.

Mignolo, W. 2011. *The Darker Side of Western Modernity: Global Futures, Decolonial Options*. Durham and London: Duke University Press.

Mignolo, W. 2012. Walter Mignolo interview by Weihua He. Accessed 25 July 2018, http://waltermignolo.com/the-prospect-of-harmony-and-the-decolonial-view-of-the-world/.

Nkrumah, K. 1965. *Neo-Colonialism: The Last Stage of Imperialism*. New York: International Publishers.

Quijano, A. 2000. 'Coloniality of power and Eurocentrism in Latin America', *International Sociology* 15 (2): 215–232.

Rao, N. 2000. '"Neocolonialism" or "globalization"?: Postcolonial theory and the demands of political economy', *Interdisciplinary Literary Studies* 1 (2): 165–184.

Sen Gupta, A.K. 2003. 'Decline of trade union power in India', *The Indian Journal of Labour Economics* 46 (4): 685–702.

Spivak, G.C. 2010. *Reflections on the History of an Idea: Can the Subaltern Speak?* New York: Columbia University Press.

Young, R. 2001. *Postcolonialism: An Historical Introduction*. Oxford: Blackwell.

CONCLUSION

Vishwas Satgar

We are at a conjuncture in world history where everything is at stake. UN reports on climate crisis, biodiversity loss, species extinction and everyday lived experiences of a world in crisis haunt our state of being. It seems like a great unravelling has begun, posing ostensibly insurmountable challenges. The power of social analysis, particularly critical and Marxist political economy analysis, is crucial to assist in explaining these realities and identifying possibilities for emancipatory transformation. In this regard, macro-analysis of big structures and processes related to capitalism and its progeny, imperialism, have to be front and centre in how we understand the contemporary world.

This volume has drawn on critical and Marxist analytical approaches to make sense of the territorial and economic logics of contemporary imperialism. A geopolitics of North versus South, embodied in a US-led bloc versus a China-led BRICS bloc, is one perception of our world. Underlying this are various assumptions about power, politics, geography and economics. At one level, the US is seen as an unchanging and structurally invincible colossus. It is the prime capitalist state, setting standards for capitalist civilisation and leading the contemporary world order. At another level, BRICS is vaunted as 'anti-imperialist', an attempt at renewing post-Bandung 'South-South solidarity' and the harbinger of an alternative for the peripheries of capitalism. This volume unsettles the simple geopolitical perceptions, images and rhetoric at work. It is critical in going beyond the accepted common sense of world order.

REMEMBERING ROSA LUXEMBURG

A crucial intellectual resource informing, either directly or indirectly, the intellectual orientation of this volume has been Rosa Luxemburg's original and pioneering work on imperialism. Luxemburg's brilliant mind was brought to an abrupt halt on 15 January 1919. She was murdered by right-wing shock troops under instruction from key members of the Social Democratic government led by Friedrich Ebert. This injustice has not been reckoned with by the Social Democratic Party of Germany. However, Luxemburg's intellectual contribution to Marxist thought and her classic *Accumulation of Capital* (1913) resonates into the present. It provides fertile and valuable resources for thinking through the form and practice of imperialism today. While Luxemburg was thinking in a different context, her attempts to explain the economic basis of imperialism and colonialism are crucial for an understanding of where we are today. While formal colonialism might have ended, imperial control of the peripheries of capitalism continues.

Revisiting Luxemburg's work and the fluorescence of fresh thinking derived from it assist in situating various contemporary dynamics of capitalism. While appreciating her limits, many critical thinkers, theorists and Marxists – beyond the scope of this volume – are using Luxemburg as a crucial starting point to understand the restructuring of global capitalism, militarism, ecological relations linked to expropriating what she termed the 'natural economy', uneven development, commodification and de-commodification, the boomerang effect of violence and the future of a terminally ill capitalism. Unearthing and reworking several of her critical historical materialist concepts are crucial for a thinking Marxism. This volume has drawn on Luxemburg as a premise or a point of departure from which to think about where we are in the contemporary world. She has impacted on contributors in this volume, some more than others, with regard to how we think about the structural divide between core/periphery, North/South and US versus the rest, that shape and condition our life world.

What the volume makes clear is that carbon extraction and control is centred in the global North, but that there are also vast amounts of carbon-based resources controlled by state corporations in the global South, in countries such as Russia, China, India and Brazil. In the context of climate change this is a crucial challenge. At the same time, water resources are stressed on a planetary scale. While water stress is exacerbated by climate change this essential resource for reproducing human and non-human life is also being commodified and tied into particular geo-economic circuits. In a country like drought-prone South Africa water conflicts are already manifesting and poised to get worse. If the imperatives of global carbon-based extraction, together with water commodification, prevail in this moment of climate-driven systemic crisis, we are heading for civilisational collapse. In this regard, Luxemburg was prescient about what could happen if capitalist accumulation engulfed the entire world. Neither BRICS nor non-BRICS countries are grappling with this challenge; rather, many are causing and contributing to the problems underpinning the trajectory of civilisational collapse.

THE AGE OF IMPERIAL CHAOS

US imperial reach, power and presence in the world is at a turning point. Financialised over-accumulation buttressed by US power is an instability wired into the circuitry of global capitalism. The roller coaster of financial instability is far from over, yet controlling global finance is crucial for the reproduction of US power. The BRICS have not succeeded in breaking this power and providing an alternative. The BRICS bank is embedded in the neoliberal financial architecture shaped and influenced by the US-led bloc. This expresses itself as subimperial relations in one moment of cooperation. On the other hand, Trump's acceleration of climate change and his repositioning of the US to push back the contender roles of Russia and China opens up conflicts with the US-led bloc. Global rivalries, partly muted through global institutions, are also emerging outside these parameters.

At the same time, Trump's belligerence towards Venezuela and Iran is showing dangerous signs of escalating. Open destabilisation of Venezuela and sabre-rattling through positioning geostrategic assets like warships close to Iran expresses both an economic and territorial logic of imperial power. It cranks up the military-industrial complex in the US for military conflict beyond the endless war on terror, which has already cost trillions of dollars, but it also disrupts global oil flows, pushing up the price of oil and benefiting shareholding-based carbon corporations in the US and the global North more generally. Increasing the price of oil also ramifies negatively through a tenuous and globalised food system. China and the other BRICS countries are not able to counter these moves of imperial overreach. In this context, China's overaccumulation challenges lock it more deeply into managing global capitalism on US terms. As has been analysed in this volume, China has skewed economic patterns in some BRICS countries for certain primary commodities (such as agricultural produce from Brazil) while at the same time Chinese overproduction of steel has impacted negatively on the manufacturing capacities of countries like South Africa. The BRICS as a bloc of countries is being pulled apart by its underlying and unequal economic dynamics, but also by the rise of extreme right-wing forces in some partner countries. It is too early to tell how this will deepen and exacerbate intra-BRICS rivalries.

In addition, complex and interconnected systemic contradictions such as climate change and growing water crises are not taken seriously within the US-led bloc. While Trump cranks up carbon extraction and pushes back against multilateral responses to climate change, its real impacts are registering in the world with extreme weather changes. Climate shocks are costing lives and money. This challenge is crossing borders. BRICS countries' investment strategies are not talking to this challenge and in the case of water resources rivalries are emerging between, for instance, India and China. Moreover, in Mozambique, which experienced two devastating cyclones (Idai and Kenneth) within six weeks of each other, Brazilian corporations are investing heavily in carbon (coal and gas) extraction and export-led agriculture.

US-led imperialism has facilitated the uneven geographic expansion of capitalism. At the same time, it has been responsible for moving crises around through spatial fixes, remaking North–South relations to ensure accumulation while dispossessing life, advancing wars and exacerbating growing global rivalry. A world of imperial chaos is in the making: US-led global capitalism is plunging the world into further barbarism, a term used by Luxemburg to characterise the capitalist world of her time. Greater violence and supremacist domination take us further away from building an emancipatory world and civilisation.

RESISTANCE AND THE FUTURE

Similar to Luxemburg, who identified various forms of resistance against imperial and colonial expansion, all the contributors in this volume identify modes and forms of resistance – mainly from below. The BRICS in the analysis of this volume is not a harbinger of an emancipatory politics and future. Its contradictions, limits and incoherence is laid bare. Some authors in the volume assess the BRICS as a sideshow for China, others reduce this configuration to subimperial relations, while others underline the incapacity of the BRICS to deal with its own contradictions. What is exciting in some of the contributions is the extension of analysis beyond the BRICS as a bloc. The optic of some contributions points to struggles from below within BRICS countries, against transnational corporations, mass defensive strikes by workers and various forms of cultural critique. Resistance to expanded reproduction and to accumulation through dispossessing life might be beneath the surface, in most instances, but is reassuringly alive and well, albeit pitched against an increasingly supremacist imperial order.

Finally, sitting at the centre of this volume is a crucial debate about the future of internationalism. One chapter reflects critically on the World Social Forum and the need for a new vessel of struggle. Another makes the call for a new Workers and Peoples International. These are not calls to repeat history or merely bring back an authoritarian left politics. There is a search going on in these pages, written by leading Marxist thinkers who want to confront the global scale of capitalist crisis, imperial chaos and worsening global rivalries. Without counter-hegemonic human solidarity and an affirmation of radical universal values, on an international scale, we are faced with a terrifying and bleak world, being made in the image of the new US imperialism.

CONTRIBUTORS

Ferrial Adam is an environmental justice activist and is presently working towards her PhD on citizen science and environmental justice in South Africa's water sector.

Samir Amin (1931–2018) was one of Africa's leading Marxists and world-systems analysts. He is well known for his work on non-Eurocentric Marxism, imperial rent, the global monopoly phase of capitalism, delinking, his call for a Fifth International of workers and peoples and his anti-imperialism.

Patrick Bond is a professor in the School of Government at the University of the Western Cape.

William K. Carroll is a professor of Sociology at the University of Victoria and co-director of the Corporate Mapping Project.

Christopher Chase-Dunn is a distinguished professor of Sociology and director of the Institute for Research on World-Systems at the University of California, Riverside.

Alexander Gallas is an assistant professor in the Department of Political Science, University of Kassel, Germany.

Ana Garcia is a professor of International Relations at the Federal Rural University of Rio de Janeiro and a visiting scholar in the Centre for Civil Society at the University of Kwazulu-Natal.

Karina Kato is a professor of the Postgraduate Programme on Development, Agriculture and Society (CPDA) at the Federal Rural University of Rio de Janeiro.

Nivedita Majumdar is an associate professor of English at John Jay College, City University of New York.

Vishwas Satgar is an associate professor of International Relations at the University of the Witwatersrand. He edits the Democratic Marxism series and is the principal investigator for the Emancipatory Futures Studies in the Anthropocene project.

Keamogetswe Seipato is the coordinator of the Southern Africa Campaign to Dismantle Corporate Power, which is based at the Alternative Information and Development Centre in Cape Town.

INDEX

Printed and bound by CPI Group (UK) Ltd, Croydon, CR0 4YY

16/04/2025

14658440-0003